KWAME NKRUMAH — A BIOGRAPHY

NKRUMAH *on* AFRICAN UNITY

- TODAY we are one. If in the past the Sahara divided us, now it unites us and an injury to one is an injury to us all.   *[Accra, 15 April 1958]*

- To many people, the unity of African states which we regard as the primary basis of our African policy appears visionary and unattainable. We do not hold this view. The unity of African states can be a reality and it will be achieved earlier than many of us suppose.   *[Dublin, 18 May 1960]*

- If we do not formulate plans for unity and take active steps to form political union, we will soon be fighting and warring among ourselves with imperialists and colonialists standing behind the screen and pulling vicious wires, to make us cut each other's throats for the sake of their diabolical purposes in Africa.
  I can see no security for African states unless African leaders like ourselves have realised beyond all doubt that salvation for Africa lies in unity.   *[Casablanca, 7 January 1961]*

- There is no time to waste. The longer we wait the stronger will be the hold on Africa of neo-colonialism and imperialism. A Union Government for Africa does not mean the loss of sovereignty by independent African states. A Union Government will rather strengthen the sovereignty of the individual states within the Union.   *[Accra, 24 May 1964]*

- I do believe (and nothing that has happened or can happen, will swerve me from my belief), that the emergence of a Continental Union Government of Africa will immediately make the independent states of Africa a mighty world influence.
  [Speech at the Fourth Afro-Asian Solidarity Conference at Winneba, 10 May 1965]

Kwame Nkrumah

A Biography

June Milne

PANAF

Kwame Nkrumah: A Biography

First published in 1999 by Panaf Books
Reprinted 2000, 2006

75 Weston Street
London SE1 3RS

ISBN: 0 901787 56 6

Cover main graphic ~ Jill Alder
Cover design and volume typesetting ~ Myrene McFee

The Author

June Milne was born 22 June 1920 in Melbourne, Australia. Educated at Cheltenham ladies' College and the University of London, she became in 1947 Examiner, and later Chief Examiner in History for the London University School Examinations Board. After lecturing for three years (1949–1952) at the University of the Gold Coast (now the University of Ghana), she became research and editorial assistant to President Kwame Nkrumah in 1957. Two years after the coup, on his instructions, she founded Panaf Books in 1968 to publish the new books he wrote during his time in Conakry, Guinea, and to keep his existing works in print. She worked closely with Nkrumah during the Conakry period, and was with him in Bucharest where he died on 27 April 1972.

June Milne continued to run Panaf until 1987 when she retired from publishing to spend full time on her work as Nkrumah's literary executrix.

Also by June Milne

Kwame Nkrumah (Panaf Great Lives Series, 1974)

Forward Ever (Panaf, 1977)

Sékou Touré (Panaf Great Lives Series, 1978)

Kwame Nkrumah. The Conakry Years: His Life and Letters (Panaf imprint of Zed Press, 1990)

CONTENTS

Chronology: Kwame Nkrumah's Life and Writings

Year	Events	Writings
1909-46		
1909	Born in Nkroful	
1935	IN USA as student and worker	*African Interpreter* (Organ of the African Students' Organization of USA and Canada)
	Lincoln University (B.A.; M.A)	
	Philadelphia University (M.A.; M Sc)	
1945	In London	*Towards Colonial Freedom*
	– West African National Secretariat; – Fifth Pan-African Congress	*Declaration to the Colonial Peoples of the World, Fifth Pan African Congress*
1946		*The New African* (Organ of the West African National Secretariat)
1946		*The Circle* document
1947-56		
1947	Return to the Gold Coast to join UGCC	
1948		*Accra Evening News*
1949	Formation of the CPP	*What I Mean by Positive Action*
1950	Call for Positive Action	
1950/51	Arrest and imprisonment	
1952	Prime Minister	
1953	Motion of Destiny	
1955	Bandung Conference	
1957-59		
1957	Independence of Ghana (6 March)	*Autobiography*
1958	First Conference of Independent African States, Accra	*I Speak of Freedom*
1958	All-African People's Conference	
1958	Ghana-Guinea Union	
1959	Sanniquellie Conference	

1960–65

1960	Republican constitution	
	President	
1960	Secret Agreement, Congo/	
	Ghana Union	
1961	Casablanca Conference	
1961	Ghana-Guinea-Mali Union	
1961	Dawn Broadcast	
1963	Foundation of the OAU	*Africa Must Unite*
1964	Seven Year Development Plan	*Consciencism*
1965	OAU Summit in Accra	*Neo-Colonialism: The Last Stage of Imperialism*
1965	UDI in Rhodesia — Ghana breaks diplomatic relations with UK	

1966-72

1966	24 February coup d 'état	*Challenge of the Congo*
1966	Fall of CPP government	*Axioms* (Freedom Fighters' Edition)
1966	Arrival in Conakry	
	Co-President of Guinea	
1967	Lt. Arthur's attempted coup	*Voice from Conakry*
1968		*Dark Days in Ghana*
1968		*Handbook of Revolutionary Warfare*
1968		*Ghana: The Way Out*
1968		*The Spectre of Black Power*
1968		*The Struggle Continues*
1969		*Two Myths*
1969		*The Big Lie*
1970		Revised edition of *Consciencism*
1970		*Class Struggle in Africa*
1970	Attempted imperialist invasion of Guinea	
1971	Left Guinea for medical treatment in Romania	
1972	Died in Bucharest 27 April	

Published posthumously

1973		*Revolutionary Path*
1974		*Rhodesia File*

Abbreviations

AACPC	All-African Committee for Political Co-operation
AAPRA	All-African People's Revolutionary Army
AAPRP	All-African People's Revolutionary Party
AATUF	All-African Trade Union Federation
AFRC	Armed Forces Revolutionary Council
ANC	African National Congress
ARPS	Aborigines' Rights Protection Society
AWAM	Association of West African Merchants
CAA	Council on African Affairs
CIA	(US) Central Intelligence Agency
CPP	Convention People's Party
CUEA	Council of African Economic Unity
CYO	Committee on Youth Organisation
FBI	(US) Federal Bureau of Investigation
FLN	National Liberation Front (Algeria)
FRELIMO	Front for the Liberation of Mozambique
GNTC	Ghana National Trading Corporation
GPC	Ghana People's Congress
ICFTU	International Confederation of Free Trade Unions
IMF	International Monetary Fund
MNC	Movement National Congolais
MPLA	Movement for the Liberation of Angola
NAACP	National Association for the Advancement of Coloured People
NASSO	National African Socialist Students' Organisation
NATO	North Atlantic Treaty Organisation
NCBWA	National Congress of British West Africa
NCGW	National Council of Ghana Women
NCNC	National Council of Nigeria and the Cameroons
NGO	Non-Governmental Organisation

NLC	National Liberation Council
NLM	National Liberation Movement
NPP	Northern People's Party
NRC	National Redemption Council
OAMCE	Afro-Malagasy Economic Co-operation Organisation
OAU	Organisation of African Unity
OCAM	Organisation Commune Africaine et Malagache
OSPAAAL	Organisation of Solidarity of the Peoples of Africa, Asia and Latin America
PAC	PanAfrican National Congress
PAWA	PanAfrican Writers' Association
PDG	Parti Démocratique de Guinée
PAIGC	African Party for the Independence of Guinea and the Cape Verde Islands
SWAPO	South West African People's Organisation
TUC	Trades Union Congress
UAC	United Africa Company
UAM	Afro-Malagasy Union
UAS	Union of African States
UDI	Unilateral Declaration of Independence
UGCC	United Gold Coast Convention
UN	United Nations
UP	United Party
UTC	Union Trading Company
WANS	West African National Secretariat
WAYL	West African Youth League
WFTU	World Federation of Trade Unions
WAS U	West African Students' Union
ZANU	Zimbabwe African National Union
ZAPU	Zimbabwe African People's Union

Illustrations

PART ONE

1

Early Years in the Gold Coast and the USA

On 7 July 1972, an Air Guinée aircraft took off from Conakry airport and landed in Accra. It bore the coffin of Kwame Nkrumah for burial in the village of Nkroful, his birthplace in Western Ghana. Nkrumah died on 27 April 1972 in Bucharest where he had gone for medical treatment and the coffin had been flown to Guinea three days later.

In Nkroful, Nkrumah's mother, Nyanibah, in her nineties and almost blind, awaited the arrival of the coffin. Ever since the 24 February 1966 coup which had led to her son's exile in Guinea, she had always believed he would one day return home, and she was determined to stay alive to greet him. When the news of his death was broken to her she at first refused to believe it. There followed nearly three months of negotiations between the Guinean and Ghanaian governments before President Sékou Touré of Guinea finally allowed the coffin to be taken to Ghana. Even then, it was only after Nyanibah was led to where the coffin rested, and her right arm was placed upon it, that she at last accepted that her son was dead.

Nkrumah, born in Nkroful, home of the Nzima people, was named Francis Nwia-Kofi. Among the Akans importance is attached to the day of the week on which a child is born, each day corresponding with a different name. As Nyanibah's son was born on a Saturday he was called 'Kwame'. He was the first and only child of his mother, and this partly explains the exceptionally close bond which developed between them, and which was lifelong. Although Nkrumah throughout his life defended the privacy of his personal life, he seemed to make an exception as far as his mother was concerned. He would often talk of her. He used to recall how, when he was very young, he once rebuked her for not providing him with brothers and sisters, and she replied: 'You see the big trees in the forest? They stand alone.' His *Autobiography*, published in 1957 which he dedicated to her, contains many tender references: 'There was something about her presence, her quiet decisive movements, that placed her above most people.'[1]

When Nkrumah was born, Ghana had not been born. It was still the Gold Coast, a colony of Britain. Living conditions for Africans were similar to those applying in most colonial territories at that time. In his book *Africa Must Unite*, Nkrumah described the social and economic environment of the colonial period:

> 'The failure to promote the interests of our people was due to the insatiable demands of colonial exploitation. However wise, enlightened and good-hearted certain individual officers may have been, their functions and authority fitted into a pattern of colonial administration itself conditioned by the central and overall need to extract the riches of the colonies and transfer them overseas. If in the process it was necessary to build some roads, to construct a harbour and to educate some Africans, well and good. The point I want to make is that any welfare activity for the benefit of our people was little more than incidental.'[2]

Certainly, life in Nkroful was much as it had been in pre-colonial days. There was no piped water. Water had to be carried in pots or pails from the nearest source. The walk there and back could be arduous and long. Housing, health and educational facilities were hopelessly inadequate.

Until he was almost three years old, Nkrumah lived alone with his mother in Nkroful, then a typical West African village 'composed of small mud and wattle houses and bamboo compounds.'[3] Then they went to join his father who was a goldsmith working in Half Assini,

---

1. *Ghana – Autobiography of Kwame Nkrumah*. First published in 1957. Panaf edition 1973, p. 5.
2. *Africa Must Unite, Kwame Nkrumah*. First published in 1963. Panaf edition 1970, p. 31.
3. *Ghana – Autobiography*, p. 4.

some fifty miles west of Nkroful on the border of Ivory Coast. There was no bus or lorry transport in those days, and only very rudimentary roads. The journey therefore had to be on foot. It took nearly three days, the nights being spent in the open, beside a fire lit to keep wild animals away.

In his *Autobiography*, Nkrumah described his father as 'a man of strong character, extremely kind and very proud of his children.'[1] It was a happy time for the young Nkrumah in Half Assini. For although he was the only child of his mother and father, there were many children born to other wives of his father. The compound was usually full of people. For apart from the immediate family of fourteen,there were usually other relatives staying there. The women used to take it in turns to cook meals and to look after the children, while others worked on the land or did petty trading to supplement the family income. 'It was a lovely time for us children with nothing to do but play around all day.... Our playground was vast and varied, for we had the sea, the lagoon and the thrill of unexplored bush all within easy reach',[2] yet he continues: 'My happiest hours were spent alone. I used to wonder off on my own and spend hours on end quietly observing the birds and the lesser animals of the forest and listening to their numerous and varied calls.'[3]

In the first school which Nkrumah attended, all grades were taught in the same room.The fees were threepence a month. The young Nkrumah thought this was a lot of money for his parents to provide. He therefore for a time reared a few chickens and sold them for sixpence each to help with the fees, and to provide some cash to buy books.

It was at primary school that Nkrumah came under the influence of a German Roman Catholic priest, George Fischer, who helped him with his studies, and acted almost as a guardian. Nkrumah's mother had been converted to Roman Catholicism. It was through her that Nkrumah was baptised into the RC Church. His father, who was 'not at all religious,' evidently had no objection. Nkrumah as he grew older, did not adhere to any religious denomination. He developed his own personal beliefs, and did not feel the need for any direction from, or attachment to, a third party in the conduct of 'such a personal matter.'[4]

---

1. *Ghana – Autobiography*, p. 5.
2. Ibid., p. 7.
3.   "   p. 8.
4.   "   p. 12.

When his years at the elementary school ended, Nkrumah became a pupil teacher at Half Assini. He was then seventeen years old. In 1926, the Principal of the Government Training College in Accra visited the school where he was teaching, and was so impressed that he recommended he should go to his college to train as a teacher. It was to mark a turning point in his life.

For apart from the obvious impact made on him of going from life in a small village to living in the busy, teeming city of Accra, it could be said to mark the start of his active interest in politics.

When he enrolled in the Accra Training College in 1927, the Assistant Vice Principal was Dr Kwegyir Aggrey, the first African member of staff, and a teacher of exceptional skill and personality.

Nkrumah wrote in his *Autobiography*: 'To me he seemed the most remarkable man that I had met and I had the deepest affection for him.'[1] Aggrey was then at the height of his powers. Apart from his teaching work, he used to address huge audiences in Accra exhorting them to realise their great African heritage, and to be worthy of it. His personality and the way in which he was able to awaken a strong nationalist fervour in his audiences impressed Nkrumah so much that he seldom missed one of his performances. Almost fifty years after the death of Aggrey, Nkrumah was able to recount almost word for word an allegory which Aggrey told during one of his mass meetings in Accra. Copying Aggrey's voice and gestures, Nkrumah related how an eagle had been captured and put among chickens. It was fed on chickens' food, and grew to behave just like a chicken. Then one day a naturalist visited the farm and asked the farmer about the eagle. The farmer said the bird was no longer an eagle. It had been fed on chickens' food and was a chicken. The naturalist disagreed. 'No, it is still an eagle'. The farmer, to prove his point, lifted the eagle into his hands and spread its wings. The eagle rose into the air, for a moment, then descended among the chickens again. The farmer repeated the experiment several times, and each time the eagle merely flew in a small circle and alighted again among the chickens. The naturalist remained unconvinced. 'No, it is still an eagle', he said. The following morning, just as dawn was breaking he said he would prove his point. Knowing the ways of the eagles, he lifted the bird high in his hands and faced it towards the rising sun. Then he told it that it was no chicken but a fine mighty eagle with beautiful strong wings, and that it should fly

---

1. *Autobiography*, p. 14.

away into the sky where it belonged. The eagle spread its wings and rose steadily into the air, flying higher and higher, into the dawn rays of the sun, until it became a tiny speck in the distance, finally disappearing from sight. After a pause, Aggrey would point at his audience and declare: 'You are an eagle. You have been put among chickens and fed with all kinds of chickens' food, but you are an eagle'. He would spread his arms wide indicating the rising eagle. At this point the crowd, Nkrumah said, which had until then been listening with deepest concentration to his every word, would break out into excited chattering and cheering.

Aggrey died suddenly in the USA while on a visit, and his death was a severe blow to his students at the Training College, and to his many friends and followers. His death occurred during Nkrumah's first year at the College and very close in time to the death from blood poisoning of his father. The loss of the two men who at that time were closest to Nkrumah affected him deeply. In honour of Aggrey, Nkrumah with other students formed the Aggrey Students' Society. It was a debating society, and soon Nkrumah began to make a reputation for himself as an able and persuasive speaker. It was at this time, and largely as a result of Aggrey's influence, that he resolved to try to further his education in the USA by gaining entry to Lincoln University, founded in 1854 to provide higher education for people of African descent. Nkrumah's plan was to finish his course at the Accra Training College, then teach for five years to save enough for the cost of his passage to America.

After graduating from the Training College in 1930, he became a primary school teacher at the Roman Catholic Junior School at Elmina where he taught Lower Class One. A year later he was promoted to the position of Head Teacher of the Roman Catholic Junior School at Axim, where he spent the next two years. It was then that he formally applied for entry to Lincoln University. On his application form in the space provided for a short account of his life giving the main facts of his scholastic record, and the reasons for wishing to attend Lincoln University he wrote:

'I neither know where to begin nor where to end, because I feel that the story of my life has not been one of achievements. Furthermore, I have not been anxious to tell people of what may have been accomplished by me.'

After a brief summary of his education, he ended:

'In all things, I have held myself to but one ambition, and that is, to make necessary arrangements to continue my education in

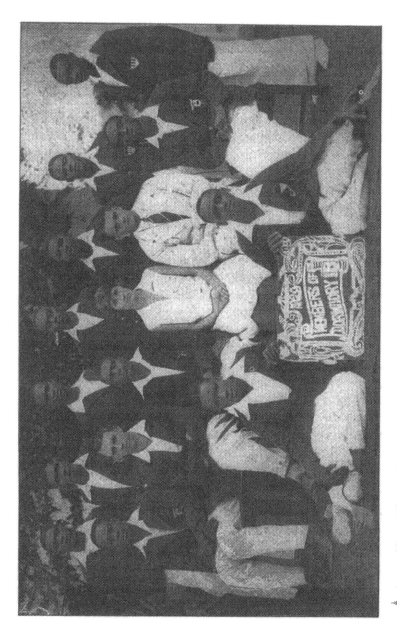

Aggrey House, Nkrumah is seated first on the left — Achimota, 1929

a university of the United States of America that I may be better prepared, and still be of better use to my fellow men. Such is the brief history of my life, and I am forced to conclude with the words: (from Tennyson's In Memoriam) "So much to do, so little done".'

News of the acceptance of his application came while Nkrumah was teaching at Amissano, near Elmina. There still remained the problem of raising sufficient money for the passage to the USA. His meagre savings were not nearly sufficient to cover the costs. He therefore stowed away on a ship to Lagos in order to visit a relative who was in a position to help. The relative gave him some money, and this together with his own savings, and a contribution from the Chief of Nsaeum, another relative, was enough for a third class ticket from the Gold Coast port of Takoradi to Liverpool in England. He had to travel via Britain in order to get a US visa since there was then no American consul in the Gold Coast.

By this time, Nkrumah's interest in politics had become firmly established. Aggrey had introduced him to the work of W.E.B. DuBois and Marcus Garvey, African Americans who had already done much to stimulate nationalist and PanAfrican movements. Nkrumah had met Nnamdi Azikiwe (ZIK), an ardent Nigerian nationalist from Onitsha, who had impressed him deeply, and whose newspaper articles in the *African Morning Post* attacking colonialism and racial inequalities, he regularly read.

Also living in Accra at this time was Wallace Johnson, the Sierra Leonean editor of the *African Sentinel*, another strongly African nationalist paper. Wallace Johnson, together with Bankole Awooner-Renner and Wuta-Ofei had founded the West African Youth League (WAYL), branches of which were established throughout the country, including Axim and Half Assini. Both Azikiwe and Wallace Johnson were then major influences in the political life of the Gold Coast. Like Aggrey, Azikiwe had studied in America. He added his encouragement to Nkrumah to complete his education there.

Nkrumah gained further inspiration from the activities of the National Congress of British West Africa (NCBWA), founded in 1920 to campaign for political, social and economic reform in all the colonial territories of West Africa, including those suffering under French colonial rule.The Gold Coast barrister J.E. Caseley-Hayford and T. Hutton Mills were founder members. The NCBWA quickly filled the gap left by the declining influence of the Aborigines' Rights' Protection Society (ARPS), formed in 1897, and regarded as the first organisation of its kind to campaign for the rights of Africans.

By the time, therefore, Nkrumah was ready to leave the Gold Coast to enter Lincoln University he was totally committed to pursue the agenda which he had developed in the exciting political environment of his youth.

When all was arranged for the journey, Nkrumah went home to spend a few days with his mother and to tell her his plans. They sat up all night the day before he left, Nyanibah giving him advice and reminding him of his family history. She told him about Chief Aduku Addaie, the first of his ancestors to settle in Nzima, whose sister Nwia gave birth to his matrilineal line. Nkrumah had claim, she said, to two chieftaincy stools, those of Nsaeum in Wassaw Fiase and Dadieso in Aowin.

The following morning, Nkrumah with his few possessions crossed the Ankobra River by canoe, on the first stage of his journey to the port of Takoradi where he was to embark on the MV Apapa destined for Liverpool. It was to be twelve years before Nkrumah and his mother were to see each other again.

An agent of George Grant, a timber merchant from Nzima, popularly known as Pa Grant, met Nkrumah when the Apapa docked in Liverpool. Nkrumah stayed in Liverpool for a week to acclimatise and to prepare for his visit to London to obtain a visa for the USA. For someone who had never been outside West Africa, the impact made by his first personal contact with western civilisation must have been immense, and in some aspects shocking. However it was minor compared with the impression made on him later when he first saw New York.

It was while he was in London that he heard of the invasion of Abyssinia (Ethiopia), as it was then named, by the forces of the Italian dictator Mussolini. The news angered him. This was yet another example of the rapacity of colonialism: 'My nationalism surged to the fore.' He wrote later in his *Autobiography* that news of the invasion made him determined 'to go through hell itself' if need be to free his country from colonial rule.

Having obtained a visa from the US authorities, Nkrumah returned to Liverpool where he stayed a fortnight with the timber merchant's family before embarking for the USA on a ship of the Cunard White Star Line. It was to be a more pleasant voyage than the one from the Gold

Coast to Britain, because Nkrumah was able to make several lasting friendships. Notable among them was with a Dutchman on his way to complete his theological studies at the Harvard Divinity School.

On his arrival in New York, on 22 October 1935 Nkrumah went straight to Harlem to the home of a Sierra Leonean, a graduate of Lincoln University, who had sent him his address. Although made very welcome, Nkrumah was only able to stay two days with him. The academic year had begun at Lincoln, and Nkrumah was already nearly two months behind schedule.

Nkrumah enrolled at Lincoln temporarily and on probation, though he soon passed the entrance examination and won a scholarship which helped him to complete his degree course. When he entered Lincoln he possessed only £40. It was necessary, therefore, to earn money to provide the full cost of his fees and to maintain himself. He helped fellow students with their essays, and by writing summaries of books for them at a dollar a time.

During vacations, and also sometimes during term-time he took whatever job he could find. It was not easy to find employment during those post-depression years in the USA, especially if one was black. Racial discrimination was rife. Non-professional black people were virtually confined to working in menial, poorly paid and often degrading jobs. Even those professionally qualified found it difficult to find work and advancement because of their colour.

Nkrumah tried selling fish from a barrow in Harlem, but had to give it up when handling the fish caused a skin complaint. He then took a job in a soap factory. His task was to load the rotting entrails and lumps of animal fat which had been dumped by lorries in the factory yard into a wheelbarrow, and to push the loads to the processing plant.

There was a time when he worked outside at night from midnight to 8 a.m., in all weather, in the Sun Shipbuilding Yard at Chester, Pennsylvania. Sometimes it was bitterly cold. He eventually developed pneumonia. He collapsed at work, was rushed to hospital and almost died.

Less hard and healthier work was found when he managed to obtain employment on a ship of the Clyde Mallory Line, sailing between New York and Vera Cruz in Mexico. He had signed on for his first voyage as a waiter, but was soon found to be unqualified for the job and was demoted to the kitchens. On subsequent trips he was given better work, becoming a steward for a time. Nkrumah's days at sea ended when the Second World War broke out. He had enjoyed his days at sea: 'The pay was reasonably good and we were always assured of three good meals a day.'[1]

Throughout his time in America, when not living in university accommodation, Nkrumah found it difficult to find lodgings which were affordable and which were available for non-whites. While in New York, he sometimes used to buy a subway ticket for a nickel and spend the night travelling backwards and forwards between Brooklyn and Harlem. Other times he had to resort to resting on a bench in a railway station or a public park until moved on by the police. If it was raining, he would shelter in doorways. But things improved when he discovered he could attend black religious and revivalist meetings, notable among them being a movement headed by Father Divine. At such meetings he could get shelter and a satisfying meal for half a dollar and a haircut for only ten cents.

When Nkrumah was studying at Lincoln he regularly spent some of his free time preaching in African American churches, which doubled as community centres. He thoroughly enjoyed the experience. His sermons, like those of most other preachers contained a strong political message.

The daunting challenges and problems faced by Nkrumah when a student and worker in the USA, seemed to act as a spur to his academic efforts. At Lincoln and then at Philadelphia University he achieved impressive examination success. At Lincoln he was consistently awarded high marks. He also excelled in other University activities. In 1936 he was placed second in the Kappa Alpha Psi oratorical contest, open to all freshmen. Two years later he won the Robert Fleming Labaree Memorial prize in social science, for a dissertation on the topic, 'Imperialism: Its Political, Social and Economic Aspects'. The following year, in 1939, he graduated with a BA degree in Economics and Sociology, coming sixth in a class of forty six.

After graduation, he enrolled at the Lincoln Theological Seminary, and also at the University of Pennsylvania for two Masters' degree courses, in Philosophy and Education. He completed his theology course at Lincoln in 1942, graduating top of the class. In the same year, he gained an MA in Philosophy, and a year later an MSc in Education from the University of Philadelphia. It was a prodigious academic record, the result of unremitting hard study.

---

1. *Ghana – Autobiography*, p. 39.

Among the titles of some of the papers written by him during his student days in the USA the following examples show the subjects in which he was particularly interested:

- Primitive education in West Africa
- The significance of African Art
- Labour problems in Africa
- A critical study of the relation of Christianity to non-Christian religions

In a letter to Dr Morrow of the University of Pennsylvania dated 5 March 1942, he wrote:

'Concerning the thesis topic under consideration, I should like to inform that on account of my previous experience and interests, I have selected the following: 'The Philosophy of Imperialism with special reference to Africa'. For many years I have accumulated material to that effect, and consequently should like to make a more detailed study of it with reference to the major thought trends of Europe in the nineteenth and twentieth centuries.'

During these years of intensive study Nkrumah found time for participation in such activities as the Fireside Club at Lincoln, described as a 'contemplative group'. He also joined the Philosophy and Science Clubs. He was a popular and much respected student. In the humorous section of the 1939 edition of *Lion*, the annual university publication, Nkrumah is described as the 'most interesting' of those at Lincoln. A verse accompanied a photograph of him:

Africa is the beloved of his dreams,
Philosopher, thinker, with forceful schemes,
In aesthetics, politics, he's in the field
Nkrumah, *très intéressant*, radiates appeal.

While at the University of Pennsylvania, Nkrumah helped to set up an African Studies Section, and to organise the African Students' Association of America and Canada. It was a PanAfrican association, its purpose being to link up the national liberation movements of Africa with the struggles of those of African descent living in the USA. A newspaper for the Association was founded called the *African Interpreter*. 'We believed that unless territorial freedom was ultimately linked up with the PanAfrican movement for the liberation of the whole African continent, there would be no hope of freedom and equality for the African and for people of African descent in any part of the world.'[1]

He was also involved with the establishment of an Institute of African Languages and Culture. Under the direction of Dr Zelig Harris, the object of the Institute was to promote the learning of African languages. Nkrumah was one of several scholars who worked with Dr Harris on the teaching of Moroccan Arabic, Swahili, Hausa and Fanti. At the Fanti summer School of 1942, Nkrumah was employed as an instructor. The course was reported a success in the *Pennsylvania Gazette*: 'Mr. Francis N. Nkrumah, a native of the Gold Coast and a graduate student of the University, was with the class the entire summer, and he is confident that any of the students could easily obtain all the necessities of daily life among speakers of Fanti'. A further achievement of the Institute was the compilation of a grammar of Fanti.

In numerous articles written at this time and at public meetings and lectures, Nkrumah urged Africans to hold to their ideals in opposing fascism and imperialism. He referred to the general statement of principles expressed in the *Atlantic Charter*, signed in August 1941 by the US President Roosevelt and the British Prime Minister Winston Churchill in which they declared their respect for the right of all peoples to choose the form of government under which they would live. Churchill later rejected the suggestion that this principle applied to African issues, but the Labour Party leader in Britain, Clement Attlee, supported the contrary view. In an article which appeared in *Educational Outlook* in November 1943, Nkrumah called on the youth of Africa to continue the fight against fascism and imperialism adhering to the principles of freedom expressed in the Atlantic Charter.

In America, Nkrumah had learned much about the problems and techniques of political organisation. He had come into contact with the work of the Council on African Affairs (CAA), the Committee on Africa, the Committee of African Students, the Special Research Council of the National Association for the Advancement of Coloured People (NAACP) and the Urban League. He was familiar with the work of Caribbean thinkers and activists, George Padmore and C.L.R. James, identifying with their left wing views and PanAfricanism. Furthermore, he had studied in depth the ideas of Marcus Garvey, Hegel, Marx,

---

1. *Ghana – Autobiography*, p. 44.

Engels, Lenin and Mazzini and others whose thoughts or actions might have relevance, or help him to prepare for the liberation struggle he intended to pursue as soon as he returned to Africa.

The book which inspired him most was *Philosophy and Opinions of Marcus Garvey* with its philosophy of 'Africa for the Africans' and the 'Back to Africa' movement. Nkrumah, however, always maintained that no mass exodus of Africans in the diaspora to Africa was either desirable or practicable until the continent was fully liberated and unified.

In March 1944, Nkrumah became one of the sponsors of a conference on 'Africa: New Perspectives', called for April 1944, by the Council on African Affairs. Among notable members of the CAA were Paul Robeson, Alphaeus Hunton, Ralph Bunche and others with strong Left-wing views. Nkrumah represented the African Students' Association at the conference which was attended by some 150 delegates. The conference resolved to call on the US government to uphold the Atlantic Charter, and to encourage the liberation and development of Africa. In addition, a decision was taken to review the PanAfrican Congresses, and to hold the next one in Britain following the end of the war. Nkrumah retained his links with the CAA until 1954 when the organisation collapsed as a result of anti-Communist pressure. At Nkrumah's invitation Alphaeus Hunton went to live in Ghana in 1961. Paul Robeson was invited at the same time but was too ill to accept.

It was while in the USA that Nkrumah wrote the first draft of *Towards Colonial Freedom*, which was later published in London soon after the Fifth PanAfrican Congress which had taken place in Manchester in 1945. In this booklet the political stand of Nkrumah is clearly stated. While some of his fellow Africans were giving priority to chasing degrees in order to get higher positions in the colonial administrative system, Nkrumah was grappling with theoretical problems, one of which was the origins of colonialism. Once he could satisfy himself as to how it arose, what factors governed its development, what forces had been thrown up in the process, then he would be in a position to know how it could be ended. Inevitably, in his researches he was drawn towards scientific socialism which he considered could provide the formula by which the problems of imperialism, colonialism, and racism, could be solved.

Nkrumah rejected outright the notion that colonialism was a result of the desire by the European nations to 'civilize' the 'barbarous' peoples of the world. Neither did he accept the view held by many in the African nationalist movement at the time, that colonisation represented simply the conquest by white nations of black people. Nkrumah examined the economics of colonialism. He observed that by the end of the nineteenth century, capitalism had reached the imperialist stage. This was the result of the development of contradictions within the capitalist system which, among other things, necessitated the export of finance capital as well as the export of commodities. This involved the political control of the areas in which investment was made. He defined colonialism as: 'The policy by which the 'mother county', the colonial power binds her colonies to herself by political ties with the primary object of promoting her own economic advantages.'[1] It followed that just as the basis of colonial territorial dependence was economic, 'the basis of the solution to the problem is political.'[2]

He did not envisage the programme of the national liberation movement just as one of the national independence, but also as a means to bring about a society in which people would be free from poverty and economic exploitation. In other words, independence was a means to an end, which aimed at social and economic justice. This wider conception of the programme of the national movement also showed itself in its composition. He did not see the movement as being confined to a few intellectuals and the privileged strata of society. He visualized it as one which would draw in the broad masses of the people. But how to achieve this? First and foremost, 'Organization of the Colonial Masses.'[3] In *Towards Colonial Freedom* he stressed the point that the organization must root itself and secure its basis and strength in the labour movement, and the youth. 'These form the motive force of the colonial liberation movement and as they develop and gain political consciousness, so the drive for liberation leaves the sphere of mere ideas and become more real.' He subsequently, when in England, ended *Towards Colonial Freedom* with a stirring call, 'PEOPLES OF THE COLONIES, UNITE: The working men of all countries are behind you.'[4]

In 1962, nearly twenty years after *Towards Colonial Freedom* was written, it was republished. In the foreword to the new edition, Nkrumah

---

1. *Towards Colonial Freedom*, Kwame Nkrumah. First published in 1962. Panaf edtition 1973, p. 2.
2. *Towards Colonial Freedom*, 1973, p. xv.
3. *Ibid.*, p. 41.
4.   "   p. 43.

wrote: 'Firstly, this booklet is exactly as it was written originally, that is, twenty years ago, no changes or corrections have been made and nothing has been added or taken from it. Secondly, the views I expressed then are precisely the views I hold today concerning the unspeakably inhuman nature of imperialism and colonialism. Furthermore, most of the points I made then have been borne out to the letter, and confirmed by subsequent developments in Africa and Asia.'[1]

Nkrumah's activities while in the USA attracted the attention of the Federal Bureau of Investigation (FBI), as their recently released records show. Initially, the Bureau had difficulty in tracing him because his name was misspelt as 'Ukrumah'. In a case report made in Philadelphia on 12 January 1845,[2] and classified as a 'Security matter,' their agent reveals that a fruitless search was made of the records of the Immigration and Naturalisation Services. A search of the Voters' Registration for the County of Philadelphia also failed to 'locate anyone bearing the name of Ukrumah.'[3] Further enquiries were made in other areas but without success.

The following month, the FBI agent examined State Department files to discover if a passport had been applied for, or had been issued to 'Ukrumah.' Once again, the search proved unproductive. In March 1945, it was finally discovered that the person they were researching was incorrectly named. From then onwards, the name appearing on FBI reports was changed to Francis Nwia-Kofi Nkrumah. In file No.100-21745 the following information appears:

'Subject registered as an alien on 10/6/40 A.R#2855567. Born 9/21/09 at Nkroful, Gold Coast, West Africa. Arrived at port of New York 10/17/35 on SS Samara with a student's visa.'

Subsequent FBI reports are increasingly censored, and this some twenty-three years after his death. Whole sentences and paragraphs are blacked out. However, it is clear from what remains that FBI surveillance on Nkrumah was kept up for the rest of the time he was in the USA. FBI agents continued to check on whether there was 'any evidence of communistic or other subversive activity.'

---

1. *Towards Colonial Freedom*, p. x.
2. File No. 100 – 21745 EPS.
3. File No. 100 – 21745 EPS 5/29/45.

Investigations at Lincoln University revealed that Nkrumah had 'attended the school from September 1935 to June 6, 1939 at which time he received an A.B Degree.He is presently teaching at the school part time, but is expected to leave for London, England, to study law. Exit Permit issued by LB#3, Coatesville, Pa, 5/14/45. He is classified 4-D'. [1]

Continuing to report on Nkrumah's record at Lincoln University, the FBI agent stated that, 'The subject had been considered a good student ... and he had not been involved in any subversive activities while on the campus....That while the subject had lacked leadership on the campus and had not shown initiative, he was considered loyal and honest.' He showed 'no radical tendencies' although a member of the African Council on American Education. [2]

Studying the FBI files on Nkrumah, one is astonished at the incompetence of the Bureau, and lack of judgement revealed in their agent's assessment of Nkrumah's potential, though it is possible that if the blacked-out parts of the report could be read, a different picture might emerge. Nkrumah was clearly a candidate for FBI interest in view of the impact he was making on African American opinion through his public speaking, and his research into racial problems in the USA. He was making an intensive study of the conditions of African Americans from a religious, economic and social standpoint. This necessitated visiting over six hundred homes in Philadelphia alone. He made similar surveys in German Town and in Reading, Pennsylvania.These surveys and his preachings, notably in the McDowell Presbyterian Church in Philadelphia, when he invariably included speaking of the struggles of the African peoples for freedom, did not go unnoticed by the authorities.

In his *Autobiography* he headed the chapter on the years he spent in America 'Hard Times'. While he makes no mention of suspecting he was under FBI surveillance, he probably realised he must be attracting hostile attention in view of the existing political and racial climate of the time.

Though largely occupied with studies and politics, Nkrumah found time for some social life. He made many friends, some of them through his preaching in 'Negro' churches which doubled as community centres. For a time he preached most Sundays. It was after preaching in a Baptist church in Philadelphia that he was introduced to Portia, who

---

1. File No. 100 – 21745 EPS 5/29/45.
2   Ibid.

became a valued friend. Nkrumah maintained that he never wanted to get too involved with a woman because he knew that marriage and a family could never be central to his life which he had dedicated to the achievement of political goals. Yet throughout his life he never lacked the company and loyalty of those women who at various times became his close companions.

One such, dating from the years he spent in America, was Christine X Johnson. In her book *Ghana Under Nkrumah*,[1] she tells how she met Nkrumah at a students' gathering in Harlem. She describes him as 'a young man wearing glasses, who was introduced as 'Kwame Francis Nkrumah'. She used to taunt him about his country still being a colony. 'Why do you say you have a country, when someone else is running it?' She found the ensuing heated exchanges stimulating and informative. 'Nkrumah,' she writes, 'was a quiet and very serious young man. His voice and mannerisms and what he said made us all stop and listen.'[2] As time went by her respect and admiration for him grew, as did their friendship. Nkrumah was a good dancer, she writes, and often took her out to dance. 'In those days there was no money. Often we walked in the park and ate popcorn and peanuts, because neither of us had the price of a movie ... we were more pals than sweethearts.'[3]

After Nkrumah left the USA in 1945, they did not communicate until 1947 when Christine Johnson wrote to him, having read in the *Chicago Defender* that there had been 'Some trouble in the Gold Coast, and Nkrumah was to blame.' It was the time of Positive Action. Subsequently, Nkrumah invited her for Independence Day on 6 March 1957, but she did not visit Ghana until the following August. There she met Mrs Marcus Garvey and Dr W.E.B. DuBois and his wife Shirley Graham DuBois, who had been invited to live in Ghana as honoured guests. Nkrumah never forgot old friends.

In every way, Nkrumah's ten years in America left indelible marks. His experiences as student, academic and worker in America in the mid-thirties and early forties gave him a profound understanding of the problems of the diaspora. It was during this formative period that the seeds of his lifelong commitment to PanAfricanism were sown.

---

1. Published in the USA by the author in 1994.
2. Ibid.
3. *Ghana Under Nkrumah*, p. 2.

Throughout his life there was seldom a time when persons of African descent from the USA and the Caribbean were not among his immediate entourage.One of the most eminent was George Padmore, who for some years was his adviser on African affairs.

There were many more from the diaspora who were in close contact with him both during the period of his government, and afterwards, during the years he spent in Conakry following the 1966 coup in Ghana. It was this rapport with peoples of African descent living beyond the shores of Africa which contributed so much to the development of his radicalism and his vision of a united Africa, the ultimate fulfilment of what he termed the African Personality.

2

In London

Nkrumah left the USA for Britain in May 1945 armed with the draft of *Towards Colonial Freedom* and firmly committed to the anti-colonial struggle. He intended to make contact with the African national movement in London, and at the same time to complete his studies. In October 1945, he arranged to attend lectures at the London School of Economics as a PhD candidate in Anthropology. But disliking the subject, he withdrew after one term, and entered University College, London, to work for a doctorate in Philosophy. The thesis he chose was 'Knowledge and Logical Positivism.' His supervisor was the renowned Professor A.J. Ayer. Nkrumah also registered as a student of Law at Gray's Inn in November 1946.

When Nkrumah arrived in London, plans were being made for a Fifth PanAfrican Congress to be held in Manchester from 13–21 October 1945. Nkrumah was already in touch with one of the organisers of the Congress, George Padmore. He wrote to Padmore before he left America, asking him if he could meet him at Euston Station on his arrival in London.

Padmore duly met him and took him to the West African Students' Union (WASU) where a room was provided for him. WASU had been founded in 1927 by a Nigerian lawyer, Ladipo Solanke and Dr Bankole Bright of Sierra Leone. It became a centre for mainly West African students, providing hostel accommodation, and opportunities for debate and discussion on political and racial issues, and to organise action.

It was at WASU, a few days after Nkrumah's arrival, that he met Kojo Botsio, who was to become a close friend and colleague. Botsio, some fifty years afterwards, still retained vivid memories of that time: 'We had not heard of him before, but were captivated by his oratory and what he had to say about the colonial struggle. His boldness and courage in assailing the colonial system was electrifying. We had come down from Oxford for the Easter holidays. A few meetings with him made me decide not to pursue any legal studies which I had planned to do, but to take to teaching in London so that I could be near him always.'[1]

Nkrumah soon found living conditions at WASU restrictive, and so set out to find suitable lodgings. In those days, after the war, accommodation was scarce, and particularly hard to find for Africans. Accompanied by his friend, Ako Adjei, they often had doors slammed in their faces. At last, however, they found a welcome at Number 60, Burghley Road, in the Tufnell Park area. They had just knocked on the door to ask if there was a room to let when opening the door to them stood Florence Manly. They could not have encountered a kinder or more sympathetic person. Nkrumah was shown a room which was to be his home for the whole of his stay in London, from June 1945 until November 1947.

There, Florence and her young daughter, Christine, treated him as a member of the family. Although he worked long and irregular hours, being seldom in before midnight, he always found food left for him. By way of return he insisted that all the washing up was left for him to do before he went to his room. There, the light often used to be on until two in the morning. Reminiscing about those days, years afterwards, Florence said that the two things she would always remember about Nkrumah were how hard he worked, and his great kindness. Not only did he help with household chores, washing up, cleaning all the shoes and so on, but he found time to help with Christine. He would carry her around on his shoulders. There was a time when Christine, recovering from illness, refused to take her tonic unless Nkrumah first had a spoonful. When Florence had a poisoned leg he used to phone her during the day to ask if she was resting it.

Within a month of Nkrumah's arrival in London, he was hard at work with Padmore, Ras T. Makonnen from British Guiana (Guyana) and Peter Abrahams, the South African writer, preparing for the Fifth PanAfrican Congress. He became joint secretary with Padmore of the

1. Kojo Botsio. Recorded interview with June Milne, London. 5 September 1995.

organisation committee. Together, from Padmore's small flat, they sent out hundreds of letters to people and organisations throughout Africa, the USA, Europe and the Caribbean, informing them of the Congress, its objectives, and inviting them to attend.

The Fifth, like the four previous Congresses, was held outside Africa. The First took place in Paris in 1919. The Second and Third were held in London in 1921 and 1923 respectively. The Fourth was in New York in 1927. The Fifth was held in Manchester in October 1945, under the joint chairmanship of Dr W.E.B. DuBois and Peter Milliard, a doctor of medicine from Guyana, one of the founders of the National Association of the Advancement of Coloured Peoples. This Congress differed from the four previous ones, which had been composed largely of members of the professions and intelligentsia:

'For the first time there was a strong worker and student participation, and most of the over two hundred delegates who attended came from Africa. They represented re-awakening African political consciousness, and it was no surprise when the Congress adopted socialism as its political philosophy.'[1]

The Congress urged Africans and peoples of African descent to organise into political parties, trade unions, co-operatives and so on to campaign for political and economic advancement. Unlike previous Congresses, it set the pattern for mass participation in the PanAfrican movement.

Two declarations, one drawn up by DuBois and the other by Nkrumah, were passed by the Congress. Both asserted the right and determination of the colonial peoples to be free, and condemned capitalism. Colonial peoples were urged to set up the necessary organisational machinery to bring about the ending of colonialism as a pre-condition for ending of all forms of oppression. The Declaration written by Nkrumah follows:

'We believe in the rights of all peoples to govern themselves. We affirm the rights of all colonial peoples to control their own destiny. All colonies must be free from foreign imperialist control, whether political or economic. The peoples of the colonies must have the right to elect their own government, a government without restrictions from a foreign power. We say to the peoples of the

---

1. *Revolutionary Path*, Kwame Nkrumah, Panaf 1973, p. 42.

colonies that they must strive for these ends by all means at their disposal.

The object of imperialist powers is to exploit. By granting the right to the colonial peoples to govern themselves, they are defeating that objective. Therefore, the struggle for political power by colonial and subject peoples is the first step towards, and the necessary pre-requisite to, complete social, economic and political emancipation.

The Fifth PanAfrican Congress, therefore, calls on the workers and farmers of the colonies to organise effectively. Colonial workers must be in the front lines of the battle against imperialism.

This Fifth PanAfrican Congress calls on the intellectual and professional classes of the colonies to awaken to their responsibilities. The long, long night is over. By fighting for trade union rights, the right to form co-operatives, freedom of the press, assembly, demonstration and strike; freedom to print and read the literature which is necessary for the education of the masses, you will be using the only means by which your liberties will be won and maintained. Today there is only one road to effective action — the organisation of the masses.

COLONIAL AND SUBJECT PEOPLES OF THE WORLD — UNITE!'

The Congress set up a working committee to organise the putting into effect of the political programme which had been agreed upon. Dr DuBois headed it, while Nkrumah was appointed general secretary. Nkrumah, Padmore, and Makonnen left Manchester for London as soon as the Congress ended, while Jomo Kenyatta the Kenyan nationalist and Dr Milliard remained in Manchester to organise the PanAfrican Federation there. The PanAfrican Federation's aims were independence for all colonial peoples and the total abolition of racial inequality.

At this point, Ashie Nikoi, Wallace Johnson, Bankole Akpata, Awooner-Renner and Kojo Botsio urged Nkrumah to establish a West African National Secretariat (WANS) to co-ordinate the anti-colonial struggle throughout the whole of West Africa, to include non-British colonial territories. Under the chairmanship of Wallace Johnson, Nkrumah was appointed general secretary, Bankole Awooner-Renner president, and Kojo Botsio treasurer. An immediate objective of WANS was to call a West African conference in London. Nkrumah went to

Paris to meet the African members of the French National Assembly, among them Sourous Apithy of Benin, Leopold Senghor of Senegal, Lamine Guèye and Houphouet-Boigny of Ivory Coast. They discussed the whole question of a Union of West African Socialist Republics, but as Nkrumah wrote later: 'It was clear to me, even then, that men such as Senghor and Houphouet-Boigny, when they spoke of socialism, meant something very different from the scientific socialism to which I was committed.'[1]

As a result of Nkrumah's visit to Paris, Apithy and M. Benoit, a representative of Senghor's attended the West African Conference held in London from 30 August to 1 September. At this conference, Nkrumah read out the text of an agreed plan of action to achieve 'a politically independent and united West Africa and the holding of a congress on West Africa within the next year.'[2] It was agreed that the anti-imperialist movement should be based on socialist principles.

A small office in 94 Gray's Inn Road became the headquarters of WANS. It rapidly became a focal point for Africans, West Indians and peoples of African descent to meet and to plan. There were students, workers, lawyers, business people and others. At meetings and discussion groups policies were worked out and strategy and tactics prepared. According to Botsio: 'We were very much attached to the Labour Party, and we often went to the house of Geoffrey Bing Q.C. (later to become Ghana's Attorney-General). There we met British left-wing personalities such as Creech Jones (Secretary of State for the Colonies in 1946), Harold Wilson (later to become British Labour Party prime minister), and others for discussions or just a social evening. We met non-Labour MPs in the House of Commons.'[3]

The Secretariat was mainly financed by African businessmen, and by Africans visiting, studying or working in Britain. But raising sufficient funds to keep the Secretariat going was a constant problem. Padmore explained the dilemma graphically: 'Lack of money is our handicap, for unlike in America, we have no rich ones among us.... All the work that has been done in all these years has been done on a purely voluntary basis ... (but) men must eat.'[4] Kojo Botsio, like many others

---

1. *Revolutionary Path*, p. 46.
2. *West Africa*, 14 September, 1946, p. 845.
3. Kojo Botsio. Recorded interview with June Milne, London. 5 September 1995.
4. *Kwame Nkrumah, The Years Abroad 1935–1947*, Marika Sherwood, Freedom Publications, Legon, Ghana, 1996, p. 147. Padmore to Professor St Clair Drake.

fortunate enough to have paid employment, regularly gave some of his pay to help with expenses. When warden of the WASU hostel, Botsio contributed half of his salary.

The Secretariat was then the only African political forum in London. 'At times we (the Secretariat) had august visitors like Leopold Senghor of Senegal, Sourous Apithy of Benin, members of the French Parliament, Jomo Kenyatta, Dr Azikiwe and members of the National Council of Nigeria and the Cameroons (NCNC).'[1] Padmore and Botsio served as aides when their delegation arrived for talks at the Colonial Office about self-rule for Nigeria.

In March 1946, Nkrumah was able to scrape together £50 to publish the first edition of the Secretariat's monthly paper called *The New African*, sub-titled 'The Voice of the Awakened African', with the motto: 'For Unity and Absolute Independence.' The Editor was Nkrumah and the Managing Editor, Bankole Akpata. This newspaper, as the official organ of the Secretariat, would, it was hoped, help to publicise the organisation's policies and attract more support. Every copy of the first edition of the paper sold within a few hours of its publication. The editorial of the first issue stated that WANS stood for 'not only equality and justice in every respect, but for complete and absolute independence for Africa, (and) we have decided to dedicate our whole lives to the cause of this great struggle.' Subsequent issues carried the same message of independence and a united Africa. After some months, in spite of strenuous efforts to achieve financial viability, the paper had to cease publication.

Nkrumah spent most days at the office in Gray's Inn Road, and often most of the evenings at meetings and discussion groups which frequently continued until late into the night. He had scarcely enough money to pay for his lodgings, and very little for food. Many a Friday, when he knew that fish would be on the menu, he went round the dustbins at the back of an hotel or restaurant to salvage the fish-heads which had been thrown away. These, which he called the best part of the fish, he would take back to the office in Gray's Inn Road and boil them to make a nourishing stew for himself and his colleagues. A liking for fish stew remained with him for the rest of his life, perhaps bringing back memories of the days in London. In Conakry, towards the end of his life, fish stew was a regular part of his diet. He would sometimes astonish a

1. Kojo Botsio. Recorded interview with June Milne, London. 5 September 1995.

guest by delving with the serving spoon into the bowl to locate a fish head which he would then place on their plate as a great delicacy.

The office in Gray's Inn Road was barely furnished, and often extremely cold, there being little money to carry on political work let alone to maintain the heating. During the winter, when no more coal could be afforded, Nkrumah and his companions would tramp the streets of London searching for the pieces which had fallen from coal lorries as they made their deliveries. These were used to keep the small fire burning in the office so that work could continue far into the night.

Most of the office typing was done by English girls, after they had finished their day's work. These girls worked for the Secretariat 'in a quiet and unassuming way and expected neither thanks nor rewards.'[1] Their selfless devotion to the work impressed Nkrumah deeply and he often referred to them later in his life when attacking those who tried to inject racialism into the socialist revolutionary struggle. At these times he would stress the point that a man or woman's contribution to the struggle should be judged least of all by their appearance, and certainly not by their words, but solely by their actions. What a person actually did was all that mattered, and their revolutionary contribution should be judged accordingly. He detested all forms of racialism: 'The foulest intellectual rubbish ever invented by man is that of racial superiority and inferiority.'[2]

Although Nkrumah found that racialism was not so blatantly practised in Britain as in the USA, it was nevertheless a fact of life which Africans and those of African descent studying or working in Britain could not ignore. In those years there were already many thousands of black people living in Britain, some of them only temporarily as students, but the vast majority had settled permanently, mainly in the large towns and ports. It was part of Nkrumah's work as Vice President of the West African Students' Union and as a member of the Coloured Workers' Association of Great Britain, formed by WANS, to try to help solve the many problems of students and workers. There were endless difficulties to be sorted out, from trouble finding lodgings to racial discrimination at work, and financial worries over college and examination fees. From time to time there were troubles involving the police.

---

1. *Ghana — Autobiography*, p. 56.
2. *Axioms of Kwame Nkrumah*, Freedom Fighters' Edition, Panaf 1967, p. 116. Speech made in Accra, 21 June 1952.

Nkrumah often had to visit courts and prisons to help solve the problems. His own experience in the USA gave him an unusual insight and
sympathy with those who found themselves up against 'the system'.
Every human problem, however trifling it seemed, was of interest to
him. No matter how busy he was, and this remained true when he was
at the height of his political life, he would be prepared to listen patiently
to any who sought his advice or help. In England, his work among
students and workers took him to the slums of not only London but of
Manchester, Cardiff and other cities. The conditions under which so
many workers lived appalled him.

As the result of a meeting of students' and workers' organisations
held in Holborn Hall, Nkrumah again visited Paris to meet African
deputies of the French Assembly. It was proposed to hold a West
African National Congress in Lagos in October 1948, to which political
organisations and peoples' movements should be invited to send representatives. A circular was sent out appealing for funds to finance the
Congress. The target figure was £25,000. The circular, addressed to
'Fellow Men and Women of West Africa' stated: 'Political power is the
only key to freedom of any sort.... A united free and independent West
Africa is the political condition for Africa's redemption and emancipation (and) for the emancipation of the Africans and peoples of
African descent throughout the world.'[1] In the words of Nkrumah in a
letter signed by him on behalf of the Secretariat: 'The future of West
Africa and her peoples rests with everyone of us. We cannot escape
from our duty and our destiny.'[2] The circular was widely printed in the
West African press. A copy was sent to, among others, the Gold Coast
nationalist, J. B. Danquah.

The appeal, though widely distributed, did not bring in sufficient
funds. The Congress had to be postponed, and then eventually
cancelled. By that time, Nkrumah had returned to the Gold Coast, and
WANS was in serious difficulty, unable to pay the office rent or to fund
its various activities. However, the organisation continued to function
until 1950, when it finally collapsed.

Although members of the West African Students' Union had done
what they could to assist the Labour Party in the general election of
1945, they had quickly become disillusioned when the Labour victory

---

1. *Kwame Nkrumah, The Years Abroad*, p. 148.
2. Ibid.

brought no real change in British colonial policy. Nkrumah and his colleagues were still continuing to meet some of the most notable members of the British Left, people such as A. Creech Jones, Dr Rita Hinden (South African secretary of the Fabian Society Colonial Bureau), Fenner Brockway, and leaders of the Communist Party such as Emil Burns, Palme Dutt and Harry Pollitt. Nkrumah's policy both in the USA and Britain was to associate with all parties and movements which, however shakily, could be called 'Progressive.' But by and large they sooner or later proved a disappointment to him. At an early stage he realised that the solution for the colonial subject peoples lay in their own hands, and would be solved only by their own efforts.

As in the USA, Nkrumah came under Intelligence surveillance while in Britain. His anti-colonialism, and particularly his connections with the Communist Party and other Left organisations, were of interest to Special Branch. The WANS office was raided and the contents of files and drawers searched. Agents of Special Branch monitored meetings. Nkrumah made no attempt to keep the activities of WANS secret. At public meetings and demonstrations in Hyde Park and Trafalgar Square he spoke openly of his political agenda. In June 1946 a Colonial office file was opened on WANS, with a request to MI5 for information on the organisation, its publications and source of funding. The Colonial Office should have been in no doubt about the work of WANS. Copies of *New African* were sent there so that they could know about the determination to end colonialism in Africa. Copies of the circular about the projected Lagos Congress were also sent to the Colonial Office, and the US Embassy in London, and to the State Department in Washington.

With so much political work to do, Nkrumah found less and less time for academic study. He had to give up his law studies and also work on his thesis. 'Such matters seemed trivial'[1] when compared with the freedom struggle which required 'prompt and concerted action.'[2] Professor Ayer apparently agreed, for he told Nkrumah early in 1947 that there was nothing more he could teach him, and that he should 'return to your country to free your people.'

---

1. *Ghana — Autobiography*, p. 60.
2. Ibid. Nkrumah took the MS of his thesis with him when he returned to West Africa in 1947 to become General Secretary of the UGCC. When he was exiled to the Northerm Territories in 1948, he returned to find the MS missing, having disappeared or been destroyed during the colonial police search of his papers.

By then it had been thought necessary to form a political cadre to train for revolutionary work in any part of Africa. Under the chairmanship of Nkrumah, The Circle was formed from among the best qualified of those who met at the office in Gray's Inn Road to discuss and to plan the liberation struggle. 'We met regularly, and organised and planned. Always, in our discussions there were two points of emphasis. First, the imperative need to organise through a vanguard party pursuing principles of socialism and based on mass participation. Second, the necessity for unification. We were at that time concerned mainly with West African unity, as the unification of British and French colonial peoples in West Africa seemed then the only practical possibility. But we always regarded West African unity as merely a first step leading eventually to the unification of the entire African continent.'[1]

A document known as The Circle contained the objectives of the organisation and the conditions of membership.

'Aims:

1. To maintain ourselves and the Circle as the Revolutionary Vanguard of the struggle for West African Unity and National Independence.

2. To support the idea and claims of the All West African National Congress in its struggle to create and maintain a Union of African Socialist Republics.'[2]

Each member was sworn to secrecy, and 'To serve, sacrifice and suffer anything for the cause for which THE CIRCLE stands.'[3] The Circle document ended with a declaration stating: 'At such time as may be deemed advisable THE CIRCLE will come out openly as a political party embracing the whole of West Africa, whose policy then shall be to maintain the Union of African Socialist republics.'[4]

In the Declaration to the Colonial Peoples of the World, Nkrumah had called on the masses of Africa to unite to end colonial rule. Again, in the Circle document, he emphasised the role of the masses, stating that an organisation such as the Circle was 'the more necessary,' to prevent 'demagogues, quislings, traitors, cowards and self-seekers,'[5]

---

1. *Revolutionary Path*, p. 47.
2. Ibid. 48.
3.   " .
4. Ibid. p. 50.
5. Ibid. p. 48.

from leading astray any section of the masses of the African people. On the question of the methods to be employed to achieve the objectives of the Circle, it was stated that violence should be avoided 'except as a last resort.'[1]

In his plans for conducting anti-colonial struggle in the Gold Coast, Nkrumah envisaged the employment of such measures as boycotts and strikes, together with other forms of pressure which did not involve actual physical violence. It was a Gandhian approach to political struggle. In later years, however, facing changed political circumstances, he declared that independence 'cannot come through delegations, gifts, charity, paternalism, grants, concessions, proclamations, charters or reformism.'[2] He wrote in *Africa Must Unite*: 'I know of no case where self-government has been handed to a colonial and oppressed people on a silver platter. The dynamic has had to come from the people themselves.'[3]

The Circle was very active for a time, but did not survive the departure of Nkrumah when, in December 1947, he left Britain to return to the Gold Coast to become general secretary of the United Gold Coast Convention (UGCC), the organisation directing the national liberation movement, which had been inaugurated at a meeting in Saltpond on 4 August 1947. Pa Grant was elected chairman.

Leading figures were J. B. Danquah, William Ofori Atta, Akufo Addo, J. W. de Graft Johnson and V. B. Annan. In his opening address at the meeting, Danquah declared that the UGCC demanded changes which would give 'the reality of power' to the chiefs and people. 'We must fight with the weapons of today, constitutional, determined, persistent, unflinching, unceasing, until the goal of freedom is obtained.'[4]

The letter inviting Nkrumah to accept the position of general secretary of the UGCC was written by Ako Adjei, the old friend of Nkrumah's whom he had first met while a student in America. The letter was followed by another, this time from Danquah. He urged Nkrumah to take up the post. By inviting Nkrumah to be general secretary, the UGCC hoped to widen their support among the people. Nkrumah had acquired a reputation as a skilful political organiser who appealed to

1. *Revolutionary Path*, p. 48.
2. *Towards Colonial Freedom*, p. xviii.
3. *Africa Must Unite*, p. 18.
4. *Kwame Nkrumah: The Political Kingdom in the Third World*, David Rooney, I. B. Tauris, London, p. 27.

the ordinary people and particularly to the youth. The UGCC needed his expertise and charisma.

When the UGCC was formed, the colonial power had decided after years of suppression to allow some measure of political activity. Under the Burns Constitution of 1944, Africans were appointed for the first time to the Executive Council. But this concession had failed to appease the growing demand of the Gold Coast intelligentsia for a greater say in the government of the country. In the changed world political climate which developed as a result of the Second World War, colonial governments had become conditioned to the idea of granting limited constitutional reforms of self-government as a process of sharing power. It was a question of tactical action. But while the ban on meaningful political activity was lifted, it was made clear that it had to take place within a certain framework, and on a time scale approved by the colonial power.

Nkrumah was at first hesitant about accepting the invitation from the UGCC. It was led mainly by members of the professional class, lawyers, traditionalists, gradualists and business men, whereas Nkrumah believed in decisive mass action by the people. He called a meeting of the West African Secretariat to put the matter before them. After much discussion, also with members of The Circle and with Padmore, it was decided that the invitation should be accepted. Although the composition and objectives of the UGCC were limited, it was considered that it was a possible vehicle through which the primary objective of gaining political power could be achieved. Nkrumah knew, however, that it might not be long before 'the basic differences between our long term objectives might make it impossible for me to continue to work for them.'[1]

Pa Grant sent funds to cover Nkrumah's passage and travelling expenses, and on 14 November 1947 Nkrumah accompanied by Kojo Botsio, left London for Liverpool, to board the Elder Dempster ship SS Accra for West Africa. In the words of Botsio: 'There was a large crowd to welcome us and bid us goodbye. People came from Manchester, Newcastle and other places which Kwame had visited. The elders took us to the house of one Mr. Duplant where a meeting was hurriedly held, and plenty of advice was given. The farewell at Liverpool was very touching. Eventually we set sail.'[2]

---

1. *Revolutionary Path*, p. 51.
2. Kojo Botsio. Recorded interview with June Milne, London. 5 September 1995.

3

Return to the Gold Coast.
Arrest and Detention

On the voyage home, Nkrumah disembarked in
Sierra Leone and Liberia where he tried to interest
political leaders in calling a West African Conference.
He spent two weeks in Freetown discussing the question of West African unity with among others Wallace
Johnson, Chairman of the West African Youth League.
He spoke at mass meetings in Freetown as well as
other parts of the country, and addressed the students
of Fourah Bay College.

He was able to spend scarcely two days in Liberia.
Nkrumah had hoped to talk with President Tubman,
whom he had met previously in the USA during the
President's visit there. But Tubman was away and
Nkrumah could not await his return. He was able,
however, to discuss the idea of a West African Conference with Liberian politicians. He found their reaction
lukewarm. As an independent state they did not think
Liberia could send a delegation to a conference composed solely of delegates from colonial territories,
though they might send an observer.

From Monrovia to the Gold Coast, Nkrumah travelled as a deck passenger, without revealing his identity to crew or fellow passengers. This was because he
anticipated a possible difficulty when his passport
was examined by immigration officials at the port of
disembarkation, Takoradi, in the Gold Coast. Information about his reputation as an anti-colonial political
activist who had associated with socialists and communists in London would have been transmitted to

the colonial authorities in the Gold Coast. However, he need not have worried. If the colonial government knew about him, so also did the African immigration officer at Takoradi. On reading the name on his passport the officer motioned Nkrumah to follow him out of hearing of other passengers and officials. Here, after shaking his hand in welcome, he told Nkrumah that they had heard so much about him, and had been eagerly awaiting his arrival. He said that immigration formalities would be quickly completed and his passport returned to him.

Thereupon, Nkrumah telephoned Mr. R.S. Blay, a UGCC Nzima lawyer, who soon arrived to drive him to Sekondi. From there he journeyed to Tarkwa where he was reunited with his mother. They had not seen each other for twelve years. Both had changed. Nyanibah's hair was grey and her eyesight was failing. To Nyanibah, Nkrumah appeared different when he smiled. The gap between his two front teeth was no longer there. In order to improve his speaking, he had undergone cosmetic dental surgery while in the USA.

Nkrumah spent two weeks in Tarkwa, resting and planning the struggle ahead. Soon, he had worked out a plan of campaign which he presented to the Working Committee of the UGCC on 20 January 1948. It involved using all the methods available to a national liberation movement operating legally in a colonial situation. He advised the immediate formation of a Shadow Cabinet. 'Membership is to be composed of individuals selected ad hoc to study the jobs of the various ministries that would be decided upon in advance for the country when we achieve our independence'.[1] At the same time, during the 'First Period' of his proposed agenda, he advocated the affiliation to the UGCC of all other organisations in the Gold Coast: for example, the trade unions, co-operative societies, women's organisations, farmers' councils, and so on. In addition, members of these organisations should be encouraged to join the UGCC on an individual membership basis. There were only two branches of the UGCC in existence when Nkrumah became general secretary. He therefore urged that new branches should be formed immediately in every town and village. He ended his recommendations for the First Period by calling for 'vigorous Convention weekend schools.... The political mass education of the country for Self-Government should begin at these weekend schools.'[2]

---

1. *Revolutionary Path, pp. 52/3.*
2. Ibid., p. 53.

Nkrumah with his mother soon after his return to the Gold Coast —1947

The Second Period of the UGCC's campaign was to be characterised 'by constant demonstrations throughout the country to test our organisational strength, making use of political crises'.[1] The Third and last period provided for the calling of a Constitutional Assembly to draw up the constitution for national independence, and the employment of demonstrations, strikes and boycotts to support pressure for self-government. Nkrumah's plan of action was approved in principle by the Working Committee of the UGCC, and Nkrumah at once began the work of implementing it.

There was fertile ground on which to work for mass participation in the anti-colonial struggle. A high degree of political awareness already existed among the people in towns and countryside. This was being expressed in a growing resentment of colonial rule. It was already widely believed that living conditions would not improve until independence was achieved.

As a result of the system of Indirect Rule which the British imposed throughout their colonies, the Gold Coast colonial government depended heavily on the power of chiefs and District Commissioners (DCs). The increase in power of the chiefs was not popular with the membership of the UGCC, nor with the youth. Large numbers gravitated to the towns in search of work. They had become impatient with a village life dominated by chiefs and elders steeped in what they considered to be outdated traditions. In 1947 the Ashanti Youth Organisation was formed. It sought the replacement of chiefs on the Legislative Council, and demanded self-government within five years. Similar youth organisations were established throughout the country.

Political unrest was fuelled by economic problems, a major one being the outbreak of swollen shoot disease which threatened the entire cocoa industry on which the economy depended. Some two and a half million trees were cut down, but the disease continued to affect millions more. Many cocoa farmers were ruined, and their work-force suffered accordingly. In the towns, with the influx of large numbers from the countryside seeking work, there was rising unemployment. Those in work had their trade unions which together formed the Trade Union Congress, another organisation dissatisfied with colonial rule. Inflation added to general discontent. While prices rose, the level of wages fell far behind.

---

1. *Revolutionary Path*, p. 53.

During the Second World War the population of Accra nearly doubled. Other cities such as Kumasi and Sekondi-Takoradi were rapidly expanding. Big changes had occurred resulting in an expanding urban work force. The Gold Coast was Britain's main source of manganese ore and bauxite. The mining of industrial diamonds, gold and valuable types of timber had seen a substantial increase during the war years. However, it was after the war ended, when some 65,000 Gold Coast soldiers who had fought as members of the British armed forces returned home, that the full impact of the war was felt. The experience abroad of the ex-servicemen in fighting fascism had broadened their political outlook, and opened their eyes to the injustices of the colonial system. They became a potent force in the national movement.

By the end of the 1940s, therefore, the bulk of the population was in the mood to support the independence movement. Leadership and organisation were needed to galvanise this potential mass support into meaningful action.

Nkrumah travelled hundreds of miles in an old car, holding meetings, organising local party branches and making speeches. Within six months over five hundred branches of the UGCC had been formed. The rapid build-up of support for the UGCC reflected the terrific pace at which Nkrumah worked. Everywhere he went people flocked to hear him speak. Never before had they heard anyone put the issues so clearly before them. Nkrumah would sometimes speak for hours, but always he would call for small breaks in the meetings to allow the people to relax; and often there would be drumming and dancing. Nkrumah spoke in everyday, easy to understand language when explaining the UGCC's aims and goals. His manner was so different from that of the business and professional leaders of the UGCC who were inclined to maintain a disdainful distance from the people, often speaking in academic terms. Nkrumah would share food and lodging with the country folk. He was equally at home with the poor in the towns. His enthusiasm and oratory had an electrifying effect. He would speak without notes, his voice deep and inspiring. His presence was such that cheering and clapping would begin sometimes before he had said a single word.

The mass rallies were joyful occasions. The political message Nkrumah conveyed was greeted as cause for celebration. Nkrumah would frequently ask the people questions, and they would enthusiastically reply. The meeting would develop into more of a discussion than a set speech occasion. Nkrumah enjoyed this kind of direct contact with the people much more than when he spoke on formal occasions. The question and answer technique came naturally to him. He loved to listen to the authentic voice of the people. It made him very happy. The people in their turn were captivated by his message and his charm. His charisma was such that he came to be named affectionately 'Show Boy'.

A typical audience response occurred in Tarkwa when Nkrumah spoke for the first time as general secretary of the UGCC, before a gathering of miners, peasants, fishermen and other working people. An elderly miner called out: 'This young man is God's greatest gift to the Gold Coast; hear ye him'. Nkrumah had been talking of the challenging struggle ahead, telling them that if they had been sleeping before, it was 'time to wake up'. He had the gift of making the most lowly and deprived feel important, by offering them the opportunity to participate in the freeing of their country. As his reputation spread news of his approach was sufficient for men, women and children to rush to escort him into the village. After hearing him speak the adults would hurry to sign UGCC membership cards.

Because of his sudden appearance in a very short space of time, often at a place hundreds of miles from where he had last been seen, he was considered by some of the superstitious among the crowd to have mystical power. It was said that at night he turned into some kind of animal or bird, and that explained his mobility. The colonial police, who were watching his every move, had a hard time catching up with him. They never knew where or when he would appear next. 'I usually travelled in the old car bought by the UGCC, but frequently had to hitch lifts on lorries, or had to trek on foot when the car broke down and there was no other means of transport. In most of the places I visited I was given food and accommodation in the homes of supporters of the movement. But there were many nights when I and my companions slept in the open by the roadside'.[1] He came to know the people of the Gold Coast as never before. He listened to their problems, sensed their discontent and frustration and understood their aspirations.

Years afterwards, those with whom he and his small entourage stayed, remembered vividly those exciting days. Nancy Tsiboe reminisced about them at the inauguration of the Kwame Nkrumah Foundation in Accra in September 1987. She told how Nkrumah always insisted

---

1. *Revolutionary Path*, p. 54.

that the drivers were fed first, then his colleagues, and finally he would say, 'Now Nancy, let us eat.' He would like to go into the kitchen to ask, 'How is it going?' Once he called her into his room to show what he had drawn. It was a spider's web. He placed his finger in the centre and said: 'This is where we are, here in the Gold Coast. You know when you touch the centre the whole web vibrates.' He was, she said, a quiet, modest man who spent long periods without speaking, deep in thought, contemplating the future of his country and the effect its independence would have on the rest of Africa.

Many women, particularly those living in urban areas, were already firm supporters of the UGCC. But on Nkrumah's return to the Gold Coast and his subsequent break with the UGCC to form the CPP, women for the first time began to play a significant, national role in the independence campaign.

As political and economic pressures mounted, even chiefs joined the national movement. Prices of not only imported goods but of locally produced products rocketed. Foreign businessmen, notably British, Lebanese, Syrian and Greek merchants were seen to prosper while the people of the Gold Coast suffered increased hardship. It was a Ga chief who emerged to lead the protest against European exploitation. The chief called for a drastic reduction of prices in foreign owned stores, threatening a complete boycott of imported goods if, by 24 February 1948, this had not been done. The foreign merchants had thought themselves in a strong position having formed an organisation, the Association of West African Merchants (AWAM), to protect their interests. But they had under-estimated the strength of the feeling against them. Chief Nii Bonne, in a New Year Message called on the people to fight and to die if necessary for their freedom. His call for a boycott coincided with a build up of the ex-servicemen's movement.

Meantime, Nkrumah, Danquah and other leaders of the UGCC kept up the countrywide campaign for the ending of colonial rule. At mass rallies they kept on repeating that only independence could bring about improvement in living conditions. A crucial point was reached when both Nkrumah and Danquah spoke at a meeting of ex-servicemen at the Palladium Cinema in Accra on 20 February 1948. A petition was drawn up to be presented to the Governor expressing their grievances. The ex-servicemen, who had fought in the Middle East or in Burma, had returned after the Second World War with high expectations that their contribution to allied victory would be suitably rewarded. Instead, they found themselves with only a meagre gratuity and suffering the same hardships as the rest of the population. They demanded the benefits which had been promised to them during the war, and assistance in finding work.

On 28 February, the ex-servicemen's march set off to present their petition to the Governor. It was originally intended to go to the Secretariat offices. But instead the procession took the road to Christiansborg Castle, the Governor's residence. Government troops and police had been put on alert, so that when the marchers reached the Christiansborg cross-roads the way was barred by armed police commanded by a British officer, Superintendent Colin Imray. After calling on the marchers to halt, and when they refused to do so, he gave the order to open fire. In the confusion which followed, three ex-servicemen were killed[1] and many others injured. The infuriated marchers turned back to the centre of Accra to join angry crowds out in the streets protesting at the failure of European merchants to lower their prices enough to meet the needs of the people. News of the shooting of the ex-servicemen sparked off days of rioting. Shops and offices of foreigners were attacked. Cars were set on fire. Shops looted. Violence continued throughout the night culminating in the breaking down of the doors of Ussher Fort in Accra, and the freeing of prisoners. Although order was eventually restored in Accra, rioting spread to other towns, including Kumasi and Koforidua. In all, it is estimated that twenty-nine people were killed in the riots and over two hundred were injured.

It had been Nkrumah's intention to affiliate the Ex-Servicemen's Union to the UGCC as part of his policy to draw all sections of the people into the national liberation movement. He was aware of their discontent. But when the march took place the Union had no direct connection with the UGCC. And it was sheer coincidence that the march took place on the very day that the Nii Bonne boycott was called off. It had lasted for about a month and had been carried out peacefully. Although the boycott was called when Nkrumah had only just arrived in the Gold Coast, it was thought by the colonial government that he must have organised it. In fact though he sympathised with it, he neither instigated it nor took part in its implementation. He was too busy setting up the UGCC office in Saltpond and preparing for the next phase in the national liberation struggle.

---

1. They were Sergeant Adjetey, Corporal Attipoe and Private Odartey Lamptey.

Faced with widespread disorder, Governor Sir Gerald Creasey declared a state of emergency and troops were called out to restore order in Accra. Police began to round up so-called trouble makers. When the rioting broke out Nkrumah was addressing a rally in Saltpond. A meeting of the Executive Committee of the UGCC was called when it was decided that Nkrumah should go at once to Accra. Immediately on arrival there he called a meeting of the Accra branch of the UGCC, and then went round the town to see for himself what was happening. The scale of the disorder and damage surprised him. Many buildings were on fire including the large stores of the United Africa Company (UAC) and the Union Trading Company (UTC).

It was decided by the Executive Committee of the UGCC that a telegram should be despatched at once to A. Creech Jones, British Secretary of State for the Colonies. Nkrumah and Danquah disagreed on the wording, so two telegrams were sent, a long one drafted by Danquah and a short one by Nkrumah. Both asked for a Special Commissioner to be sent to the Gold Coast with power to form an interim government of chiefs and people, and to call a Constituent Assembly.

On hearing that the police were seeking the six leaders of the UGCC, Nkrumah took refuge for two days in the house of two women supporters. He then slipped back to Saltpond. It was not long, however, before he and other leaders of the UGCC were arrested. The 'Big Six' as they were called, were J.B. Danquah, Ofori Atta, Akufo Addo, Ako Adjei, Obetsebi Lamptey and Nkrumah. Of those, Nkrumah alone did not come from the privileged sector of society. Dr Danquah was a brother of the late Nana Sir Ofori Atta I, chief of the Akim Abuakwa people. William Ofori Atta was the son of the old chief, and Eric Akufo Addo was his son-in-law. Obetsebi Lamptey was a wealthy lawyer. Ako Adjei, a longstanding friend of Nkrumah, identified with the UGCC business and professional hierarchy.

Nkrumah was flown to Kumasi and imprisoned there for three days in the same cell with the other five members of the Big Six. While Nkrumah hoped to make use of the opportunity to discuss future tactics, the others spent most of the time bemoaning their fate, blaming Nkrumah for their predicament. Danquah, apparently 'began to sob noisily'.[1] They did, however, manage to consider plans for a future constitution if and when the Burns Constitution was abolished. But throughout their

---

1. *Autobiography*, p. 82.

discussions it became obvious to Nkrumah that his views were far apart from those held by the other five. They made it clear that they regretted inviting him to become general secretary of the UGCC, even blaming Ako Adjei for recommending him. They had wanted to conduct the liberation struggle in an orderly manner, step by step, under conditions prescribed by the colonial government. While they wanted Nkrumah to broaden support for the UGCC, they did not want the movement to be swept along by mass mobilisation of the people. The UGCC leaders were content with the slogan 'self-government within the shortest possible time'. Nkrumah was intent on achieving 'self-government NOW'.

In the early morning of the third day, the prisoners were suddenly told to prepare to leave. They later learned the reason. Some of the Ashanti youth, under the leadership of Krobo Edusei, planned to attack the prison to release the prisoners. The Big Six were at once taken by bus to Tamale, capital of the Northern Territories, a journey of eight hours. They were taken to a bungalow on the outskirts of the town where they remained under close guard for three days. Then they were split up, each prisoner being taken to a different destination in the Northern Territories. Nkrumah found himself in Lawra, where he was placed in a hut closely guarded night and day. There he remained in solitary confinement for about six weeks, allowed to read books and to receive letters after they had been censored by the District Commissioner. But he was denied newspapers. He later wrote in his *Autobiography*, 'It was a very lonely existence but surprisingly enough I enjoyed it. It was the first time in thirteen years that I had been able to remain quiet and undisturbed in one place for any length of time and also, after the recent bickerings of my five companions in this plight, I was really thankful to be away from them.'[1] He went on to describe how a mongoose used to visit his hut each night, arriving at dusk and staying with him throughout the night. The creature was the pet of a doctor who was on leave. The mongoose used to nestle up to Nkrumah and sleep beside him.

After six weeks, Nkrumah was transferred to Accra to appear with the other prisoners before a Commission of Enquiry which had been set up by the Governor under Aiken Watson KC to enquire into the disorders. The first thing the Commission did was to call for the release of the prisoners to enable them to appear before them as free men. Fortunately, other members of the Executive Committee of the UGCC

---

1. *Autobiography*, p. 83.

had managed to obtain the services of a British lawyer, Dingle Foot, to defend the Big Six. When the Commissioners cross-examined each prisoner separately the isolation of Nkrumah from the rest of the leaders of the UGCC was soon apparent. The other five were quick to disassociate themselves from the recommendations which Nkrumah had put before the Working Committee when he became general secretary of the UGCC. As a result of their interrogations the Watson commissioners came to the conclusion that Nkrumah was largely to blame for the disorders. In their report, issued in June 1948, they stated that 'the UGCC did not really get down to business until the arrival of Mr Kwame Nkrumah on 16 December 1947.'[1] The report continued:

'Mr Nkrumah appears to be a mass orator among Africans of no mean attainments. Nevertheless he appears before us as a 'Humble and obedient servant of the Convention' who had subordinated his private political convictions to those publicly expressed by his employers. From the internal evidence we are unable to accept this modest assessment of his position. As appears from the Minute Book, the warmth of his welcome is reflected in the enthusiastic invitation from one member of the Working Committee to Mr Nkrumah to 'Use the organisation as his own'. From this it is clear that, for the time being at all events, he was occupying the role held by all party secretaries in totalitarian institutions, the real position of power.... Mr Kwame Nkrumah has never abandoned his aims for a Union of West African Soviet Socialist Republics and has not abandoned his foreign affiliations connected with these aims.'[2]

A copy of the Circle document had been found among Nkrumah's papers when he was arrested. The word 'Soviet' did not appear in the document but was inserted deliberately by the commissioners to give added force to their report. They were flashing the warning light that Nkrumah was a dangerous man and had to be closely watched. For if his ideas triumphed in the Gold Coast it would mean not only the end of colonial rule, but possibly an eventual socialist transformation of society.

---

1. *Autobiography, p. 85.*
2. Ibid., *p. 86/7.*

▲ Nkrumah reading letter of resignation from UGCC, 30 July 1949, after the foundation of the CPP on 12 June 1949

In their report, the Watson Commissioners recommended that a committee should be set up to consider the drafting of a new constitution which would replace the outmoded Burns Constitution of 1946. As a result, in December 1948, a committee known as the Coussey Constitutional Committee[1] was appointed by the Governor. It consisted of forty members all of them nominated by the Governor. All were from the elite. Not one represented the ordinary working people of the country.

Soon after the Watson Report was published, Obetsebi Lamptey and William Ofori Atta ransacked Nkrumah's office in Saltpond while he was away addressing a party meeting. Searching through files and papers they seized every document which they considered might help to prove that he was a communist. Letters containing the word 'Comrade' were considered vital evidence.

Nkrumah grew increasingly convinced that the time had come to break with the UGCC and to form his own party. It had become obvious that the leaders of the UGCC no longer trusted him, and were determined to block his plans for drawing the youth and rank and file of the people into genuine participation in the liberation struggle. They objected to his founding of the Ghana College, established by him to accommodate pupils who had been expelled from schools because they went on strike in support of the Big Six when they were detained in the Northern Territories. Nkrumah had managed to hire a hall in Cape Coast to accommodate the students. The three teachers with which the college started had lost their jobs for the same reason as their pupils. These teachers agreed to work for no pay until the college finances were on a sound basis. Nkrumah himself contributed £10 of his £25 monthly salary to purchase basic equipment.

At the Ghana College opening on 20 July 1948, Nkrumah urged all present and future students to consider laziness a crime: 'Think! Study hard! Work with sustained effort. As never before we want thinkers — thinkers of great thoughts. We want doers of great deeds. Of what use is your education if you cannot help your country in her hour of need?' He said that he envisaged similar colleges being established throughout the country, leading eventually to the founding of a University of Ghana.

---

1. Under the Chairmanship of Mr. Justice Coussey.

A year later, from its very humble beginnings, Ghana College had more than two hundred pupils, and over a thousand on the waiting list. More schools and colleges were founded in other parts of the country.

Growing personal support for Nkrumah, particularly among the youth, alarmed the more cautious members of the UGCC hierarchy into appointing him treasurer instead of general secretary. The change was met with a deluge of protests which poured into the office of the UGCC.

Another cause of mounting friction between Nkrumah and the UGCC was his founding of the Committee on Youth Organisation (CYO) which embodied the Ashanti Youth Organisation and the Ghana Youth Association. Nkrumah intended the CYO to be the youth section of the national movement. The Working Committee of the UGCC strongly resented its formation, regarding it as a pressure group supporting Nkrumah's objectives of 'self-government NOW'. Arrangements were made by the CYO to hold a Ghana Youth Conference in Kumasi from 23–26 December 1948. Fearing disorder, this was banned by the police. Instead, an informal meeting was held at which the Ghana Youth Manifesto was drawn up and published under the title 'Towards Self-Government'. Another conference of the CYO was arranged as tension between the CYO and the Working Committee of the UGCC grew. A few months later, at a meeting in Saltpond, the UGCC Committee dismissed Nkrumah's private secretary, and decided not to reinstate Nkrumah as general secretary.

In addition, the Working Committee of the UGCC objected to Nkrumah's founding of a newspaper, the *Accra Evening News*, in September 1948. In Nkrumah's words: 'The inevitable split was imminent'.

Nkrumah was then in a strong position to form a new party. His stand before the Watson Commission had confirmed the people's opinion of him as a man of courage who expressed their aspirations. He alone of the prisoners had stood up to the commissioners and had never for a moment wavered. The mass of the people and the youth had come to know him as they never knew the other leaders of the UGCC. His obvious integrity, his deep concern for the ordinary folk and his complete confidence in the outcome of the struggle were an inspiration to all with whom he came into contact.

4

The Convention People's Party (CPP) and Positive Action

The decision to break away from the UGCC was taken at a conference in Tarkwa of the CYO. With the youth firmly behind him, and with the certainty of mass support, Nkrumah could confidently resign from the UGCC. He launched the Convention People's Party (CPP) before a crowd of some 60,000 in Accra on 12 June 1949.

In his speech, Nkrumah outlined the events which had led to the break with the UGCC. 'The time has arrived', he declared, 'when a definite line of action must be taken if we are going to save our country from continued imperialist exploitation and oppression.'[1] He explained the necessity for demanding 'self-government NOW' rather than the UGCC objective of 'self-government within the shortest possible time.' He pointed out that the Labour Government then in power in the United Kingdom could be expected to be more favourably disposed towards their demand for self-government, than would a Conservative government which might be returned the following year. He

---

1. Speech in Accra on June 12 1949 when launching the Convention People's Party (CPP). *Revolutionary Path*, p. 57.

spoke of plans for a programme of Positive Action employing non-violent methods of agitation, the use of newspapers, political education campaigns and the calling of strikes, boycotts and non- co-operation.

The CPP was to be a mass-based disciplined party with, according to the Constitution of the Party,[1] the following 'Aims and Objects':

NATIONAL

(I)   To fight relentlessly to achieve and maintain independence of the people of Ghana (Gold Coast) and their chiefs.

(II)   To serve as the vigorous conscious political vanguard for removing all forms of oppression and for the establishment of a democratic government.

(III)   To secure and maintain the complete unity of the people of the Colony, Ashanti, Northern Territories and Trans-Volta/Togoland regions.

(IV)   To work with and in the interest of the Trade Union Movement, and other kindred organisations, in joint political or other action in harmony with the constitution and Standing Orders of the Party

(V)   To work for a speedy reconstruction of a better Ghana (Gold Coast) in which the people and their Chiefs shall have the right to live and govern themselves as free people.

(VI)   To promote the Political, Social, and Economic emancipation of the people, more particularly of those who depend directly upon their own exertions by hand or by brain for the means of life.

INTERNATIONAL

(I)   To work with other nationalist democratic and socialist movements in Africa and other continents, with a view to abolish imperialism, colonialism, racialism, tribalism and all forms of national and racial oppression and economic inequality among nations, races and peoples and to support all action for World Peace.

---

1. For the full text of the CPP Constitution, see *Revolutionary Path*, pp. 58–71.

(II)   To support the demand for a West African Federation and of PanAfricanism by promoting unity of action among the peoples of African descent.

The party was to establish branches in all towns and villages, each branch to be governed by an elected Branch Executive Committee. As regards the central administration of the party, there was to be a National Secretariat under the direct supervision and control of the Central Committee of the National Executive Committee of the party. The Secretary of the Central Committee would serve as a liaison between the National Secretariat and the National Executive Committee of the party. Members of the first Central Committee of the CPP were Nkrumah (Chairman), Kojo Botsio (Secretary), K. A. Gbedemah, N.A. Welbeck, Kwesi Plange, Kofi Baako, Krobo Edusei, Dzenkle Dzewu, and Ashie Nikoe.

The colours of the party would be red, white and green. Its tricolour flag would be in horizontal form with red at the top,[1] and the party's motto, FORWARD EVER-BACKWARD NEVER.

The CPP's campaign was publicised in the party's newspaper *The Accra Evening News*, founded by Nkrumah in 1948, the first issue of which appeared on the 3rd of September, the day he ceased to be general secretary of the UGCC. Each day, through the columns of this paper, Nkrumah and his associates hammered home the message of 'self-government NOW' and exposed injustices of the colonial administration. Nkrumah was frequently threatened with libel action. The claimants were mostly civil servants and included the Commissioner of Police. Supporters of the CPP were able to collect enough money to settle the claim of the Police Chief and some others who demanded immediate payment. Other claims were settled over a period of time. At one stage claims against Nkrumah amounted to around £10,000. 'I was not worried. I had no property to be impounded. I had nothing for them to seize except two suits, a couple of shirts and a pair of shoes. There was no bankruptcy law in the country.'[2]

Demand for the *Evening News*, as it came to be generally known, rose dramatically. Its stirring mottoes headed each issue:

— We have the right to live as men

---

1. Subsequently, the white section was replaced by gold. During the Conakry period, however, in a flag to be adopted in the event of his return to the country, Nkrumah reverted to the original flag colours of the CPP, restoring white in the place of gold.
2. *Autiobiography*, p. 96.

— We prefer self-government with danger to servitude in tranquillity
— We have the right to govern ourselves

Soon 'self-government NOW ' as well as other slogans printed in the newspaper began to appear on walls and buildings throughout the country.

It had been a struggle to launch the newspaper. The Cropper machine, on which the paper was first printed, had to be paid for by instalments. An Accra printer allowed Nkrumah to set it up in his Ausco Press premises. At first, it was only possible to print a single sheet containing feature articles, editorial, an agitator's column, and the most provocative column headed 'Rambler'. It was this column which caused the colonial authorities the most embarrassment. 'Rambler' reports revealed knowledge of most secret and intimate happenings among those in position of authority and trust. The eyes and ears of 'Rambler' were everywhere. 'Rambler' had no hesitation in publicising injustice no matter how powerful the offender. A threat of legal action against the paper often resulted in a repetition of the alleged slander or libel. The identity of 'Rambler' was never revealed though an American journalist visiting the Gold Coast at that time, was said to have offered £1,000 to meet 'Rambler'.

So popular did the *Evening News* become that it was sometimes impossible to satisfy the demand because of lack of funds and limited printing capacity. Copies of the paper would be shared among many readers. Those unable to read, gathered in groups to hear the columns of the newspaper read aloud to them by a literate person. The paper made no profit, having to limit the price and not accepting advertisements in case pressure was brought to influence policy. Nkrumah, with his considerable experience of editing newspapers and journals in the USA and Britain, knew the value of editorial freedom. In political struggle he rated the written word more important than the spoken.

A typical editorial, headed 'Bullets or No Bullets' appeared in the paper on 13 January 1949. It drew attention to the number of British troops arriving in the country, as if a pitched battle was soon to be expected:

'With the present upsurge among the masses of the people for full self-government, the British Government is manoeuvering feverishly to delay what must eventually come to pass.... We have no arms, but we have tremendous weapons at our disposal which neither steel nor bullets can vanquish....'Britons never shall be slaves'. Yet imperialist Britain wants to enslave others. Colonisation is nothing but slavery....

Bullets or no bullets, British troops or no British troops, there is nothing that can deter us from our determined march towards the goal of complete self-government and independence.'[1]

Encouraged by the success of the *Evening News*, Nkrumah launched the *Morning Telegraph* in Sekondi in January 1949 with Kwame Afriyie as editor. This was soon followed by the establishment of the *Daily Mail* in Cape Coast, edited by Kofi Baako.

When the CPP was launched, the Coussey Committee had been at work for about six months. During that time the *Evening News* had carried repeated warnings against the Committee drawing up a constitution which would be unacceptable to the people of Ghana. 'We as a people in our own God-given land must be given a clear chance to act freely, and live freely', wrote Komfo Atta in the paper on 11 December 1948. In referring to the country as 'Ghana' rather than the Gold Coast, the *Evening News* reflected the growing momentum of the independence movement. Eventually, the *Accra Evening News* was to become the *Ghana Evening News*. Nkrumah in speeches and in writing had always used the name 'Ghana' instead of the Gold Coast, so that when independence was won in 1957, the people already thought of themselves as 'Ghanaians'.

By the time the CPP was founded, the newspaper campaign for 'self-government NOW' had prepared the ground well. Besides the *Evening News*, other papers also pressed for independence. The *West African Monitor* with its motto, 'Service not servitude' was influential at that time. So also was the *Cape Coast Daily Echo*. In an editorial of 16 September, economic arguments were expressed: 'West African cocoa earns five times as many dollars in a year as Britain receives from sales to America of motor-cars, ships and locomotives. Last year the total dollar earnings from cocoa sales in the United States amounted to US$140,000,000. But the goose that lays the golden eggs is being strangled'.[2]

It was necessary to keep up pressure on the colonial government.

---

1. *Revolutionary Path*, p. 76.
2. *I Speak of Freedom*, Kwame Nkrumah, first published in 1961. Panaf edition 1973, p. 11.

For while the Coussey Committee continued to sit, self-government could be indefinitely delayed. Nkrumah pointed out that there were two ways of achieving independence, by armed struggle, or by non-violent methods, the nature of which he described as Positive Action. This involved peaceful political agitation similar to the methods employed in India by Mahatma Gandhi. 'We had no guns. But even if we had, the circumstances were such that non-violent alternatives were open to us, and it was necessary to try them before resorting to other means'.[1]

Although Nkrumah had used the term Positive Action at the launch of the CPP in June 1949, and had previously often used the term in the *Evening News*, he had never defined in writing the full meaning of what he meant by it. This omission was remedied in 1949 as a result of pressure from the Ga State Council which had summoned him to appear before it to discuss 'the unfortunate lawless elements in the country and any possible solution'.[2] Having explained what he meant by Positive Action, Nkrumah then worked throughout the night to define the term in writing. The result was a detailed statement entitled *What I Mean by Positive Action*. Five thousand copies were then printed on the *Evening News* Cropper printing machine. He read the statement to a mass meeting of supporters the following morning. The preamble began:

> 'In our present vigorous struggle for self-government, nothing strikes so much terror into the hearts of the imperialists and their agents than the term Positive Action. This is especially so because of their fear of the masses responding to the call to apply this final form of resistance in case the British Government fails to grant us our freedom consequent on the publication of the Coussey Committee report.
>
> The term Positive Action has been erroneously and maliciously publicised, no doubt, by the imperialists and their concealed agents-provocateurs and stooges. These political renegades, enemies of the Convention People's Party for the matter of Ghana's freedom, have diabolically publicised that CPP's programme of positive action means riot, looting and disturbances, in a word, violence.... By Positive Action we mean the adoption

---

1. *Revolutionary Path*, p. 86
2. Ibid., p. 85.

of all legitimate and constitutional means by which we can cripple the forces of imperialism in this country. The weapons of Positive Action are:

   (1)   Legitimate political agitation;

   (2)   Newspaper and educational campaigns and

   (3)   as a last resort, the constitutional application of strikes, boycotts, and non-co-operation based on the principle of absolute non-violence'.[1]

In the final paragraph, Nkrumah outlined the circumstances in which a call for Positive Action would be made:

'Positive Action has already begun by our political education, by our newspapers agitation and platform speeches and also by the establishment of the Ghana Schools and Colleges as well as the fearless and legitimate activities of the CPP. But as regards the final stage of Positive Action, namely Nation-wide Non-violent Sit-down-at-home Strikes, Boycotts and Non-co-operation, we shall not call into play until all the avenues of our political endeavours of attaining self-government have been closed. They will constitute the last resort. Accordingly, we shall first carefully study the Report of the Coussey Committee. If we find it favourable, we shall accept it and sing alleluya. But if we find it otherwise, we shall first put forward our own suggestions and proposals and upon refusal to comply with them, we shall invoke Positive Action straight away on the lines indicated above.[2]

The editorial in the *Evening News* of 10 March 1949, carried the headline 'The Dawn of Positive Action'. But it was not until the end of October 1949 that the Report of the Coussey Committee was published. It provided for a Legislative Assembly consisting of eighty-four elected members and included three ex-officio members to be nominated by the Governor. These were the Minister of Defence and External Affairs, the Minister of Finance, and the Minister of Justice. The constitution was considered unsatisfactory by the CPP Central Committee and by the rank and file of the people. Real power still resided with the Governor who retained the right to veto any decision taken by the Assembly. In

1. *Revolutionary Path*, p. 91–94.
2. Ibid., p. 95.

essence, all that was provided for in the Coussey Constitution was a small measure of African participation in government. The Constitution virtually assumed that the colonial system would remain for an indefinite period.

Nkrumah's response was to call together a Ghana People's Representative Assembly. The object was to mobilise all sections of the people to oppose the Coussey Report and to demonstrate the readiness of the people for full self-government. Over fifty public organisations took part, including trade unions, the co-operative movement, youth, women and ex-servicemen. Apart from the statutory Territorial Councils, the only two organisations which refused the invitation were the executive committee of the UGCC and the Aborigines' Rights Protection Society. The Assembly passed a resolution stating that the Coussey Report was unacceptable to the country as a whole, and declaring that self-government should be granted immediately. The assembly also drew up a memorandum outlining the structures of central and local government which must be incorporated in a new constitution.

After calling a meeting of the Executive Committee of the CPP, Nkrumah was empowered to send a letter to the Governor Sir Charles Arden-Clarke on 15 December 1949. This informed him that if the administration 'continued to ignore the legitimate aspirations of the people as embodied in the amendments to the Coussey Committee's Report by the People's Representative Assembly, then the CPP would embark on a campaign of Positive Action based upon non-violence and non-co-operation.'[1] On the same day, Nkrumah printed on the front page of the *Evening News* a rousing article headed: 'The Era of Positive Action Draws Nigh'. Then, in front of a large crowd in the Arena, he warned the British government that if nothing had been done within two weeks concerning the CPP request for a Constituent Assembly, Positive Action would begin. The colonial government responded with a wave of arrests. Editors of newspapers founded by Nkrumah were imprisoned, and Nkrumah himself was charged with contempt for an article which appeared in the *Sekondi Morning Telegraph*. He was given the alternative of a fine of £300 or four months imprisonment. The fine was paid by party members, and Nkrumah continued the work of organising party and people for Positive Action. At last, after several meetings with the colonial authorities, when it was clear that no progress was being made

---

1. For the full text of *What I Mean by Positive Action*, see *Revolutionary Path*, pp. 91–95.

on the question of calling a Constituent Assembly, Nkrumah called a mass meeting in Accra and on 8 January 1950 proclaimed the start of Positive Action. He then travelled to Cape Coast, Sekondi and Tarkwa to declare that Positive Action had begun.

He called for a general strike. It was to include all but those engaged in maintaining essential services, such as hospitals and water supplies. Shops and offices closed. Road and rail services came to a standstill. The government responded by banning public meetings. Newspapers were censored, and through its own sponsored newspapers, namely the *Gold Coast Bulletin* and the *Gold Coast Weekly Review* the government attacked the CPP, accusing the leadership of causing violence and economic ruin.

Nkrumah was invited to meet with the Joint Provincial Council of Chiefs to discuss a peaceful settlement. Accompanied by three other members of the CPP central committee, he explained to the chiefs that Positive Action must continue until self-government was achieved. He warned the chiefs that unless they supported the liberation movement they might be compelled to flee 'and leave their sandals behind them'.

On 10 January, after a CPP mass meeting in Accra, the situation became so tense that the Governor declared a state of emergency and imposed a curfew. The offices of CPP newspapers were raided and closed down. CPP leaders throughout the country were arrested. On 15 January, Kojo Botsio, general secretary of the party, was taken into custody. His office was ransacked and all party literature confiscated. The situation reached a climax when two African policemen were killed by a crowd of CPP supporters.

At a meeting of the Legislative Council on 20 January, Sir Tsibu Darku deplored the 'disruption of the country's peace' and supported the emergency measures imposed by the colonial government. His motion was supported by other African members of the Council, including Dr Danquah, Vice-President of the UGCC.

By the night of 21 January 1950, all CPP leaders except Nkrumah had been arrested. He happened to be visiting a party member in Labadi when the police raided party headquarters, so was not picked up until the following morning. He was taken to James Fort Prison in Accra after being charged with inciting people to take part in an illegal strike in an attempt to coerce the government. He was held in custody until his trial, which lasted about a week. For inciting the strike he was sentenced to two years' imprisonment. He was then taken to Cape Coast in handcuffs to face a second trial, this time on a charge of sedition for an article in the *Cape Coast Daily Mail* headed: 'A Campaign of Lies'. This article denounced the government for broadcasting the lie that Positive Action was over and that the people should return to work. Nkrumah was found guilty and sentenced to another year in prison, making three years in all, to run concurrently.

It was only the end of the beginning. Positive Action had not succeeded in its immediate aim of forcing the government to call a Constituent Assembly, but it had shaken it to its foundations. For in Nkrumah's words: 'The people had seen with their own eyes the economic life of the Gold Coast brought to a halt by unified people's effort in the form of a general strike. Never again would they accept that it was hopeless to attempt to attack a seemingly mighty power structure as that represented by the colonial administration.... The political revolution in the Gold Coast had begun in earnest, and it was only a question of time before the decisive confrontation would take place.'[1]

1. *Revolutionary Path*, p. 91.

5

From Prisoner to Prime Minister
and The Motion of Destiny

The arrest and imprisonment of Nkrumah and
other leaders of the CPP in 1950 had the effect of further strengthening the Party. They were recognised as
men prepared to suffer for the people, and as such
they attracted tremendous personal loyalty. For under
colonialism, to serve a prison sentence for political
activities was in itself a qualification for leadership.
Any national liberation leader of any calibre would
sooner or later find himself in prison. In Ghana, such
leaders were awarded the honour of being named
'prison graduates'. It was recognition that they had
sacrificed for the people.

Conditions in James Fort Prison in Accra, where
Nkrumah was imprisoned, were very bad even by colonial standards. He shared a small cell with ten others,
the only sanitation being a bucket in one corner. Food
was scarce and poor, and had to be eaten in the cell.
But Nkrumah at once set to work to organise the CPP
prisoners in order to discuss and to formulate Party
plans for the general election due to take place under
the Coussey Constitution in February 1951. It was
vital for the CPP to contest every seat in order to win
a majority in the Legislative Assembly.

Right from the start of his prison sentence,
Nkrumah had managed to get messages smuggled
out to party headquarters. These messages, written on
sheets of toilet paper, were mostly written in the small
patches of light made on the floor by a street light
which shone into the cell. A friendly warder then took

them to party headquarters where Komla Gbedemah and others, keeping in touch with Nkrumah, were carrying on the work of the CPP. One of Nkrumah's notes, written on ten small sheets of toilet paper, has survived. It is Nkrumah's reply to Gbedemah who had sent him a copy of an election manifesto drawn up by himself and his colleagues for the general election campaign.

Headed IMPORTANT, Nkrumah wrote on the first two pages as follows:

> 'I have read the draft of the manifesto. It is good work done and much labour has been expended on it. You and Lamptey deserve my congratulations for such comprehensive document. However, it is too elaborate to serve as a manifesto for an election campaign; that for an election campaign should be short, brief, simple, direct, popular and attractive, stating in concise paragraphs and headings just what the people and country want, especially in the economic and social spheres. The kind of programme and manifesto the party needs is just a two-leaf leaflet (4 or 8 page) like that of *What I mean by Positive Action.*'

He went on to advise Gbedemah to discuss the printing of a new manifesto with 'Mr Ankrah' chief printer at the *Evening News* press. Nkrumah said that he was preparing a new manifesto 'more concise and cheap to print, and will let you have it by Wednesday or Thursday. When you get it, please act quickly on it'. He ended, 'I am well and wish you the same'. In a postscript he thanked Gbedemah for the £2 sent to his mother.

A new concise manifesto, drawn up by Nkrumah was duly delivered on time to party headquarters. Nkrumah's name was already registered on the election roll. There remained the processing of the required electoral papers. This was arranged with the prison superintendent. The papers were signed and the deposit paid. Nkrumah was then qualified to stand as official CPP candidate for the Accra Central constituency.

The election was a resounding victory for the CPP. The Party won thirty-four out of a possible thirty-eight elected seats and also had a majority in the Assembly over the nominated candidates. Nkrumah was elected for Accra Central with 22,780 votes from a possible 23,122, the largest individual poll so far recorded. The colonial government, temporarily dismayed, had to allow the Executive Committee of the CPP into James Fort Prison to consult with Nkrumah. Support for the CPP had been very much stronger than the government had anticipated. Nkrumah as leader of the CPP would have to be released from prison and asked to become Leader of Government Business.

On 12 February 1951, having served only fourteen months of his three-year sentence, Nkrumah was released from prison and driven among cheering crowds to party headquarters. The following day he was invited by the Governor, Sir Charles Arden-Clarke, to form a government. The colonial power, in line with its policy of making concessions only when faced with irresistible pressure, had been forced to recognise that the CPP had the support of the vast majority of the people.

On the day after his release from prison, Nkrumah called a press conference at which he declared that the constitution under which he was to act as Leader of Government Business was 'bogus and fraudulent' but that it would serve temporarily as a stepping-stone towards self-government. A situation in which Africans had an overwhelming majority in the Assembly and in the Executive Council, yet the few members nominated by the Governor held the real reins of power, could not be tolerated for much longer. The ex-officio members, nominated by the Governor, controlled defence, external affairs, finance and justice. Furthermore, the Governor had the right to veto any legislation and the power to prorogue or dissolve parliament. All the ministries held by Ghanaians were dependent on the Ministry of Finance. This Ministry, controlled by an ex-officio member, was in a position to decide which sector of the economy should be given funds and which should be denied them. Difficulties were bound to develop.

Nevertheless, the CPP could make use of the radio, the press and other institutions to politicise the people. The CPP leadership was no longer at the mercy of the colonial police. It would be difficult, for example, for them to raid the offices of the *Evening News* and to charge its editor with sedition. The CPP could promote economic, social and educational advancement as a prelude to the implementation of a long-term policy of Africanisation of the civil service and other key sectors of the economy and administration. Priority would be given to an extensive programme of education, and the implementation of a Five Year Development Plan.

Through the Women's section of the CPP, the party's politicisation programme was carried into every home. Among notable women supporters at that time were Mabel Dove Danquah and Akua Asabea Ayisi who worked with Nkrumah on the *Accra Evening News*.

Women had taken an active part in the Positive Action Campaign, some being imprisoned, among them Letitia Quaye, Akua Asabea Ayisi and the elderly Ardua Ankrah, convicted for "unruly behaviour" in court during the trial of some of the activists. It was while Nkrumah was himself in prison that he was told of a CPP rally in Kumasi during which a woman who named herself "Ama Nkrumah" got on the platform and ended a fiery speech by slashing her face with a razor blade. Smearing blood over her body she challenged men to be prepared to shed blood in the cause of independence.

In May 1951, the CPP appointed four women to become Propaganda Secretaries. They were Mrs Letitia Quaye, Mrs Hanna Cudjoe, Madame Ama Nkrumah and Madame Sophia Doku. These and others travelled throughout the country holding rallies, enrolling new members into the CPP Women's Section and Youth League, stressing the great improvement in living conditions which independence would bring. For example, new schools, hospitals and roads would be built, and better drinking water provided. Women particularly had much to gain by independence, having for so long been discriminated against in education, employment, political and family life.

In the Accelerated Development Plan for Education, drawn up while Kojo Botsio was Minister of Education, provision was made for the introduction of universal free primary education, and for an increase in teacher training and technical education. Soon, more than half a million pupils were attending primary and middle schools throughout the country. A £2 million endowment fund was granted to the University College of the Gold Coast, situated at Achimota, a few miles from Accra. Plans were afoot for the College to become a fully-fledged university, and to move to a new site at Legon where building had begun on the first two Halls of Residence, Legon and Akuafo. Ultimately, there were to be five halls to accommodate over a thousand students.

Kumasi Hospital was built, providing over five hundred beds and many specialist departments. The project included a training college for some three hundred nurses to serve hospitals in the Ashanti area. Throughout the country, medical services were improved with the opening of more clinics with trained staff. Later, a medical school was founded to train doctors, and Korle Bu Hospital was built in Accra.

As far as economic development was concerned, two measures undertaken during the life of the First Legislative Assembly, were of exceptional potential importance. There were plans for the construction of a town and harbour at Tema to be linked to Accra by a new railway, and a farsighted scheme known as the Volta River Project. This envisaged the construction of a huge dam on the Volta to provide hydroelectric power to produce aluminium from local deposits of bauxite, and to generate electricity for an industrialisation programme. No longer would there be dependence on a single crop, cocoa. Ghana was to develop her own industries and agriculture as part of the general policy of self-reliance.

In 1953, the Gold Coast and British governments, together with British and Canadian business interests, set up a Preparatory Commission to make a thorough investigation of the Project. But it was not until 1956 that the Report was published. It stated that the Project was technically sound, and that it could be constructed and operated successfully. By then the estimated cost had risen from £114 million to £230 million. It was decided that there should be a 'breathing space' to allow all parties to consider the Report. Meantime, a model was made of the proposed dam, and a travelling exhibition with maps and diagrams toured the country to explain the Project to the people.

In a series of meetings and rallies throughout the country, Nkrumah himself spoke of CPP policies. At Anomabu, birthplace of Kwegyir Aggrey, he reiterated some of the principles by which the CPP stood. 'My hatred of imperialism can never dwindle, but what I want everyone in this country to remember is that we are fighting against a system and not against any individual, race or color'.[1]

Soon afterwards, in May 1951, Nkrumah and Kojo Botsio visited the United States. Nkrumah had received an invitation from the President of Lincoln University to accept a Doctor of Laws degree. It was an opportunity to visit his old university, and to carry out other engagements giving him the chance to explain the situation in the Gold Coast and to seek technical assistance for the development of the country. En route, they spent two days in London in the company of George Padmore. 'Together we went to George's flat where, seated around the old kitchen table, we related our activities since our last meeting'.[2]

1. *I Speak of Freedom*, p. 24.
2. *Autobiography*, p. 158.

Nkrumah receiving honorary degree of Doctor of Law, Lincoln University —
USA, 5 June, 1951 [L to R] The Hon. Kojo Botsio, Dr. Nkrumah,
Dr. W.H. Johnson and Dr. Horace Bond, President of the University

In America, Nkrumah was enthusiastically welcomed by Gold Coast students and businessmen, as well as by American government officials. In Philadelphia, he was presented with the keys of the city. There, Nkrumah took the opportunity to visit his old lodgings to see Mrs Borum, his landlady. She was surprised and delighted to see him. So too was Portia, whom he visited later. Nkrumah had left his small library of books in Portia's care when he left America for England in 1945. 'I lost no time in going to the bookcase, fingering each volume affectionately and remembering the struggle it had been procuring them. Each volume, I recalled, represented a sacrifice of some kind, mostly a meal or a bed for the night'.[1]

After receiving the Doctor of Laws degree at Lincoln University, Nkrumah returned to New York where he and Botsio called on the Mayor; afterwards spending some time at the United Nations headquarters where they attended a meeting of the Trusteeship Council. They talked with Trygve Lie, Ralph Bunche, Wilfrid Benson and others, discussing the possibility of help with planning the Volta River Scheme and other economic development projects.

There followed a brief visit to Washington where Nkrumah took the opportunity to discuss political and economic problems in the Gold Coast, and the struggle to achieve self-government. They left the USA on 10 June 1951, returning home determined to press ahead with the campaign for constitutional reform.

In view of the massive CPP election victory in 1951, the post of Leader of Government Business was clearly inappropriate for the leader of the predominant party in the legislature. No provision had been made in the Coussey Constitution for the position of a Prime Minister. But on 5 March 1952, the Governor announced in the Legislative Assembly that the British had decided that the position of Leader of Government Business should disappear from the constitution, and the office of Prime Minister should be formally recognised. Nkrumah thereupon became the first African Prime Minister. The Executive Council promptly resigned to be reconstructed as the Cabinet. The way had been cleared for the final steps to be taken towards independence. Discussions were held with the Governor and with Oliver Lyttleton, Secretary of State for the Colonies during his visit to the Gold Coast in June 1952.

---

1. *Autobiography*, p. 162.

The Cabinet consisted of seven members from the Legislative Assembly. They were:

Kojo Botsio, Minister of Education and Social Welfare
K.A. Gbedemah, Minister of Commerce and Industry
A. Caseley-Hayford, Minister of Agriculture and Natural Resources
E.O. Asafu-Adjaye, Minister of Local Government
J.A. Braimah, Minister of Communications and Works
T. Hutton-Mills, Minister of Health and Labour
Ansah Koi, Minister of Housing

Nkrumah, as Prime Minister, became also Minister of Development. There were thus eight Ghanaians in a Cabinet of eleven, the other three being ex-officio members nominated by the Governor. These members responsible to the Secretary of State for the Colonies, held the key ministries, and therefore the real power in the Executive.

Cabinet ministers were surprised to find on their assumption of office that the Budget estimates had been already prepared, and that they were expected to push the Budget through parliament as if it came from them. These, and other instances led to open conflict between the ministers and ex-officio members. Nkrumah saw that the basis of this conflict lay in the nature of the diarchy itself, for both sections represented opposite interests. It was imperative that a showdown be avoided, however, for this would have given the Governor an excuse to suspend the Constitution.

The composition of the Legislative Assembly was another matter for concern. In addition to three ex-officio members, it consisted of six special members of whom only two had the vote, and 75 other members. Of the 56 members representing the Colony, Ashanti and Southern Togoland, one third represented the chiefs and traditional authorities. These were elected not by universal adult suffrage but by the Joint Provincial Council and the Trans-Volta Southern Togoland Electoral College. The nineteen members representing the Northern Territories were elected by a system peculiar to the Northern Territories.

Clearly, there was need for a Commission of Enquiry to consider representational and electoral reform. In a statement in the Legislative Assembly in October 1952, Nkrumah declared: 'It is for the chiefs and people to consider whether the Assembly as at present constituted affords the best representation of the country which can be devised'. He questioned whether the three ex-officio members should be retained in the Cabinet, or be replaced by representative ministers. He called on chiefs and people, 'To place at the disposal of the government the best advice that they can give'. Months of consultation and discussion followed, leading to the publication of the 1953 government White Paper on Constitutional Reform.

Meantime, Nkrumah toured the country to see for himself how CPP organisation was progressing, and to stress the importance of the new local councils in building a vigorous, independent local government. For this would form the basis of free and democratic independence. Everywhere he went, Nkrumah took note of the people's urgent needs for basic amenities such as housing, dispensaries, water supplies, schools and so on.

On his return to Accra, he called a delegates' conference of the CPP to report on his countrywide tour, and to discuss the next phase in the struggle for independence. He informed the delegates of the decision of the party's National Executive to demand that an Act of Independence be simultaneously passed by the British Parliament and the Gold Coast Legislative Assembly declaring that the Gold Coast, under the new name of Ghana, be proclaimed a sovereign and independent state.

On 10 July 1953, Nkrumah introduced into the Legislative Assembly the historic 'Motion of Destiny'. This called upon Britain to make constitutional and administrative arrangements for independence so that all members of the Assembly be elected directly by secret ballot, and Cabinet members be members of the Assembly and directly responsible to it. 'If there is to be a criterion of people's preparedness for self-government, then I say it is their readiness to assume the responsibility of ruling themselves. For who but a people themselves can say when they are prepared?'[1]

Nkrumah's 'Motion of Destiny' speech was one of his finest. Every seat in the Assembly was filled, and large crowds had gathered outside. He spoke at length of events leading up to the demand for an end to colonial rule. 'We have travelled long distances from when our fathers came under alien subjugation to the present time. We now stand at the threshold of self-government and do not waver. '[2] After summarising the history of the Gold Coast he said, 'In the future we would doubtless make mistakes, as all nations had done. But the mistakes would be our

---

1. *I Speak of Freedom*, p. 31. For the full text of 'The Motion of Destiny' see *Revolutionary Path*, pp. 100–115.
2. Ibid.

own mistakes, and it would be our responsibility to put them right'.[1] Loud cheering followed. He went on to remind members that independence was not an end it itself, but a means to an end, 'The building of a good life to the benefit of all, regardless of tribe, creed, colour or station in life. Our aim is to make this country a worthy place for all its citizens, a country that will be a shining light throughout the whole continent of Africa.'[2] He ended by quoting:

'Man's dearest possession is life, and since it is given to him to live but once, he must so live as not to be besmeared with the shame of a cowardly existence and trivial past, so live that by dying he might say; all my life and all my strength were given to the finest cause in the world — the liberation of mankind.'[3]

The Motion of Destiny took Britain by surprise. It demanded self-government now, and a clear commitment by Britain to a date for full independence. The colonial planners had not expected such a Motion so soon. At most, they anticipated a Motion on self-government. But Nkrumah, having felt the pulse of the people, wanted to telescope the entire period of preparation to a few years. In doing so, it was Nkrumah who was setting the pace. Yet as in 1951, Britain could do nothing about the matter beyond insisting on another election; for Nkrumah was following the rules of the game by using the constitutional machinery available to him to put forward his programme.

Britain conceded the demand for self-government but insisted on another election. There was to be a Legislative Assembly of 104 members, all members being directly elected by secret ballot. In addition, all cabinet ministers were to be directly responsible to the Assembly. Two portfolios, those of Finance and Interior, were handed over to Ghanaians. But Britain kept the portfolios of External Affairs and Defence.

The UGCC which had stood against the CPP in the 1951 election, had lost support, as the decisive CPP victory demonstrated. Some of these opposition elements, however, regrouped to form the Ghana People's Congress (GPC). Against the CPP demand for self-government now, they said they stood for self-government soon. Regional and openly religious parties surfaced to contest the elections. At the last moment,

---

1. *I Speak of Freedom*, p. 31.
2. Ibid., p. 31–32.
3. Ibid., p. 32.

the Northern People's Party (NPP) emerged to the dismay of Nkrumah, for it announced its plans at the last moment, when the CPP had no time to campaign in the North. The Muslim Association made no secret of its religious foundation and its aim to uphold chieftaincy. Britain, however, had great faith in those renegade CPP members who having failed to gain a party nomination now stood as independents.

Outwardly, the opposition parties looked quite formidable. But the results of the June 1954 elections were a severe jolt to the colonial power. Again, the strength of the CPP had been under-estimated and the strength of the opposition over-estimated. The CPP won 72 out of the 104 seats in the Assembly and polled 391,817 votes. The second largest group were the Independents, who managed to get 156,401. The GPC, on which Britain had pinned so much faith, secured only one seat with a total vote of 32,168. The CPP emerged as the only national party with 38 seats in the Colony, 18 in Ashanti, 8 in Trans-Volta and 8 in the Northern Territories. The Independents won 20 seats, but within two years of the election seven Independents had joined the CPP. This election gave the Gold Coast its first all-African Assembly.

The great CPP victory was in Ashanti, the home of powerful chiefs. It was only in the Northern Territories that the CPP failed to get a majority. Neither of the opposition parties were able to win seats outside their particular areas.

Faced with the clear verdict of the people, opposition elements emerged under a new name, the National Liberation Movement (NLM). Although described as a 'national' movement it was largely Ashanti-based. The issue of cocoa prices was key to NLM policies, and this they linked with federalism. There had been unrest in the cocoa-growing area of the country since 1951 when, in an attempt to stop the spread of swollen shoot disease, the New Deal for Cocoa was announced. Cocoa farmers resisted attempts to persuade them to cut down diseased trees, until eventually it became necessary to compel them to do so.

A Cocoa Duty and Development Funds Amendment Bill in August 1954 guaranteed the price to be paid to cocoa farmers, and made funds from cocoa sales available for the development of the country as a whole. Anti-CPP elements, particularly in Ashanti, made use of the Bill to stir up regional animosities by alleging that the government in Accra was spending too much on developing the coastal or Colony region. The Asanteman Council, headed by the Asantahene, joined forces with the NLM. The NLM claimed that Ashanti, as the main cocoa-producing region, was not getting its fair share of the funds from cocoa sales. Ashanti should therefore manage its own affairs and utilise cocoa revenue for its own needs.

It was at this time that the British press began what came to be a relentless campaign to discredit Nkrumah. Open support was shown for the NLM while Nkrumah was portrayed as a dictator. Members of the NLM referred to the CPP as the 'Communist People's Party.' For a time, the rate of progress towards independence was slowed while CPP supporters and the NLM contested the question of whether Ghana should be a unitary or a federalist state.

During the next eighteen months, violence periodically erupted in various parts of the country, mostly stirred up by NLM supporters. Some chiefs loyal to the CPP were destooled. CPP members were intimidated and some physically assaulted. The sister of Krobo Edusei, a founder member of the CPP, was shot and killed. An attempt was made to assassinate Nkrumah when a bomb was placed against his house in Accra. Nkrumah, two party colleagues and Erica Powell (his secretary) were upstairs in the home when the bomb exploded in the yard outside. Nkrumah at once rushed down the steps from the verandah to see if his mother was all right. 'Every window in the house had been blown in and the brickwork was chipped. It seemed a miracle that no-one had been killed or hurt'.[1]

In spite of the tireless efforts of Nkrumah to reach agreement on the federation question, leaders of the NLM declined an invitation to discuss the matter at a Round Table Conference. They refused the invitation on the excuse that it had come from the four members of the Legislative Assembly and not from the government. Nkrumah therefore sent them an official invitation, but this was also refused. Three times the NLM turned down invitations to discuss the matter, and whenever the subject was raised in the Assembly the NLM members walked out. Finally Nkrumah on 5 April 1955 introduced a motion into the Assembly calling for the setting up of a Select Committee to examine the question of the federal system of government in the Gold Coast. Once again, the NLM walked out of the Assembly and refused to take part in the work of the Select Committee. Nevertheless, the Select Committee held twenty-two meetings and considered some 279 petitions. Eventually, on

---

1. *Private Secretary (Female) Gold Coast*, Eric Powell, C. Hurst, London 1984, p. 97.

26 July 1955 it issued a Report rejecting the idea of a federal form of government, and recommending the setting up of Regional Councils which would take over certain powers and functions from the central government.

The total area of Ghana is about 92,000 square miles and the population before independence was only in the region of six million. Yet the NLM, born only in the final stages of the independence struggle, called for a federal constitution.

Nkrumah invited Britain to send out a constitutional adviser to help draw up a suitable constitution. Sir Frederick Bourne was sent and arrived in the Gold Coast on 26 September 1955. He travelled widely throughout the country, sounding opinion at every level and consulting most of the national organisations. Once again however, the NLM were unco-operative and refused to discuss the matter. Nevertheless, on 17 December, Sir Frederick Bourne delivered his Report to the Governor in which he recommended the devolution of certain powers to the Regional Councils, but left all legislative power with the central legislature.

Still, the colonial power prevaricated. The CPP electoral victory in 1954 was a clear indication that a substantial majority of the people wanted independence; but the Secretary of State declared that independence would not be granted until a substantial majority of the people had shown that they wanted independence in the very near future, and had agreed upon a workable constitution. If these conditions were fulfilled the British government would be prepared to fix a firm date for independence. To satisfy these conditions, Nkrumah declared that he was ready to hold another election 'when circumstances demanded', and proceeded to call a conference of all the major political, social and territorial organisations of the country to meet on 16 February 1956 to consider Sir Frederick Bourne's Report and the constitutional question. Again, the NLM and the Ashanti Council refused to participate. But the conference was attended by delegations from the Brong-Kyempem Council, the CPP, the Ex-Servicemen's Union, the Muslim Council, the Joint Provisional Council of Chiefs, the Trades Union Congress, the Trans-Volta/Togoland Council and Local Government Councils in the Northern Territories.

Despite the representative nature of the conference, the Secretary of State declared that it was not representative enough because the NLM had not participated. Undaunted, Nkrumah drew up constitutional

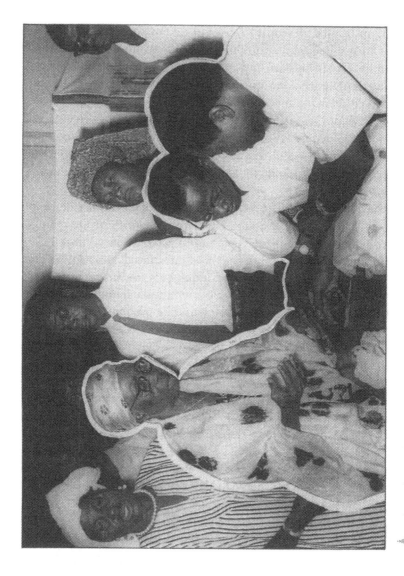

Nkrumah's mother Nyanibah voting by fingerprint — Accra, 1956

proposals for the sovereign and independent state of 'Ghana', and put them before the Assembly on 15 May 1956. The Assembly was then dissolved and a general election announced for July. The Secretary of State thereupon declared: 'If a General Election is held, Her Majesty's Government will be ready to accept a motion calling for Independence within the Commonwealth passed by a reasonable majority in a newly elected Legislature and then to declare a firm date for attainment of this purpose.'

This was a shrewd move. The British government challenged the CPP to go to the people once more. As far as Nkrumah was concerned, he had confidence in the people and knew that the CPP would carry the day as it had in 1951 and 1954. But the situation had changed since the last election. There had been the unrest and violence of the previous eighteen months, and a hostile press campaign had to some extent succeeded in confusing issues.

Faced with this situation, Nkrumah made a characteristic move. With one decisive blow he cut straight through the confusion and the lies and appealed directly to the people, putting before them the straightforward question: 'Do I want independence in my lifetime? or Do I want to revert to feudalism and imperialism?' This was his election manifesto summed up in just seventeen words. Nkrumah was determined not to allow the election campaign to drift away from the issue which had provoked it: that is, a unitary versus a federal structure of government. The election was decisive in the struggle for final political freedom for Ghana and the point had to be made clear to the people. With a mass rally in the Accra Arena, the CPP election machinery swung into action. Nkrumah himself travelled hundreds of miles, addressing meetings in support of CPP candidates. Time and again he pointed out to the people that this was no ordinary election. The whole future of the country was at stake.

During the evening of election day, as results were being announced on the radio, and signs indicated another sweeping CPP victory, Nkrumah telephoned his secretary, Erica Powell, to join him. She, however, was about to have her evening meal and in any case was hesitant to drive through the excited crowds thronging the streets of Accra. Nkrumah therefore invited himself to join her. Together they listened to the radio describing the jubilant crowds gathering at the Polo Ground, where a large board had been erected to display the results as they came in. Nkrumah wanted to be out in the streets among the people, so when

Erica offered to drive him there in her little 500cc Fiat, he immediately agreed. Someone had left a red beret in Erica's car. Nkrumah put it on, pulling it down almost to his eyebrows. Then he sat beside her, arms folded, smiling but not saying a word as they edged through the crowds. 'The disguise was perfect. I had a job to convince myself that it was really Kwame Nkrumah sitting there'.[1]

When she drove him back to his house, the place was filled with people laughing and chatting as they awaited his arrival. The time had come for him to go to the Polo Ground to appear before the people who had returned him to power with such a massive majority. Erica drove back to her home alone. 'But for the very cheap red beret lying on the seat beside me, it might well have been a mad dream. '[2]

The leader of the NLM, Dr Kofi Busia, had been confident of winning the election. He actually sent a note to the Governor asking him to call on him to form a government if his party succeeded in winning 52 seats. But again, as in 1951 and 1954, the electorate rejected his policies. The CPP in 1956 won a victory as impressive as those in 1951 and 1954. The CPP had the same majority as in 1954. It had won every seat in the Colony and in Accra itself, obtaining 82 per cent of the votes cast. In Trans-Volta/Togoland, the CPP won eight seats out of thirteen, and polled a clear majority of the total votes. In the Northern Territories, the result were eleven seats out of a possible twenty-six. Even in Ashanti, where the NLM was strongest, the CPP won eight of the twenty-one seats with 43 per cent of the total votes. It had been proved once more that the CPP was the only party which had support from all parts of the country. It was now impossible to assert that the CPP did not have the support of a 'reasonable majority' in the Assembly. The issue of independence could no longer be delayed.

However, in spite of the clear verdict of the electorate, Busia was intent on causing further delay. He called a press conference in Kumasi to announce that since the CPP had not obtained overall majorities in Ashanti and the Northern Territories, the need for a federal form of government had been proved. Later, on the occasion of the formal opening of the Assembly, the Opposition failed to attend to hear the Governor announce that the British government would within the week set in

1. *Private Secretary (Female) Gold Coast*, Eric Powell, C. Hurst, London 1984, p. 41.
2. Ibid.

motion a Bill declaring the Gold Coast a sovereign and independent state within the Commonwealth. The very next day the NLM tabled an amendment stating that the proposal was 'premature' until a further effort had been made to secure an 'agreed constitution'. The amendment was rejected, and the NLM then announced that its members would not attend the Assembly when the Independence motion came before it. They were therefore absent when the final vote for independence was given in the Assembly.

In one last attempt to prevent Independence, Busia flew to London to appeal to the British government, stating that the Gold Coast was not ready for parliamentary democracy. 'We still need you (the British) in the Gold Coast. Your experiment there is not complete. Sometimes I wonder why you seem in such a hurry to wash your hands of us'.

He was unsuccessful. On 17 September 1956, in response to a formal request from the CPP to the Secretary of State to fix a firm date for independence, the Governor informed Nkrumah that 6 March 1957 had been decided upon. Amid scenes of great jubilation, the news was given to the Assembly by Nkrumah on the following day 18 September 1956.

Thereafter, events moved swiftly. In Accra, as preparations were made for Independence Day, the building of State House was completed. A monumental arch was constructed bearing the inscription 'Freedom and Justice', the motto on the crest of independent Ghana. The Ambassador Hotel was built to accommodate the hundreds of guests expected. Throughout the country, plans were made in every town and village so that everyone could join in celebrating the forthcoming historic occasion.

6

Independence

On leaving the Assembly on 18 September 1956 after the dramatic announcement of the date for Ghana's independence, Nkrumah was carried shoulder high into the street outside where crowds were celebrating, singing the CPP song, 'There is victory for us'. It was Nkrumah's forty seventh birthday, a strange coincidence and a day which he came to regard as one of the happiest of his life. Congratulations poured in from all over the world. At Independence, it would be one hundred and thirteen years since the Bond of 1844 which had led to the British colonial government of the Gold Coast.

Amid the celebration it was typical of Nkrumah to remember the role the Governor had played in helping to secure a firm date for Independence. During the afternoon of the 18th, Nkrumah and his ministers called at the Castle 'to share with him the victory'.[1]

Two months later, on 12 November 1956, Nkrumah placed before the Assembly a Motion for the Approval of the Government's Revised Constitutional Proposals. In his longest speech before independence, Nkrumah set Ghana's historic struggle for freedom within the context of PanAfricanism. 'We have a duty not only to the people of this country, but to the people everywhere in Africa who are striving towards independence. If we can make a success of our independence, we shall have made an incalculable contribution

---

1. *Autobiography*, p. 286.

towards freedom and progress throughout Africa.'[1] He spoke of the tasks ahead, for example, the need to Africanise the administrative machinery of government. Fundamental human rights would be respected. There would be free elections, free speech, freedom for all citizens to join any trade union, political party or other association, freedom of religion, a free press and an independent judiciary. Although all these provisions could not, for practical reasons, be included in the Independence Order in Council, they would be implemented once independence had been achieved.

Meantime, Accra was already being seen as an appropriate centre for PanAfrican occasions. On 14 January 1957, the All-African Regional Conference of the International Confederation of Free Trade Unions (ICFTU) was inaugurated in Accra. Nkrumah had experienced membership of a trade union when in the USA. As a student worker he had belonged to the National Maritime Union. In welcoming delegates to the conference, he emphasised the need to develop a strong trade union movement in Africa as part of the struggle within the so-called Third World to attain economic and social justice.' Unfortunately, wealthy industrial countries often fail to realise that the source of their prosperity is bound up with the progress and economic development in the less fortunately developed countries who produce the primary products, and from which come the raw materials essential to modern industry'.[2]

Later, the All-African Trade Union Federation (AATUF) was founded. This PanAfrican organisation, unlike ICFTU and the World Federation of Trade Unions (WFTU) both of which were non-African dominated, was developed 'to give our working class a new African consciousness and the right to express themselves in the councils of the World Labour'.[3]

All those years ago, Nkrumah was warning of World Bank and International Monetary Fund (IMF) policies, saying that they would be counter-productive to Africa's progress, bringing disastrous social and

---

1. *I Speak of Freedom*, p. 71.
2. Speech in Accra on 14 June 1957 at the Inauguration of the All-African Regional Conference of the International Confederation of Free Trade Unions (ICFTU). *I Speak of Freedom*, p. 86.
3. *Africa Must Unite*, p. 128. Subsequently, AATUF gave way to the Organisation of African Trade Union Unity (OATUU) with headquarters in Ghana. This organisation has remained weak and dependent on foreign aid. The World Seventh PanAfrican Congress, held in Kampala in April 1994, mandated the formation of a new workers' organisation designed to meet post Cold War conditions.

economic results. In the face of a world economic network of industrialised powers and multinational corporations, the building of a strong
PanAfrican trade union organisation to act in the interests of African
labour, was essential. Nkrumah saw in AATUF 'a dynamic and positive
instrument for drawing together the people of the African countries....
It can become an immediate practical union, bringing together the Labour movements existing in the independent African states and leaving
room for others to join as they became free. We in Africa must learn to
band together to promote African interests or fall victims to imperialist
manoeuvres to recolonise us'.[1]

Ten days before Independence, on 24 February 1957 a CPP conference was held at Saltpond. Addressing the meeting Nkrumah was again
thinking ahead. 'With independence won, where do we go next?'[2]
Critics have accused him of always being in too much of a hurry, of seeing visions of distant horizons instead of concentrating on the immediate landscape. It is a criticism commonly levelled at those considered
to be 'ahead of their time', as though this was a fault and not a quality
distinguishing statesman from politician.

As Independence Day approached, thousands gathered in Accra.
Apart from Ghanaians, there were representatives of fifty six countries
and of the United Nations Organisation. Vice President Nixon headed
the US delegation. The British government sent R. A. Butler, Lord Privy
Seal and Home Secretary, the Duchess of Kent to represent the Queen,
and a parliamentary delegation. Liberia sent her Vice President, W.S.
Tolbert Jnr accompanied by members of the House of Representatives
and the Senate. The prime minister of Tunisia Habib Bourguiba attended.
The Soviet Union, Poland, Rumania, Yugoslavia and the Republic of
China sent delegations, as well as Japan, India the Philippines, Canada,
Ceylon, Sierra Leone, Greece, Iran, Italy, Portugal, Spain, Sweden, the
Vatican, Germany, Pakistan, Switzerland, and the Sudan. The High Com-
missioner of French West Africa and French Equatorial Africa was there,
and even the Spanish Governor of Fernando Po. Representatives were
sent by South Africa, Austria, Brazil, Haiti, Holland, Iceland, Israel,
Mexico, New Zealand, Peru, Czechoslovakia and Nigeria. Then there
were those personally invited by Nkrumah: among them, the widow of
Dr Aggrey, George Padmore, Martin Luther King, Fenner Brockway, and

1. *Africa Must Unite*, p. 128.
2. *I Speak of Freedom*, p. 90.

the Reverend A.G. Fraser, first headmaster of Achimota School. In addition, representatives of students' organisations in Ghana, Britain and the USA were invited. So also were leading figures in Africa and the West Indies, including the Kabaka of Buganda King Fred Mutesa II and Sir Alexander Bustamente of Jamaica.

Among media representatives were correspondents representing radio and TV, news agencies and many newspapers ranging from *Pravda* to the *Eastern Nigerian Catholic Herald*, from South Africa's *Die Burger* to the *Manchester Guardian*. Also in Accra were Leslie Murby and Van Milne of Thomas Nelson and Sons, publishers of Nkrumah's *Autobiography* timed to be launched in Ghana at Independence.[1]

It was an incredible feat of organisation for Ghana to host such a huge gathering. Accommodation and services were stretched to the limit; many delegations turned up with more members than expected. But there was scarcely a hitch in the arrangements. Ceremonies were carried out with precision in a fitting atmosphere of solemnity and joy.

On the 5th of March, the eve of Independence, Nkrumah made a major policy statement before the prorogation of the last Assembly of the Gold Coast. His speech ranged over domestic and foreign policies which the government of Ghana intended to pursue. 'Every step in the government's power, both internally and in its external relations, will be taken to further the development of the nation's resources for the common good.... The government hopes that, as a free, sovereign and independent state, Ghana can become the centre for the discussion of African problems as a whole... Our aim is to work with others to achieve an African Personality in African affairs'.[2] Ghana would apply for membership of the United Nations, and would remain in the Commonwealth. The foreign policy of Ghana, he said, would not be dictated by the need to seek assistance from other countries. He pointed out that the material basis already existed for independence. 'We can stand on our own feet.'[3] It did not mean that western influence, techniques and methods were not applicable to Africa, or that Ghana would not need foreign investment. But it did mean 'that in Ghana we must look at every problem from an African standpoint.'[4]

1. On inscribing a copy of his *Autobiography* for Van Milne, Nkrumah wrote (in green ink): 'It is far better to govern or misgovern yourself than to be governed by anybody else.'
2. *I Speak of Freedom*, p. 98.
3. Ibid., p. 99.
4. ", p. 101.

At midnight, outside the Assembly building, where a large crowd had gathered, the Union Jack was lowered and the new red, green, and gold flag of Ghana was raised. The appearance of Nkrumah at the door of the House was greeted with loud cheering, calls of 'Freedom', 'Show Boy' and the singing of 'There is victory for us'. Nkrumah was carried shoulder high to the nearby Polo Ground where tens of thousands had gathered. There, he stood on a small wooden platform draped with a cloth of the new Ghana colours. With him, wearing, like him, Northern Territory dress and 'prison graduate' caps, stood Cabinet colleagues A. Caseley-Hayford, Minister of Communications, Kojo Botsio, Minister of Trade and Labour, and A. K. Gbedemah, Minister of Finance.

With great emotion, Nkrumah began to speak: 'At long last the battle has ended. And thus Ghana your beloved country is free for ever.' After a minute's silence to remember all those who had contributed and sacrificed so much to end colonial rule, the Ghanaian national anthem was played again and again. 'We shall no more go back to sleep', Nkrumah said, 'Today, from now on, there is a new African in the world.'[1] Ghanaians had won their political battle for freedom. Other battles, social and economic lay ahead. Above all, there remained the need 'to re-dedicate ourselves in the struggle to emancipate other countries in Africa; 'For our independence is meaningless unless it is linked up with the total liberation of the African continent.'[2]

The following morning, the Duchess of Kent opened the first session of the Parliament of Ghana. In reply to her goodwill message from the Queen, Nkrumah repeated the long-term objectives expressed on the Polo Ground the night before. Ghana's future was inextricably linked with that of 'those millions in Africa who put their trust in us.... By our actions the whole future of Africa must be affected.'[3] He was indicating the next stages in a struggle which had only just begun, the building of a new society in Ghana based on socialist principles, and an active commitment to the total liberation and unification of Africa. No-one hearing him at Independence could have been left in any doubt about the policies of the CPP government.

Among the foreign visitors attending the ceremonies there were probably some who thought Nkrumah's objectives unrealistic. Though

1. *I Speak of Freedom*, p. 107.
2. Ibid.
3. ", p.110.

to judge by the high-powered delegations from Africa and overseas who travelled to Ghana from all over the world in March 1957, Ghana's independence was taken very seriously.

At a press conference, the first since Independence, Nkrumah again took the opportunity to outline domestic and foreign policy aims. Correspondents questioned him closely, particularly about his PanAfricanism. Nkrumah denied that Ghana would interfere in the internal affairs of African countries. 'We shall help others by our example.'[1] Answering a question about the Volta project, Nkrumah replied: 'It is my baby and my ambition.'[2] He would do anything to achieve it, but the government would need a year or more to consolidate before embarking on major development projects. There were lighter moments. When somebody asked about the post of a Deputy Prime Minister, Nkrumah asked, 'Do I look so old as to need a Deputy?'[3]

The atmosphere was relaxed throughout, a good start to Nkrumah's relations with the international press. They reported him charming and confident, refusing to be drawn into rash statements. Having been a newspaper man himself he enjoyed meeting pressmen. In later years, however, he became increasingly less willing to talk with foreign correspondents, particularly those from western countries whom he considered dishonest in their reporting. Time and again he was exasperated by their hostile presentation, often misquoting him or printing excerpts from his statements taken out of context.

He particularly disliked any attempt to intrude on his home and family. It was on the evening of 30 December 1957 that Ghana radio announced that Nkrumah had married an Egyptian, Fathia Rizk, at a private ceremony in Christiansborg Castle. The news came as a complete surprise to all but the few who attended the wedding. The bride, who had only recently arrived in Ghana, had been chosen by President Nasser as a suitable wife for Nkrumah. She spoke little English. Nkrumah did not speak Arabic or French. Nor had the couple met before, though photos had been sent from Cairo. To many it seemed a strange arrangement, though explicable in terms of Nkrumah's PanAfricanism. The offspring of such a union, inheriting North African and sub-Saharan

---

1. *West Africa* magazine, 16 March 1957, p. 241.
2. Ibid.
3. " .

cultures, would symbolise Nkrumah's vision of a united Africa. Others thought the marriage was designed to put an end to speculation among Ghanaians as to whom he would marry. As prime minister he was required to host an increasing number of public occasions. It was desirable for him to be accompanied by a hostess. A Ghanaian bride might have stirred up tribal jealousies. Then there were those who thought the marriage had been advised on medical grounds. Nkrumah's health was of concern. There had been scares attributed to overwork. It was thought by some that he needed the relaxation a normal family life could provide.

Nkrumah seldom spoke of his personal life. He regarded his wife and children as 'purely private', having nothing to do with his official and public life. For example, when the publishers of his book *Neo-Colonialism*, Thomas Nelson & Sons, prepared notes on the author to appear on the dust jacket and mentioned that Nkrumah was 'married with three children',[1] he scored out the passage as totally irrelevant. In a letter written in November 1964 to Shirley DuBois, the head of Ghana's television service, he wrote: 'People in general seem to be insatiably curious about the family and private lives of those who are in the public eye. It has always been my strong conviction that my domestic affairs — my home, my family — are purely private matters which should not be mixed up with my official and public life. I see no reason why I should exhibit my wife and children in order to satisfy public curiosity.'[2]

In the history of all countries there are landmark dates when decisive events happen, and conditions are never the same again. Unquestionably, the landmark date for Ghana is 6 March 1957. The unique importance of this date lies in the fact that it is not only a landmark in Ghana's history, but in the history of Africa as a whole, and in the history of PanAfricanism. For from that time, until 1966 when the CPP government was ended by a military coup d'état, Ghana's example and Nkrumah's leadership generated a remarkable succession of developments throughout the continent of Africa, and in the diaspora.

---

1. Gamal, the elder son of Fathia, was named after President Abdel Gamal Nasser of Egypt. There followed a daughter, Samia, and a second son, Sékou, named after President Ahmed Sékou Touré of Guinea. Nkrumah had a son, Francis, in the Gold Coast (Ghana) before he left to complete his education in the USA. Francis was to become a distinguished doctor of medicine.
2. *Private Secretary (Female) Gold Coast*, Erica Powell, pp. 125–126.

At Independence the world spotlight was on Ghana. Nkrumah's openly declared vision of a genuinely free and unified continent, and his determination to build a just society, ensured that it would remain on. For the independence of Ghana ushered in far reaching historical processes which have continued to be relevant and ongoing throughout Africa and the diaspora, indicating that the PanAfrican political philosophy which inspired them has stood the test of time.

Driving to Accra Stadium, Independence Day, 6 March 1957.
[L to R] Komla Gbedemah, Kwame Nkrumah, Kojo Botsio

7

"Africa Must Unite"

Soon after Ghana's independence, invitations were sent to all the independent states of Africa to attend a conference in Accra early in 1958. There were then only eight independent states. They were Ghana, Ethiopia, Libya, Tunisia, Morocco, Egypt, Liberia and Sudan. It was to be the first conference of its kind, and to mark the reactivation of PanAfricanism on the soil of Africa, its true home.

In a speech at the opening of the conference on 15 April 1958, Nkrumah outlined the purpose of this historic conference:

> 'We are here to know ourselves and to exchange views on matters of common interest; to explore ways and means of consolidating and safeguarding our hard-won independence; to strengthen economic and cultural ties between our countries to find workable arrangements for helping our brothers still languishing under colonial rule; to examine the central problem which dominates the world today, namely the problem of how to secure peace.'[1]

He said that free and independent states should avoid entanglement in the quarrels of the great powers by following a policy of non-alignment so that they could implement social and economic development programmes to raise the standard of living of their

---

1. *I Speak of Freedom*, pp. 126–127.

peoples. This could best be achieved in an environment of world peace. He appealed to the great powers to resolve their differences, and to cease spending astronomical sums on piling up stocks of weapons which, if employed, 'Will wipe out mankind and leave this earth barren and desolate.'[1] He was referring here to nuclear weapons and in particular to French plans to use the Sahara as the testing ground. 'Radioactive winds know no international frontiers, and it is these tests — in a period of so-called peace — which can do more than anything else to threaten our very existence.... We vehemently condemn this proposal and protest against the use of our continent for such purposes.'[2]

Subsequently, when the French did carry out a test in the Sahara, the independence movement in Africa had spread, and Nkrumah was in a stronger position to take the initiative to express the voice of the independent African states. As a direct result of his leadership, France was compelled to end the testing of nuclear bombs on African soil. The authentic voice of Africa was beginning to be heard in world affairs.

At the 1958 Accra Conference, the eight independent states agreed to co-ordinate their economic planning; to improve communications between their states; to exchange cultural, scientific and educational information; and to assist liberation movements by providing training and other facilities for them. But for Nkrumah, 'Probably the most important single achievement of the Conference was the adoption of the formula of one man, one vote, as an objective of the African Revolution. This gave the liberation movement direction and cohesion.'[3] The resolutions passed at the Conference defined a new and positive approach to the problems of Africa, an All-African approach, embodying the determination to liberate the entire African continent and to work towards continental unification. It was decided that the 15th April each year should be designated 'Africa Freedom Day' to mark the progress of the liberation movement.

Six weeks after the Conference ended, Nkrumah visited all the countries which had taken part. His purpose was to familiarise himself with the particular conditions and problems of the separate countries, and to cement relationships which had developed during the conference. As always, he attached great importance to the time factor, and

1. *I Speak of Freedom*, p. 130.
2. Ibid.
3. *Revolutionary Path*, p. 126.

Nkrumah welcoming Nigerian politician Nnamdi Azikiwe (ZIK) — Accra, c. 1958

Nkrumah with his Egyptian wife, Fathia Rizk — Accra Stadium, 1958

was anxious to prevent the independent states from slipping back into narrow, national positions. Nkrumah wished to speed up the liberation process and the unification process which he considered interdependent. On this, the first of his major trips abroad after Ghana's independence, Nkrumah and his entourage travelled over 20,000 miles. It was a political success in that it helped to establish a precedent for meetings between heads of independent states and resulted in an impetus being given to PanAfrican processes. But it was more than that. It marked the beginning of a period in Africa's history which was to be characterised by rapid and dynamic change. The example and leadership of the Nkrumah government in Ghana began to permeate every part of the African continent, and emerged as a factor of increasing importance on the world political scene.

It was during this exciting year that I first met Nkrumah and agreed to help, as and when required, in the work of assembling material for his books and seeing them through the press. The success of his *Autobiography* had led the publishers (Nelson) and party (CPP) officials to press Nkrumah for another book. The latter was to be a collection of his speeches in what was to be his second book *I Speak of Freedom*. As a person who had some knowledge of Ghana, having worked for three years in the History Department of the (then) University College of the Gold Coast, now the University of Ghana, I was considered suitably qualified for the work. We met in London while as Prime Minister, Nkrumah was on an official visit. Nkrumah said that he could arrange for texts of speeches to be posted to me. Some of them had been published separately in Ghana by the government printer or had appeared in local newspapers. The speeches were to be selected and arranged with a connecting narrative.

From that time onwards I became involved in the processing of all his subsequent books, except *Consciencism*, which originated from the thesis Nkrumah was working on when a PhD student in London under the supervision of Professor Ayer.

My work involved frequent visits to Ghana researching, and liaising with Nkrumah's UK publishers, Nelson and later Heinemann Educational Books Ltd, checking galleys and page proofs with Nkrumah. All this gave me a wonderful opportunity to witness developments taking place in Ghana during the period of CPP government.

In December 1958, Nkrumah followed up the Conference of Independent African States with an All-African People's Conference. This

Conference represented freedom fighter movements, nationalist parties, as well as trade unions, co-operative and youth movements from all over Africa. Some three hundred delegates attended. It was the first time that members of freedom movements from British, French, Portuguese, Spanish and the racist minority regimes had met together to discuss common problems and to formulate plans. It was a major move to end Balkanisation, the delegates seeing clearly that their struggles were inextricably linked and were part of the continental struggle for total liberation and unification.

History was also made when the conference endorsed the right of the unliberated to use all methods of struggle available to them to obtain their objectives, including armed struggle. According to the provisional agenda, the conference members were to work out strategy and tactics for a 'non-violent' revolution. But one of the national movements invited to the conference was the FLN of Algeria. Frantz Fanon was a member of the five-man delegation, and he and his colleagues were received by Nkrumah as highly-honoured delegates. Nkrumah's example was noted by the rest of the conference members who also enthusiastically welcomed the Algerian patriots. Unlike other national movements represented at the conference, the FLN had embarked on armed struggle. But in the very receptive political atmosphere of the conference, it was able to put forward its point of view and to receive warm support. The result was that the conference was able to evolve a very important principle, that the oppressed have the right to use violence against the oppressor if all non-violent methods have failed. This cleared the way, and set a precedent for other national movements, for example, in the Portuguese colonies, Rhodesia (Zimbabwe) and South Africa. Freedom fighters in these areas were soon to follow the road of the FLN in Algeria. All-African People's Conferences held in Tunis in 1960, and in Cairo in 1961 went further. Resolutions were passed to support both morally and materially the FLN and other such movements employing the armed method of struggle.

Present at the 1958 All-African People's Conference in Accra were Patrice Lumumba, Julius Nyerere, Kenneth Kaunda, Kanyama Chiume, Tom Mboya, Oginga Odinga, Joshua Nkomo, and many others who were to become notable political leaders. Lumumba was head of the MNC (Movement National Congolais). He was soon to become the country's first democratically elected prime minister. After his own government was overthrown through the use of UN troops, he too decided that the only course left open to him was to launch an armed struggle to win back the independence of his country from the forces of neo-colonialism. Conference members returned to their respective countries determined to end colonial rule. On independence, African governments followed Ghana's example in making their territories base areas for freedom fighters.

A significant first step towards African unification was taken when Ghana and Guinea formed a political union in November 1958. The Ghana-Guinea Union was intended as a pilot scheme for a wider Union of African States. As Nkrumah stated, it was the intention of himself and President Sékou Touré of Guinea to start the unification process by setting up an embryo organisation which other states could join as and when they wished. Nkrumah had found in Sékou Touré a man after his own heart - a man who had led his country to obtain independence from French rule and who had shown remarkable courage and confidence in rejecting General de Gaulle's call for Guinea to remain a member of the French community. In 1958, at a time of severe crisis in Guinea's history, when Sékou Touré was facing immense economic pressure to give in to the French government, Nkrumah, in a magnificent practical demon-stration of PanAfricanism, made Guinea a loan of £10 million. Guinea, under the leadership of Sékou Touré and PDG (Parti Démocratique de Guinée), intended following a similar path of development, and like Ghana, also supported PanAfricanist policies. So began a close and continuing unity of purpose between Ghana and Guinea, and a deep personal friendship between Sékou Touré and Nkrumah which was to reach a climax in March 1966 after the reactionary military coup in Ghana, when Sékou Touré welcomed Nkrumah to Conakry and took the unprecedented step of proclaiming him Co-President of Guinea.

The Ghana-Guinea Union of 1958 provided for resident ministers to be exchanged, who were then recognised as members of both the gov-ernments of Ghana and Guinea. Such was the impact of this Union that the following year, in July 1959, at a conference held in Sanniquellie, attended by Nkrumah, Sékou Touré and President Tubman of Liberia, a Declaration of Principles concerning African States was formed. Un-like the Ghana-Guinea Union which was a political union of states, the Community was an economic, cultural and social organisation designed to advance the unification process by building up a free and prosperous African Community for the benefit of its peoples and the peoples of the world. One of its main objectives would be to support the continental liberation movement. Membership of the Community was open to any independent African state. The motto adopted for the community was 'Independence and Unity'. Although Nkrumah was convinced that unification could only come through the setting up of All-African political institutions, he nevertheless supported any genuine efforts at cooperation of a PanAfrican basis, since these would inevitably serve to speed up the progress towards political unification.

On 14 June 1960, almost a year after the Sanniquellie Conference took place, the Declaration was submitted to a conference in Addis Ababa of independent states, and states which were shortly to become independent. At this conference, decisions taken at the 1958 Accra Conference of Independent African States were confirmed, and resolutions were passed calling for increased assistance to be given to the liberation movement. On the question of the political unification of Africa, however, there was already disagreement about how this should be achieved. While no African would argue against an eventual Union Government for Africa, there were differing views on procedure. Progressive governments supported Nkrumah's view that the setting up of All-African political organisations must receive top priority, while the less progressive governments advocated a gradualist approach involving economic and cultural unity before the establishment of any continental political institutions.

The Ghana-Guinea Union was soon broadened. In April 1961, the Ghana-Guinea-Mali Union was formed when President Modibo Keita of Mali joined Sékou Touré and Nkrumah in Accra and agreed upon a Charter for the Union of African States (UAS). Provision was made for the admission into the UAS of other African states which might wish to join. The Charter of the UAS provided for regular meetings between the Heads of State of the UAS, and the supreme executive organ was to be the quarterly conference to be held in turn in Accra, Bamako and Conakry. At the UAS Conference held in Bamako in June 1961, the member states once again reaffirmed their support for the liberation movement and, in addition agreed on a common policy towards the European Common Market and the establishment of an African Common Market.

Nkrumah was determined to demonstrate in a practical way 'the workability of union between African states.'[1] In Sékou Touré and Modibo Keita he had comrades who saw the problems of Africa in much

---

1. *Africa Must Unite*, p. 143.

Meeting of the Ghana-Guinea-Mali Union leaders [L to R] Sékou Touré, Modibo Keita, Kwame Nkrumah — Accra, 1961

Soviet Union (Russian) Prime Minister Nikita Kruschev congratulating Nkrumah after his speech at the United Nations — New York, 23 September 1960

the same way as himself, and the various conferences of the Ghana-Guinea-Mali Union were characterised by an identity of view on most of the problems examined in an atmosphere of perfect understanding.[1] In the immediate post-independence era in Africa such a degree of unity between states with differing colonial backgrounds, different languages, culture and institutions, was a great achievement. It demonstrated in a practical way the truth of Nkrumah's dictum: 'The forces that unit us are intrinsic, and greater than the superimposed influences that keep us apart.'[2] He expressed the same truth in a more explicit way when he declared: 'I am convinced that the forces making for unity far outweigh those which divide us. In meeting Africans from all parts of the continent I am impressed by how much we have in common. It is not just our colonial past, or the fact that we have aims in common, it is something which goes far deeper. I can best describe it as a sense of oneness in that we are *Africans*.[3]

The 'sense of oneness' experienced by Nkrumah, Sékou Touré and Modibo Keita stemmed not only from their PanAfrican policies of liberation and unification, but also from their commitment to socialist reconstruction. Their vision and grasp of the realities of the African situation were rare at that time among heads of state of the newly-independent countries. Most of them were content to step into the shoes of their colonial masters and to continue the structures which characterised the colonial period. In their countries, neo-colonialism had replaced the old-style colonialism, and political independence was a sham. When these nationalist leaders spoke of African liberation and unification they meant something quite different from the leaders of the progressive states. They had in mind changes in government, but not a basic change of social and economic structures. Such leaders in the post-independent political climate of Africa were compelled to pay lip service to the ultimate Pan-African goals of the total liberation and unification of the African continent, and most of them in time found it necessary also to declare some kind of support for the socialist ideals. But their actions showed clearly their true alignment.

In view of this fundamental difference between the outlook of radicals and non-radicals it was not surprising that different groupings

---

1. *Africa Must Unite*, p. 143.
2. Ibid., p. 221.
3.   " p. 132.

of African states emerged. The radical states consisting of Ghana, Guinea, Mali, Libya, Egypt, Morocco and the Algerian FLN came to be known as the Casablanca Powers, after the Casablanca Conference held from 3 to 7 January 1961. The Monrovia conference sponsored by Nigeria, Cameroon, Liberia and Togoland, took place on May 1961 and led to the emergence of another group of powers which advocated the setting up of economic associations between African states before any political unification was attempted.

The Casablanca Conference was attended by the Heads of State of Ghana, Guinea, Mali and Egypt. The FLN was represented by Ferhat Abbas, and Libya by her Foreign Minister. In the Chair was the convenor of the conference, King Mohammed V of Morocco. The main topic for discussion was the situation in the Congo, and it was agreed that the African states should withdraw their troops from UN command unless Lumumba's legitimate government was immediately restored. In addition, the Conference recommended the disarming of Mobuto's army; the expulsion of Belgians from the Congo; and the calling of the Congolese parliament. The question of French atomic tests in the Sahara, and the policy of apartheid in South Africa were also discussed and resolutions passed. But the most significant outcome of the Conference was the publication of the 'African Charter of Casablanca' which bears the unmistakable stamp of Nkrumah.

The Charter provided for the establishment of a permanent African Consultative Assembly and three permanent functional committees, the first political, consisting of Heads of States; the second economic, comprising Ministers of Economic Affairs; and the third cultural, consisting of Ministers of Education. In addition, there was to be a joint African High-Command composed of the Chiefs of Staff of the independent states. In his closing speech to the conference, Nkrumah summed up the arguments for the Charter. 'I can see no security for African states unless African leaders, like ourselves, have realised beyond all doubt that salvation for Africa lies in unity... for in unity lies strength, and as I see it, African states must unite or sell themselves out to imperialist and colonialist exploiters for a mess of pottage, or disintegrate individually.'[1]

When the Monrovia Conference took place in May 1961 the discussions centred on vague topics concerning peace and stability in

---

1. *Africa Must Unite*, p. 145.

Africa, ways and means to achieve better understanding between states, and the setting up of economic and cultural organisations. Among the political resolutions passed were those declaring the principle of non-interference in the domestic affairs of any state, and the freedom to accept or reject political unions. The conference members condemned South Africa's apartheid policies, supported independence for Algeria, pledged support for the United Nations and condemned all nuclear tests.

However, both the Casablanca and Monrovia conferences resulted in progress being made in the direction of greater economic and cultural cooperation between African states. At a follow-up conference in Conakry, experts from the Casablanca countries agreed on the ending of customs barriers over five years from 1 January 1962, and the ending of quota systems and preferential treatment from the same date. They furthermore proposed the creation of a Council of African Economic Unity (CUEA) and a Development Bank and proposed the formation of joint air and shipping lines.

Similarly, experts from the Monrovia group, meeting in Dakar, recommended the setting-up of a Development Bank, regional customs unions, the co-ordination of various development policies, and joint shipping and air lines. But although both the Monrovia and Casablanca powers had similar aims in economic and cultural spheres, they were poles apart when it came to procedures and to fundamental objectives. While both might be said to have aimed ultimately at some kind of unity for Africa, the Casablanca group were convinced of the need to find political solutions before integrated plans for economic and social development could be worked out, while the Monrovia group advocated the priority of economic and regional associations. The ultimate objective of the Casablanca powers was an All-African Union Government administering a totally liberated continent, pursuing policies based on the principles of socialism. In general, the Monrovia group envisaged a very loose policy of co-operation between states, with considerable powers left to the individual states, and with basic social and economic structures left intact.

It was a great source of disappointment to Nkrumah that no matter how hard he tried to reconcile differences, he was throughout his period of rule, always confronted with splits between African states even on issues on which he might reasonably have expected a united approach, such as the Rhodesian issue and the question of dialogue with South

Africa. While he was prepared at all times to make allowances and even concessions in the interests of a united African stand, he would never compromise over principle. 'One can compromise over programme, but not over principles. Any compromise over principle is the same as an abandonment of it.'[1] He saw in the attitude of those states which soft-pedalled the African Revolution the legacy of a colonial mentality and the pressures of neo-colonialism. While he accepted that there were differences between the independent states of Africa, he was convinced that they could be resolved within the context of African Unity.

'The notion that in order to have a nation it is necessary for there to be a common language, a common territory and a common culture, has failed to stand the test of time or the scrutiny of scientific definition of objective reality. Common territory, language and culture may in fact be present in a nation, but the existence of a nation does not necessarily imply the presence of all three. Common territory and language alone may form the basis of a nation. Similarly, common territory plus common culture may be the basis. In some cases, only one of the three applies. A state may exist on a multinational basis. The community of economic life is the major feature within a nation, and it is the economy which holds together the people living in the territory. It is on this basis that the new Africans recognise themselves as potentially one nation, whose dominion is the entire African continent.'[2]

In the political and economic climate of the period in which he worked, Nkrumah had to depend much on personal relationships with brother heads of state. Few, on meeting him, could fail to be won over by the strength of his commitment to PanAfricanism, his trust in the common man and his immense faith in Africa's future. He inspired great respect and confidence. The result of one short meeting between Nkrumah and Patrice Lumumba, then prime minister of the Congo, in August 1960 resulted in the signing of a secret Agreement to form a political union between Ghana and the Congo. This 'Union of African States' was to have a republican constitution within a federal framework. The federal government was to be responsible for foreign affairs, defence, the issue of a common currency, and economic planning and

---

1. *Consciencism*, Kwame Nkrumah. First published in 1964. Panaf edition, 1970, p. 57.
2. *Class Struggle in Africa*, Kwame Nkrumah, Panaf 1970, p. 88.

development. There would be no customs barriers between any part of the federation, and the capital of the Union would be Leopoldville (Kinshasa), a striking indication of Nkrumah's lack of personal ambition. Finally, as in the other political unions of states organised by Nkrumah, provision was made for any other state or territory in Africa which might wish to join the Union. It was a typically imaginative and bold Agreement which unfortunately was never implemented owing to the fall of Lumumba's government the following month, and his subsequent assassination.

Recollecting these events years later in Conakry, Nkrumah wrote about them in his final work, *Revolutionary Path*. In this book he examines not only the early attempts at political unification, but also the many economic and regional groupings and organisations which were formed. These included the Afro-Malagasy Economic Co-operation Organisation (OAMCE) set up as a result of the Brazzaville Conference in December 1960; the Afro-Malagasy Union (UAM) established in September 1961; the Organisation Commune Africaine et Malagache (OCAM) formed in February 1965; the East African Community of Uganda, Kenya and Tanzania, formed by a treaty signed in Kampala on 1 December 1967. He pointed out that it had been, in general, the French speaking independent states which had 'consistently advocated a gradualist approach to African liberation and unification, insisting that economic and regional co-operation must precede any form of political continental unification.'[1] In his opinion, not one of the groupings and organisations had resulted in a significant improvement in the standard of living of the African masses. They represented just another form of Balkanization. In retrospect, he was more firmly convinced than ever of the need to set in motion actual political machinery on an All-African basis, if independent Africa was to survive and to realise the aspirations of the African people.[2]

A high-water mark in Nkrumah's efforts to establish the political machinery for unification occurred with the foundation of the Organisation of African Unity (OAU) in Addis Ababa on 25 May 1963.

---

1. *Revolutionary Path*, p. 218.
2. Julius K. Nyerere, when President of Tanzania, was foremost of those who urged the setting up of regional, economic organisations before attempting to establish political machinery for African Unity. But in a speech in Accra on 6 March 1997 marking the 40th anniversary of Ghana's independence, he declared that in the light of what had happened in Africa since Nkrumah's time his view had been wrong and 'Nkrumah was right'. Political steps towards African unity took priority over economic measures.

This was the year of the publication of one of Nkrumah's most important books, *Africa Must Unite*. Copies of the book were given to all delegates at the Conference of Heads of Independent States meeting in Addis Ababa in the hope that any members who were not yet convinced of the need for unification would absorb the overwhelming case for unity by reading the book, and would support the Charter of the OAU. The book undoubtedly made a considerable impact not only in Addis Ababa, but throughout Africa and indeed the world. But in spite of Nkrumah's urgent appeal for definite All-African political machinery to be created then and there, the Charter of the OAU, as agreed in 1963, was as Nkrumah later remarked, 'a Charter of intent, rather than a Charter of positive action.[1] All agreed on the general principle of African liberation and unification, but there were differing opinions on the nature of the organisation to be set up. Differences developed along the lines of the old power groups and alliances. The result was that the OAU was born with serious inherent weaknesses. For one thing, the failure to set up an All-African High Command, which Nkrumah considered essential if the OAU was to have any strength, meant that it was reduced right from the start to the position of an organisation without the authority or the means to enforces its decisions. While the OAU was an advance on anything that had gone before, it fell far short of Nkrumah's hopes.

Article Two of the Charter containing the 'Purposes' of the OAU expressed general intentions, not definite plans. Member states would 'co-ordinate' and 'harmonise' policies 'to achieve a better life for the people of Africa.'[2] There would be political, economic and diplomatic co-operation; education, health, defence and security, communication, scientific, technical and cultural co-ordination. Under Article Three, headed 'Principles,' the equality of member states was affirmed, together with the principle of non-interference in each other's affairs. Disputes were to be settled peacefully, and there was to be 'absolute dedication' to the total liberation of Africa. A policy of non-alignment as regards 'all blocs' was agreed. As far as OAU institutions were concerned, there was to be an assembly of Heads of State and Government, a Council of Ministers, a General Secretariat, and a Commission of Mediation, Conciliation and Arbitration.

1. *Revolutionary Path*, p. 249.
2. For the full text of the OAU Charter, see *Revolutionary Path*, pp. 251–259.

The OAU Charter was signed by the heads of states and governments of thirty-two African States. This in itself was an achievement bearing in mind that in 1957, only some six years previously when Ghana became independent, there were only eight African independent states.

Nkrumah, while disappointed with the failure to establish even a rudimentary All-African governing body and a joint High Command, nevertheless left Addis Ababa in 1963 determined to work ceaselessly to achieve this as soon as possible at a future conference of the OAU. He saw in the formation of the OAU an expression of the determination of the African states to achieve total liberation and unity, and considered that the intensification of the liberation movement would lead inevitably to a unified military command. In a speech to the National Assembly of Ghana on 21 June 1963 on the occasion of the ratification of the Charter of the OAU, he said: 'We have proved at Addis Ababa that we are ready to build to a united Africa... Until Africa achieves its total independence and national unification, the African revolution will not have completed its destined task. When we talk of African Unity, we are thinking of a political arrangement which will enable us collectively to provide solutions for our problems in Africa.'[1] He went on to warn against groupings, saying that they were a serious threat to the unity of Africa, and as always, urged the need for speed. 'Time is everything in our march. We must in Africa crowd in a generation the experience and achievements attained through centuries of trial and error by the older nations of the world.'[2]

No sooner had the OAU been formed than it was put to the test and found wanting, and for the very reasons foreseen by Nkrumah when he warned the member states of the dangers in delaying the establishment of unified political machinery and a joint High Command. There were disputes between Ethiopia and Somalia, between Morocco and Algeria, and between Somalia and Kenya. Fighting continued in the Congo. In Rhodesia and South Africa, racist minority regimes stepped up their oppression. In the areas still ruled by colonial powers, freedom fighters complained about the ineffectiveness of the OAU Liberation Committee.

---

1. *Revolutionary Path*, p. 272.
2. Ibid., p. 274.

▲ Nkrumah with Emperor Haile Selassie — Addis Ababa, 1963

▲ Nkrumah urging Africa to unite. Conference of African Heads of State, Addis
Ababa 1963. In foreground [L to R] Algerian Premier, Ahmed Ben Bella;
President Yameogo (Burkina Fasso); President Abdel Gamal Nasser (Egypt).
[For text of the Address, see Appendix Two]

At the Summit Conference of the OAU held in Cairo in July 1964, Nkrumah put forward detailed and firm proposals for a Union Government of Africa. Once again, he argued the case for urgent action in view of the world situation and the pressing problems of Africa which could not await gradual or piecemeal solutions. 'Time indeed is the crucial factor, time acts for those who use it with purpose, and not for those who let it slip by. Those who do not use time as their agent give the advantage to those who do.'[1]

He pointed out the failure of the OAU to make any significant improvement in the position of African freedom fighters. Imperialists and neo-colonialists were, in fact, continuing to pour vast sums of money and armaments into Africa in support of colonial and minority regimes. The Liberation Committee set up by the OAU in 1963 had failed to provide sufficient supplies and training facilities for freedom fighters, who had become 'disappointed, disgruntled and frustrated.[2] Ghana would not, therefore, make its contribution to the Liberation Committee until the Committee had been reorganised to allow more effective and positive action.

In appealing to the conference members not to let down the freedom fighters of Africa, Nkrumah was using the one firm unifying argument on which all had been agreed at the time of the setting up of the OAU. All wished to see the total liberation of Africa. Seeking to build on this common aspiration, Nkrumah showed how events had clearly demonstrated the hopelessness of trying to achieve total liberation without the necessary unified political and military machinery. 'The imperialists regard our Charter of Unity as token unity, they will not respect it until it assumes the form of a Union government... We have not yet made the imperialists believe that we can set our continent in order.'[3] He went on to re-state the other basic argument for a Union Government, the need for an All-African economic plan: 'We must unite for economic viability.'[4] Then, with a detailed review of the year since the founding of the OAU he reminded the conference members of the many border disputes, the lost opportunities for development, and the increasing problems brought about by Balkanization and continuing imperialist and neo-colonialist pressures. 'All over Africa, the essential economic pattern developed

1. *Revolutionary Path*, p. 279.
2. Ibid., p. 280.
3.   "   p. 281.
4.   "   p. 283.

under colonialism remains. Not one of us, despite our political independence, has yet succeeded in breaking, in any substantial measure, our economic subservience to economic systems external to Africa.'[1]

Nkrumah not only stated problems clearly, but he proposed solutions. The formation of the OAU was a declaration of intention to unite: now the time had come to act. A Union Government of Africa had to be established NOW. The specific fields of common action he had in mind were; defence, foreign policy and economic development (including a common currency for Africa). In addition, he proposed the foundation of a permanent headquarters for the OAU and a permanent Secretary General, and in case anyone should think that he had ambitions for Ghana in this respect, he stated that Ghana was not interested in either. As far as the machinery for a Union Government was concerned, he proposed: 'This Union Government shall consist of an Assembly of Heads of State and Government headed by a President elected from among the Heads of State and Government of the Independent African States. The Executive of the Union Government will be a Cabinet or Council of Ministers with a Chancellor or Prime Minister as its head, and a Federal House consisting of two Chambers. The Senate and a House of Representatives. If you agree, we can appoint our Foreign Ministers, assisted by experts, to work out a constitution for a Union Government of Africa.'[2]

While he realised that some of the heads of states would not agree to the setting up of a Union Government there and then, he implored them not to leave Cairo without at least agreeing to the idea in principle, and to a further meeting within six months 'to adopt and proclaim to the world the Federal Union Government of Africa.[3] Again, Nkrumah was faced with procrastination and timidity. The question of a Union Government was referred to the next meeting of the OAU due to take place in Accra in 1965.

By then, Nkrumah's progressive policies were causing domestic and external pressures against him to mount. As his reputation among freedom fighters rose, as Ghana showed signs of breaking through to economic independence, as his exposure of the workings of neo-colonialism in his speeches and writings became more vociferous, so did the strength of reactionary forces against him grow.

---

1. *Revolutionary Path*, pp. 286–287.
2. Ibid., pp. 295–296.
3.   " p. 296.

Not surprisingly, therefore, the news that the next OAU Conference was to take place in Accra, and that Nkrumah intended to achieve the formation of a Union Government however rudimentary, sparked off feverish hostile activity to try to prevent the conference taking place in Ghana, and if this could not be prevented, then to make sure that it did not make any significant progress in the direction of African unification. The initiative was taken by former French colonies, namely Ivory Coast, Cameroon, Upper Volta (Burkina Fasso), Dahomey (Benin), and Niger. These states, and Togo, objected to the OAU Conference being held in Accra on the grounds that Ghana was sheltering political refugees from their territories. A meeting of OAU Foreign Ministers was held in Lagos under the chairmanship of Kenya's External Affairs Minister, Joseph Murumbi, with the result that Ghana agreed to expel all refugees named by the objecting states. However, representatives of the five governments then met in Upper Volta (Burkina Fasso) and proclaimed that they still refused to attend the Accra Conference because it was claimed that Ghana had not sent away all the families of 'subversive elements'. It was apparent that these five governments intended to sabotage the Accra Conference by boycotting it and they proceeded to block every effort made by the Ghana government and other OAU member governments to persuade them to attend.

When the Conference opened in Accra on 21 October 1965, the Entente states and Togo were absent, which meant that the number of states attending was reduced to twenty-eight. They met in an atmosphere of high tension brought about by the Rhodesian crisis. Ian Smith's Unilateral Declaration of Independence (UDI) appeared imminent and the case for unified African action was more glaringly obvious than ever before.

After the formal opening speeches, a move was made by Somalia and others to obtain the immediate adoption of a resolution on Rhodesia (Zimbabwe) which had been prepared by the meeting of foreign ministers which had preceded the conference. The only objection came, predictably, from Dr. Banda of Malawi (formerly Nyasaland) who advised against a hasty decision, and asked for the debate to be held in secret. The conference thereupon went into private session, and remained thus, except when formal announcements were made, until the concluding session.

Resolutions were passed on Rhodesia (Zimbabwe), calling on the British Government to suspend the 1961 constitution and to take all measures necessary concerning the administration of the territory, including the calling of a constitutional conference with the participation of representatives of the entire population. The conference should aim at adopting a new constitution based on 'one man, one vote', free elections, and independence on that basis. There were resolutions also on South Africa's policy of apartheid; the question of political refugees; the stepping-up of support for liberation movements. But on the key question, the question of the OAU transforming itself into a Union Government of Africa there was once again no real progress made.

Nkrumah had prepared plans for the setting up of a full-time Executive Council of the OAU with a Union President, and a number of Union Vice-Presidents to meet periodically during the year to review the work of the Executive Council when the OAU General Assembly was not in session. It was a modest enough proposal, but received only twenty-two votes in favour of its immediate adoption. This was two votes short of the necessary two-thirds vote of the total membership required to pass the resolution. Instead, it was agreed that the proposal should be referred back to the governments of the member states for further consideration, and a report be submitted to the next session of the Assembly. Similarly, there was a resolution passed agreeing to the principle of co-ordination in the military field, but Nkrumah's call for the setting up of a single African High Command was not successful.

Looking back to the Accra Cconference of 1965, and to Nkrumah's address at the opening session, the exactness of his predictions for Africa if unification was delayed any further is all too apparent. The OAU, he said, faced the choice of going forward to progress 'through an effective African Union or step backward into stagnation, instability and confusion — an easy prey for foreign intervention, interference and subversion.'[1] Continuing Balkanization would result in increased aggression by the forces of reaction, and the independent states would be 'picked off one by one'. Again, Nkrumah stated clearly the overwhelming arguments in favour of unification; again, his brother leaders of the independent states failed to give the necessary support as Nkrumah remarked: 'It is courage that we lack.'[2]

Within a few months of the Accra Conference, Ian Smith had proclaimed UDI; there was a military coup in Lagos; and in February 1966

---

1. *Revolutionary Path*, p. 307.
2. Ibid.

the Ghanaian people suffered the worst setback in their history when a military coup succeeded in toppling the Nkrumah government. A chain reaction followed; but the reverse of the chain reaction which had followed Ghana's independence in 1957. Then the sequence of events when so many of the African states had achieved independence was forward. After the 24 February 1966 coup in Ghana, it was as though the African Revolution had been stopped dead in its tracks, and was going into reverse as military coups, almost all of them neo-colonialist inspired and supported, followed quickly one after the other throughout most of the African continent. There was to follow 'recolonisation' through non-governmental organisations (NGOs) such as the IMF and World Bank.

Nkrumah was disappointed, though not surprised at the failure of his proposal for an Executive Council to receive the necessary two-thirds vote. But he never retreated from his firm conviction that a Union Government would one day be formed. 'I am more than ever convinced that Africa should unite into one state with a Union Government. This is the view which I stated at Addis Ababa in 1963 and in Cairo last year, and I still hold to this position.'[1]

---

1. *Revolutionary Path*, p. 308.

8

Development Plans and Problems of Neocolonialism

In the years before independence, Nkrumah concentrated on winning the battle for the political freedom of Ghana. It was largely a fight on a single front. But as soon as independence was achieved on 6 March 1957, the next stage of struggle began in earnest, the fight on two fronts. In Ghana there was to be a restructuring of the economy and the building of a just society. Concurrently, Ghana was to become actively engaged in the Pan-African struggle. In Nkrumah's words: 'This is not an easy task. Many splendid armies in history have been known to go to pieces for trying to fight on two fronts at once. The Convention People's Party, however, is a different type of army. It is the people's own political army, built by their sweat and labour .... We are determined to conquer and we shall conquer on both fronts. But first we must sacrifice everything for the victory.'[1]

For Nkrumah, the attack on both fronts must be simultaneous and rapid. Just as he insisted that political independence was the necessary prerequisite for the socialist reconstruction of Ghana, so also he was convinced that Africa's problems of economic development could only be solved when the continent was totally liberated and when the African states were politically united in an All-African Union Government. Political solutions had to be found before economic

---

1. The Fight on Two Fronts. Speech by Nkrumah on assuming office of General Secretary of the CPP.

problems could be solved. A unified Africa was a political kingdom which could only be gained by political action. Under the conditions of neocolonialism, there was no time to spare if the young African states were to survive and to develop their human and material resources to the full for the benefit of their peoples. Pan-African political policies were comparatively straightforward to pursue. More complex was to resolve the domestic and Pan-African problems of neocolonialism.

A popular CPP slogan during the electoral campaign of 1951 was, 'Seek ye first the political kingdom and all things will be added unto it.' For Ghanaians the 'things' to be added were advances in their standard of living. Ghana inherited at independence almost complete trade dependence on the West. The economy was mainly foreign or locally capitalist owned. A colonial mentality permeated the professions, the army, police, and civil service. As Nkrumah wrote in later years: 'Those who would judge us merely by the heights we have achieved would do well to remember the depths from which we started.'[1]

Nkrumah had to start virtually from scratch when the First Development Plan was launched. The First and Second year Development Plans covered the periods 1951-56 and 1959-64, and the Consolidation Plan bridged the two year gap between these Plans (1957-59). Then in March 1964, building on the foundations of the previous Plans, the Seven Year Development Plan was launched. 'Our aim, under this Plan, is to build in Ghana a socialist state which accepts full responsibility for promoting the well-being of the masses.'[2]

The long-term objective of a socialist state was to be achieved by stages. There was to be a period of mixed economy when a limited private sector would be allowed to operate and when vigorous public and co-operative sectors would rapidly expand, particularly in the strategic productive areas of the economy. Eventually, with the full implementation of Development Plans, the private sector would be eventually eliminated.

The very first programme of the CPP, contained in the party constitution drawn up in 1949, clearly stated that the objective was the establishment of a 'socialist state in which all men and women shall have equal opportunity and where there shall be no capitalist exploitation.' Later, in the Party's *Programme for Work and Happiness* launched

---

1. *Dark Days in Ghana*, Kwame Nkrumah, Panaf 1968, p. 76.
2. Speech to launch the Seven Year Development Plan, 11 March 1962. *Revolutionary Path*, p. 190.

in 1962, it was again declared that 'the principles upon which the party is pivoted' were those of socialism. But the most specific declaration of socialist objectives came with the launching of the Seven Year Development Plan. 'The main tasks of the Plan are: firstly to speed up the rate of growth of our national economy. Secondly, it is to enable us to embark upon the socialist transformation of our economy through the rapid development of the state and co-operative sectors. Thirdly, it is our aim, by this Plan, to eradicate completely the colonial structure of our economy.'[1]

Ghana was to develop a self-sustaining economy, balanced between industry and agriculture, 'providing a sufficiency of food for the people, and supporting secondary industries based on the products of our agriculture.'[2] In other words, Ghana's economy was to be diversified in order to lessen the heavy dependence on cocoa, and to develop the infrastructure necessary for industrialisation and for the achievement of a satisfactory level of integration of industry and agriculture.' The people, through the state, should have an effective share in the economy of the country and an effective control over it.'[3]

During the period 1951-64 considerable progress was made in laying the foundations for a modern state. A network of roads, considered to be among the most modern in Africa was constructed. Houses, schools, colleges, hospitals, clinics were built. Many state enterprises and corporations were set up, and a State Management Committee established to supervise them. By 1966 there were sixty-three enterprises in existence. Among the new industries founded were two cocoa-processing plants, two sugar refineries, a textile printing plant, a glass factory, a chocolate factory, a radio assembly plant, a meat-processing plant and a large printing works at Tema. In addition, work was well advanced on a gold refinery at Tarkwa, asbestos, cement, shoe and rubber tyre factories at Kumasi, and a factory for the manufacture of prefabricated houses. Ghana was beginning to supply local demand for many basic consumer goods, using locally-produced raw materials. During the first year of the Seven Year Development Plan some £48.9 million was spent on development projects. The harbour at Takoradi was extended, and an entirely new artificial harbour constructed at Tema. A piped water supply was provided to villages which had never before known such an

1. Speech to launch the Seven Year Development Plan, p. 189.
2. Ibid.
3. " , p. 190.

amenity. Agriculture was diversified, and where possible mechanised. State farms cultivated 24,000 acres of rubber, oil palm, banana, urena, lobata and citrus. The agricultural wing of the Workers' Brigade alone farmed 12,500 acres of cereals and vegetables. Work was almost completed on the Volta River Project which was designed to provide enough electrical power for the whole of Ghana as well as for neighbouring states.

But perhaps nowhere was the progress more marked than in the sphere of education. In the first ten years of his administration, Nkrumah was able to claim that more had been achieved in education than during the whole period of colonial rule. The education Act of 1961 made education compulsory for school-age children. By 1965/6, the 1951 figures of 1, 700 primary schools enrolling some 226, 000 children had increased to approximately 11, 000 schools with nearly 1.5 million pupils. The access of girls to education increased dramatically so that by 1965/6 girls constituted nearly 44 per cent of total primary school enrolments, 35 per cent at middle school and 25 per cent at secondary level. It was CPP policy to advance women's social, political and economic roles in nation building. Nkrumah saw women as key architects. To educate women was to educate a nation. In his words: 'The degree of a country's revolutionary awareness may be measured by the political maturity of its women.'[1]

All education from primary to university level was made free. In addition, all textbooks were supplied free to pupils in primary, middle and secondary schools. By 1966 Ghana had one of the highest literacy rates in Africa, among the best public services and the highest living standards per capita in Africa.

As part of CPP policy of enhancing the political and civic rights of women, provision was made for the election of women to the National Assembly. Ten women parliamentarians took their seats at the first session of the First Republic of Ghana in 1961. 'Nkrumah catapulted women onto the political scene in a way that was new both in Ghana and Africa. For him, this was part of the attempt at projecting the African Personality and at raising the status of African womanhood.'[2]

---

1. *Axioms*, p. 132.
2. *Women and their Organisations during the CPP period.* Paper presented by Takyiwah Manuh at Symposium organised by the Institute of African Studies, Legon. Published in *The Life and Work of Kwame Nkrumah*, edited by the Director, Kwame Arhin, and published by SEDCO Publishing Ltd. in 1991.

Women were appointed to serve on boards of corporations, schools and town councils. A few women served on the Central Committee of the CPP. Increasing numbers of women entered courses of higher education, many pursuing training courses abroad qualifying them to occupy most of the positions previously held exclusively by men. In addition, discriminatory provisions relating to women's work were abolished, and equal pay instituted for equal work. Maternity leave on full pay was assured. Women underwent pilot training in the Ghana Air Force Training School at Takoradi. Women were encouraged to enrol in the army to train alongside men in the infantry, in the intelligence and service corps, and to become electrical and mechanical engineers.

Among the most enthusiastic supporters of the CPP were the market women, always a very strong voice in the country. Not only did they contribute generously to party funds, but together with local government councils they controlled much of the trading life of their communities. Nkrumah had the greatest respect for them, ever mindful of their power and good sense. Demonstrations of market women would be quickly organised on occasions when it was deemed necessary, or when their interests were perceived to be threatened.

The National Council of Ghana Women (NCGW) was inaugurated by Nkrumah on 10 September 1960 as an integral wing of the CPP. The NCGW, with branches throughout the country, was to be the only recognised women's organisation, and to be represented on the party's Central Committee. With the formation of the NCGW the Women's Section of the party ceased to exist. Members of the Council frequently formed part of Nkrumah's entourage on his travels overseas when they studied the position of women and their organisations abroad.

Two months before the inauguration of the NCGW, the Conference of Women of Africa and of African descent was held in Accra. In his opening address, Nkrumah spoke of the mission the women of Africa had to fulfil in working actively with men in liberating and unifying the continent, and projecting the African Personality. At the time of the Ghana-Guinea-Mali Union, a Council of Women of the Union of African States was formed. At the second conference in Accra, Nkrumah called attention to the sufferings the people of the Congo, Angola, Mozambique, South Africa and Namibia, urging Africa's need for 'a new woman', dedicated and inspired by the high ideals of patriotism and African unity.

Through party organization, Nkrumah sought to draw on all sectors of the population, men, women and young people in all walks of life, to become actively involved in achieving CPP domestic and PanAfrican objectives.

As regards industrialization, there were three broad aspects of CPP development plans. First, industries were to be established which would be large consumers of power and for which raw materials would be locally available. Second, there were to be industries which would utilise cash crops, and which would provide employment in rural areas. Third, light industries were to be set up for the production of such goods as textiles, shoes, clothing and furniture. For each programme of industrialisation, hydro-electric power had to be provided on a massive scale, and this was the purpose of the Volta River Project. Nkrumah described the Volta Dam as 'the greatest of all our development projects'[1] since it was designed to make possible the development of 'the full industrial potential of Ghana'[2] and the provision of power for neighbouring states. Ghana was estimated to have sufficient bauxite to last for 200 years, and this would be processed by a new aluminium smelter at Tema using Volta hydroelectric power. The initial power output of the Volta Dam was estimated at (512,000kw at full load), and for the ultimate power output at 768,000kW (882,000 kw at full load). The giant scheme, which cost £70 million to complete was financed 50 per cent by Ghana. The rest of the money was provided by raising international loans.

The participation of foreign interests in the Volta Project illustrates the problems and difficulties faced by Nkrumah in most of the major economic developments throughout the whole period of his rule. He was faced with having to allow the continuance of a private sector in the economy, and to make use of international companies to carry through projects essential for Ghana's economic development. There were obvious dangers, which Nkrumah was very well aware of, and he took what he considered to be a justifiable risk in the interests of the Ghanaian people and the African people as a whole. For if Ghana was to become the powerhouse of the African Revolution an economic breakthrough had to be achieved with maximum speed before neocolonialism, which he maintained was a greater threat than the old colonialism, became too entrenched to be removed.

---

1. *Dark Days in Ghana*, p. 82.
2. Ibid.

Nkrumah did well to secure on favourable terms half the funds needed for the Volta Project. Nevertheless, some have criticised the deal made with the Volta Aluminium Company (Valco). Briefly, the terms were that Valco, which was owned 90 per cent by Kaiser Aluminium and Chemical Corporation and 10 per cent by Reynolds Metal Company, would construct an alumina smelter and in return for tariff and tax concessions would guarantee to use a specified amount of Volta power at a fixed price. The agreement has been criticised on two counts. First, the price of power was effectively little more than cost. Secondly, Valco would import bauxite mined abroad instead of using Ghanaian deposits and developing an integrated aluminium industry in Ghana. Nkrumah would have liked an integrated aluminium industry in Ghana. However, it suited the quite different multinational economics of Edgar Kaiser, the head of the US Kaiser Corporation, to restrict his investment in Ghana for the time being to a smelter, and Nkrumah was reluctantly compelled to agree for the smelter to operate on imported bauxite.

Kojo Botsio, then Minister of Development, was a member of Ghanaian entourage accompanying Nkrumah to the USA in connection with the Volta Dam Project. As a personal witness of the negotiations, and one who enjoyed the full confidence of Nkrumah, he was in a position to comment on the project when visiting London in 1995. He confirmed that 'the aim of Osagyefo regarding the Dam was twofold: first to have a plentiful supply of electricity to spearhead the industrialisation of Ghana; and second, to have an integrated aluminium industry to be the flag bearer in his industrialisation programme.'[1]

According to Botsio, the highlight of the visit was the meeting between Nkrumah and President Kennedy. 'Despite opposition from some members of the American establishment, especially Vice-President Lyndon Johnson, President Kennedy gave his blessing to the project. No doubt he did not want to repeat the Aswan Dam fiasco which had gone to Russia.'[2]

As regards the Agreement, the project had to be reduced in size because of the huge cost. Furthermore, the cost of power for Valco was fixed very low, 'one of the lowest of the time, in order to induce American investors to participate. Even then, the cost of production of power at Akosombo was much below that of oil-generating plants then widely

---

1. Kojo Botsio. Recorded interview with June Milne, London, 5 September 1995.
2. Ibid.

used in Ghana. Valco was given five years' grace within which to bring alumina from outside, i. e the West Indies, before setting up its own alumina plant in Ghana, to be supplied from the enormous bauxite deposits in Ghana, which was the primary objective of the whole project. Provision was also made in the Agreement for a periodic review of the cost of power to Valco.'[1]

Within a month of the commissioning of the Akosombo power project, the 1966 coup took place, and with the frequent changes of government it seemed that the two salient provisions of the Agreement were forgotten, namely, the periodic review of the cost of power to Valco, and the establishment of the alumina plant within five years. By 1995, only the cost of power to Valco had been reviewed. The setting up of an alumina plant had still not been realised. In the words of Botsio, 'The alumina plant is still a dead dream, because there has been no government since Kwame to champion it.'[2]

The 'electrification' of Ghana was to make possible the building of a modern industrialised state whose citizens would also be able to enjoy the domestic benefits which the provision of electricity would provide. It was a memorable occasion when, sitting beside Nkrumah one evening on a drive to Tema, he suddenly noticed in the outskirts of Accra a schoolboy sitting beneath a street lamp. Excitedly he pointed him out: 'See, June, he is doing his homework, because he has no light at home. Soon it will not be necessary. Every house in Ghana will have electric light.' It was this kind of vision which drove him.

It is now generally agreed that the deal with Valco was a good decision in the circumstances of the time. Nkrumah towards the end of his life, in looking back over the period wrote: 'The undertaking of joint projects with already operating capitalist concerns was better than the alternative of economic blockade by the West and the consequent lack of development until the assistance of socialist states could be procured and become operational.'[3] It was a dash for growth. Nkrumah was not prepared to risk delaying the construction of the dam at Akosombo because the building of an alumina plant had to be delayed. The successful implementation of the Seven Year Development Plan depended on the power project.

---

1. Kojo Botsio. Recorded interview with June Milne, London, 5 September 1995.
2. Ibid.
3. *Revolutionary Path*, p. 182.

Nkrumah had no illusions about multinational corporations. Even before the inauguration of the Volta River Project in January 1966, he had published a thoroughgoing exposure of the operations of international companies in his book, *Neo-colonialism: The Last Stage of Imperialism*. 'The less developed world will not become developed through the goodwill or generosity of the developed powers. It can only become developed through a struggle against the external forces which have a vested interest in keeping it underdeveloped. 'Of these forces, neocolonialism is, at this stage in history, the principal.'[1] He went on to define neocolonialism: 'The essence of neocolonialism is that the state which is subject to it is, in theory independent and has all the outward trappings of international sovereignty. In reality, its economic system and thus its political policy is directed from outside.'[2] Publication of this book in 1965 so infuriated the US government that $35 million of American 'aid' to Ghana was immediately cancelled.

When Nkrumah published the book, the workings of the multinational corporations in Africa had not previously been spotlighted. His exposure of them was based on his own practical experience as head of a government engaged on a socialist path of development. His purpose in compiling the book was to make available to the African people an analysis of the workings of neocolonialism, and how it could be overcome. Although the activities of multinationals operating in Ghana were strictly limited, their very presence tended to undermine the CPP government. They strengthened the private sector which was allowed to function during the transition phase of the mixed economy. In this sector, particularly where a large volume of investment was required, foreign investors were welcomed in a spirit of partnership. 'We did not allow them to operate in such a way as to exploit our people. They were to assist in the expansion of our economy in line with our general objectives, an agreed portion of their profits being allocated to promote the welfare and happiness of the Ghanaian people.'[3] The state controlled strategic branches of the economy including public industries, raw materials, and heavy industry. The state also participated in light and consumer goods industries in which the rates of return on capital

---

1. *Neo-Colonialism: The Last Stage of Imperialism*, Kwame Nkrumah. First published in 1965. Panaf edition 1971, pp. xix–xx.
2. *Neo-Colonialism*, p. ix.
3. *Dark Days in Ghana*, p. 80.

were highest. The intention was for the state to own those industries which provided the basic living needs of the people.

Three categories of Ghanaian businessmen were recognised. The first category employed their capital in trade or industry which fulfilled a public need, and these businessmen had for the time being no restrictions placed on their activities. In the second category were those who acted as middlemen and who used their capital for speculative purposes, for example, buying essential commodities such as salt and sugar cheaply and selling them at high prices. This category was given no encouragement by the government, and steps were taken to see that banks did not give them credit facilities. The third category comprised those who acted as agents for foreign companies. They had no place in the Seven Year Development Plan. No Ghanaian would be allowed to take up shares in any enterprise under foreign investment. Instead, Ghanaians would be encouraged to save by investing in the state sector and in co-operative enterprises.

Nkrumah in pursuing a socialist path of development had chosen to phase out the private sector of the economy through the expansion of the public sector rather than attempt an all-out programme of nationalization. Immediate nationalization would have run the risk of an economic blockade by the West. Many important development projects, chief among them the Volta River Dam, would have had to be shelved. In addition, Ghana was venturing along an uncharted road in that no other newly independent African country, with similar economic conditions, had attempted such far-reaching socialist objectives. There was, therefore, no experience on which to draw. Ghana was in this respect a pace-setter.

The other problem was one of economic scale. Ghana in common with most of the independent African states was then too small an economic unit in terms of population and resources to be viable. Nkrumah expressed the dilemma and prescribed the solution. 'The optimum zone of development for the African people is the entire continent of Africa. Until there is an All-African Union Government planning the economic development of Africa as a whole, the standard of living of the African masses will remain low.'[1]

In a broadcast to the Ghanaian people of 24 December 1957, the year of Independence, Nkrumah declared: 'We shall measure our progress

---

1. *Revolutionary Path*, p. 183.

by the improvement in the health of our people; by the number of children in school, and by the quality of their education; by the availability of water and electricity in our towns and villages, and by the happiness which our people take in being able to manage their own affairs. The welfare of our people is our chief pride, and it is by this that my government will ask to be judged.' He could not have foreseen then that the CPP government would have a mere nine years in which to carry out its radical policies. Though even if he had, it is doubtful if he could have achieved more in that short period, given the circumstances of the time. In the words of the great Pan-Africanist, Dr W.E.B. DuBois, 'Time is long.' Yet no regime in Ghana since 1966 has yet been able to solve Ghana's economic and social problems. In fact with the additional problems brought by 'recolonization, 'conditions have deteriorated. The judgement of the people of Ghana on their standard of living, the yardstick by which Nkrumah wanted the CPP performance to be judged, may well be that they had 'never had it so good,' or travelled so hopefully, as during those years of CPP rule.

9

A Race against Time

When he was living in Guinea, between 1966 and 1971, Nkrumah often reflected on the years between independence and the overthrow of the CPP government in 1966. He said that possibly Ghana's independence had been achieved too easily. The majority of Ghanaians had not needed to take up arms or to sacrifice for their freedom. Perhaps if they had, they might have valued it more highly, defending it more robustly when the military seized power in 1966. He believed that an armed struggle to achieve freedom inevitably builds during the course of the campaign a freedom-fighter mentality, a politicisation both of guerrillas and the people on whom they depend for support.

In retrospect, Nkrumah also wondered whether, in the circumstances of the time, it would have been possible to implement CPP policies any faster. He wrote in his *Autobiography*: 'What other countries have taken 300 years or more to achieve, a once dependent territory must try to accomplish in a generation if it is to survive. Unless it is, as it were, 'jet propelled' it will lag behind and thus risk everything for which it has fought.'

But as he remarked on several occasions: 'Socialism cannot be built without socialists.' The CPP, a mass-based Party, had won power through the ballot box. It was able to do this as a result of organisation and leadership which brought such pressure on the British colonial government that it had no alternative but to surrender power. At that time, the CPP had a clear-cut central target, the ending of colonial rule. For that task, a mass Party embracing all sectors of the population was required. After 1957, however, the CPP had to adapt to a much more difficult situation. While maintaining as broad a base as possible, the Party needed to develop into a Party of dedicated members prepared to build in Ghana a progressive society and to pursue a vigorous Pan-African policy. For this, it was necessary to enhance the political awareness of the people.

Nkrumah's problem was where to begin. He found the answer in the nation's youth. They were not weighed down by 'colonial mentality' and by traditions of tribalism and regionalism. Nkrumah had already experienced their political awareness in the CYO, and they in their turn had shown that they also stood for the society which Nkrumah was trying to build.

In 1958, Nkrumah founded the Ghana Young Pioneer Movement. The purpose was to widen the school curriculum to include political education so that each pupil was equipped to become an aware, responsible citizen. Through activities and training, Young Pioneers were taught CPP policies of social and economic reconstruction, and of the wider PanAfrican objectives. It became compulsory for each pupil to join the Movement and to pledge loyalty to it. Young Pioneer scarves and badges were worn on all school and state occasions. If the 1966 coup had not occurred, every pupil would have been supplied with a Pioneer uniform, just as free books were provided.

In addition, Nkrumah encouraged the National African Socialist Students' Organisation (NASSO) to organise study groups all over the country. NASSO had within its ranks some of the most politically-conscious sections of Ghana and its members went about after independence as a band of dedicated and selfless individuals. NASSO was one of the five organisations of the CPP. The others were the Trades Union Congress, the United Farmers' Council, the National Co-operative Council, and the National Council of Ghana Women. Nkrumah entrusted NASSO with the vital task not only of Party political education, but also of being the custodian of Party ideology. They were the 'torch bearers' of the Party's ideals and principles.

In June 1959, in a speech on the occasion of the tenth anniversary of the founding of the CPP, Nkrumah said that the composition of the Party had become heterogeneous and that there was a danger that socialist objectives might be clouded by opportunist accommodation and adjustment. Nevertheless, it would have been a tactical mistake to dissolve the CPP in 1957 simply because it could not, as it stood, adequately adjust to the conditions of post-independence Ghana. The Party had acquired immense prestige and an organisational framework which could be utilised. The task was to transform it, though this would not be easy.

As a first step, Nkrumah established the 'vanguard activists.' These were similar to the political cadres he had in mind when he formed the Circle. But unlike members of the Circle, the vanguard activists had political power behind them. They were to live and work among the people, explaining the Party's policies and objectives. Through them, a vast programme of political education of the masses was to be carried out. When NASSO had prepared sufficient cadres fit to be vanguard activists, Nkrumah announced that the Central Committee had decided that the work of political education should in future be taken over by the Party. NASSO had done its work well in stirring up great enthusiasm in the field of political education. As a result of its efforts, the general level of political awareness among the rank and file of the Party had been considerably raised. The situation was sufficiently in hand for the Party to assume full responsibility.

In February 1961, the Ideological Institute at Winneba was founded 'to provide a steady flow of ideologically-sound cadres to carry on the work of politicisation of the masses. In addition, such an institution was needed as a centre where Party members from the Central Committee to local official level could undergo courses of study, and hold discussions on Party organisation and objectives.'[1] Soon, the reputation of Winneba spread far beyond the borders of Ghana, and attracted students from most parts of Africa and elsewhere. Nkrumah hoped that in this way a part of the old Party apparatus could at least be neutralised, if not completely won over. This could be employed in the transition period until a real vanguard Party emerged. Several times, Nkrumah himself went to Winneba to address students and to take part in discussion groups. On more than one occasion, ministers of the CPP government and top Party officials attended special re-education seminars at Winneba, conducted by Nkrumah himself.

In his address at the laying of the foundation stone at Winneba on 18 February 1961, Nkrumah said: 'This day is historic because it is the positive beginning of the end of reaction in Ghana through conscious

---

1. *Revolutionary Path*, p. 161

ideological education.'[1] Present on that occasion was Leonid Ilyich Brezhnev, then President of the Praesidium of the USSR.

The Institute comprised two sections: the ideological education training centre and the Positive Action training centre. There was to be no excuse for any Party member who had passed through a course at Winneba not to know the Party's aims and policies. Men and women from every section of society were to receive training there. In a special warning to top Party officials and members of the government, Nkrumah said: 'We must eschew ridiculous ostentation and vanity when the Party has charged us with eminent offices of state, and remember constantly that we hold such offices not in our own right, but in the right of the total membership of the Convention People's Party, the masses of the people who really matter ... It is a travesty of trust, therefore, for any one of us to consider that we are privileged to install ourselves as masters of the people instead of servants of the masses.'[2]

In his address at the first seminar held at the Ideological Institute in Winneba on 3 February 1962, Nkrumah stated that there were still members who did not appear to understand the Party's policies. It was his suggestion, therefore, that the Secretariat of the Bureau of Party Education should 'go to the people; it must go to the ward, town and village branches as well as to the special branches created in the offices, shops, factories, state farms, corporations and other places of employment, carrying its work to our general membership. It must go to the primary schools through the Young Pioneers; it must go the secondary schools, colleges and universities ... I suggest that Education Secretaries should be appointed wherever a Party branch is established, and these should undertake Party educational work in addition to their normal duties.'[3] Periodically, meetings of all Branch Education Secretaries should be held at Nkrumah's residence, Flagstaff House, so that Party matters could be discussed and talks could be given by members of the Party on appropriate subjects.

Referring to Nkrumaism he pointed out that this was just the application of scientific socialist principles to African realities. Of particular significance, however, was the stress he laid on the techniques of the neo-colonialist period. This, he warned, was the most dangerous form of exploitation because it was concealed.

---

1. *Revolutionary Path*, p. 162.
2. Ibid., p. 167–168.
3.   "   p. 173.

In the press, notably in *The Spark* newspaper, CPP objectives were publicised. Editors of *The Spark* published a booklet in 1964, *Some Essential Features of Nkrumaism*, which summarised Nkrumah's political philosophy.[1]

It was a race against time. The ordinary membership of the Party had to be armed ideologically to make possible the removal of unsound members of the top leadership before they sabotaged the Party's programme through their ineptitude and backsliding. Nkrumah fired the first shots against them in the famous 'Dawn Broadcast' of 8 April 1961. It was a 'call to action to revitalise the CPP, to end self-seeking, to energise the efforts of the people towards socialism.'[2] He continued: 'Some Party members in Parliament pursue a course of conduct in direct contradiction of our Party aims. They are tending, by virtue of their functions and positions, to become a separate social group aiming to become a new ruling class of self-seekers and careerists.'[3] He gave these people a choice. They must either give up their business interests or quit the Party. Nkrumah went on to warn against ostentatious living, and laid down a code of behaviour for those who did not own businesses, but whose outlook and aspirations were elitist.

More often than not, ostentatious living was associated with corruption. Nkrumah took the bull by the horns, knowing that it would mean exposing some of the founder members of the CPP. He instituted a Commission of Inquiry into assets of all leaders of the CPP, including ministers, Party officials and members of the Assembly. The report showed that some of them were in possession of property far in excess of what they could have acquired honestly. As a result, some were asked to resign and others were instructed to surrender their properties. In this way, many of the old guard CPP came under the axe, men who had played an important part in the independence struggle, often undergoing great personal sacrifice. They had come to the parting of the ways. The separation was painful to Nkrumah, who was aware of the contributions they had made in the past. But if anything, he was even more strict with his personal friends than with his enemies.

In striking contrast to some of his ministers, Nkrumah lived in a small two storey house, modestly furnished. His whole manner of

---

1. This was republished by Panaf in 1970. with an additional section to take account of the books written by Nkrumah after 1966 in Guinea.
2. *Revolutionary Path*, p. 153.
3. Ibid., p. 155.

living was ascetic. He was a light eater and neither drank alcohol nor smoked. The food he enjoyed most was the plain food which might be found in the home of the humblest Ghanaian. While he would occasionally wear traditional Kente cloth when state occasions demanded, he was happiest in a simple tunic-type jacket and trousers. After 1966 he never wore anything but this. His typical daily routine would begin at 4.30 to 5.00 a.m. when he would rise and take exercise, playing tennis, riding or walking sometimes as much as four miles. He would sometimes eat the yolk of an egg for breakfast; sometimes nothing at all. Then into the office where he would work through until 2 or 2. 30 p.m. when he would have a light lunch. After a short rest, he would return to the office and often work through without a break until late at night. More often than not, he would only have five hours sleep.

Nkrumah as he said himself took a 'calculated risk' in tolerating for a time the continued presence in the CPP of those who were unable, or did not wish 'to understand the political and social purpose of the state.'[1] He did so in order that his policies for the total liberation and unification of Africa might go ahead without interruption. But after the 1966 coup he declared that: 'The conduct of many of those in the higher Party leadership has demonstrated to the people of Ghana that one can no longer trust in a broad coalition of interests. The old civil service and the judiciary went over almost to a man to the usurping regime. By so doing, they were of course serving personal interests ... The lesson, however, which their conduct provides, is that they have no loyalty to the state or understanding of the social purposes which we were attempting to achieve ... the coup has achieved something which it would have been impossible to achieve without it, namely, a complete and public exposure of the impossibility of continuing along old lines.'[2]

Again, in retrospect, Nkrumah pin-pointed the source of many of the difficulties the CPP government experienced between 1957 and 1966, namely the continuance of old colonial structures and personnel in the armed forces, police and civil service. While Africanisation proceeded and unsuitable personnel, on the grounds of commitment, not of race, were phased out as soon as practicable, it would be some time before a radical transformation could be effected. It was not until 1961, for example, after the army was involved in suppressing a strike of workers in

---

1. *Dark Days in Ghana*, p. 73.
2. Ibid. pp. 73–74.

Takoradi and then in Accra, that Nkrumah dismissed the British army commander, General Alexander. Nkrumah had been in the Soviet Union when the strike occurred. The Party leadership and army commander who acted in his absence with such incompetence in handling the crisis further illustrated the dilemma faced by Nkrumah in trying to forge ahead with insufficient resources in terms of trained, dedicated man power.

Even before independence, in 1956, when Geoffrey Bing QC, an eminent English lawyer became Constitutional Adviser to the Ghanaian government, the condition of the Civil Service was precarious. One quarter of all the senior posts were vacant because the British officials occupying them, facing Africanisation of the service, decided to retire early in order to receive maximum compensation in addition to their pensions. There were at that time insufficient Ghanaians trained to replace them. On Independence Day, only 519 pensionable officers remained. On the same date a year later, 1958, the total was down to 400. 'Of these, 285 were in the technical and professional grades, agriculturalists, architects, civil engineers and so on who could not be replaced immediately by Ghanaians.'[1] Although contracts were drawn up to encourage expatriates to stay until 1959 to enable training programmes to produce a sufficient number of trained officers to replace them, the problem remained. The CPP Africanisation programme was not based on racism. Expatriates were welcome to remain as long as they were needed. Expertise, integrity, and a sincere commitment to basic objectives of the CPP were what counted. There were Ghanaians who failed to qualify on these counts; and expatriates who identified completely with CPP policies.

Between 1956 and 1966, Geoffrey Bing was totally committed to the domestic and PanAfrican policies of the CPP. He worked for many years closely with Nkrumah and the Cabinet. Soon after Independence, Bing was appointed Attorney-General, having been advised by Nkrumah to apply for the post. It was Bing who played a key role in drawing up the Republican constitution for Ghana. Proposals for a republican constitution were published in March 1960 as a White Paper. A plebiscite was then held in April, the result of which made it clear that the people of Ghana welcomed the new constitution, and by an overwhelming vote made Nkrumah the first President. On the first of July 1960, the

---

1. *Reap the Whirlwind: An Account of Kwame Nkrumah's Ghana 1950–66*, Geoffrey Bing. McGibbon and Kee, 1968, p. 183.

Governor-General, Lord Listowel, performed his last duty, the prorogation of Parliament.

The Republican constitution was not copied from that of any other country. Furthermore, it contained a unique provision 'that the independence of Ghana should not be surrendered or diminished on any grounds other than the furtherance of African unity, that no person would suffer discrimination on grounds of sex, race, tribe, religion or political belief, and that chieftaincy in Ghana would be guaranteed and preserved ... freedom and justice would be honoured and maintained.'[1]

Nkrumah was installed as President at State House on 1 July 1960. Standing at his side on that great occasion was President Sékou Touré of the Republic of Guinea. The two presidents then drove in an open car through the streets of Accra. That Ghana's republican constitution provided for a surrender of sovereignty in the interests of African unity further illustrates the consistency and vision of Nkrumah's PanAfricanism. The two presidents celebrating in Accra on that historic 1 July 1960 did not speak the same language. This was no barrier to their communication. Already, their two countries were linked in the Ghana-Guinea Union. They spoke the same language of socialist planning and PanAfricanism. Their brotherhood was both personal and political.

In a final 1 July ceremony held on the race course in Accra, Nkrumah again accompanied by Sékou Touré and other African leaders lit the flame of African freedom. This was to be kept burning to symbolise the continuing struggle for African emancipation.

A few days later, Sékou Touré speaking in Accra confirmed 'the genuine solidarity that binds the people of Ghana and the people Guinea together in one and the same struggle, whose aim is to shape the historic destiny of all the peoples of Africa within the framework of peace, based upon social freedom and democratic progress.'[2]

The lifelong brotherhood of Nkrumah and Sékou Touré was a unique practical expression of the African Personality, a concept so dear to Nkrumah. He described it as a 're-awakening consciousness among Africans and people of African descent of the bonds which unite us — our historic past, our culture, our common experience and our aspirations.'[3]

---

1. *I Speak of Freedom*, pp. 235–236.
2. Ibid., pp. 243–244.
3. *Revolutionary Path*, p. 205.

It was at this time that the title of 'Osagyefo' meaning 'Victorious Leader', was bestowed on Nkrumah by the Asantehene, King of the Ashanti people. It had been used for one of the greatest Ashanti warrior chiefs. The Asantehene considered that Nkrumah well deserved the title, having achieved so much for Ghana and for Africa. It was considered fitting that Nkrumah should be addressed as Osagyefo rather than as President, a non-African title. The matter was put before the Cabinet, and approved as suitable to mark the historic declaration of the Republic.

The word Osagyefo has frequently been translated by non-Ghanaians to mean Redeemer, as proof that Nkrumah encouraged a personality cult. Nothing could be further from the truth. He did not seek the title of Osagyefo. In fact, he spoke in Cabinet against the adoption of the title. On no occasion did he initiate or support measures to enhance his personal position. His modesty was a byword. Often he had to restrain the enthusiasm of Party members wishing to build up his image. Nor would he accept a life-Presidency, though the Party tried several times to persuade him to do so. Time and again, he showed that his personal position and the sovereignty of Ghana were not important. He was sincerely prepared to serve in a Union Government of Africa in any capacity.

10

An African Voice in World Affairs

One of the most remarkable of Nkrumah's achievements was his successful projection of an African
voice in world affairs. This was something new. At no
time before, or since, has any African leader made
such an impact on a PanAfrican level or internationally. It was not that he consciously sought the role of
spokesman for the African people, but it was something which developed naturally from his complete
identification with the basic aspirations of the people
of Africa and with people of African descent throughout the world. The fact was that Nkrumah, whether
he was speaking at the United Nations Organisation,
at an OAU or Commonwealth Conference, at a CPP
rally, or anywhere else, came to be regarded as the
authentic mouthpiece of the African people. When
any major crisis occurred affecting Africa, all eyes
were on Accra, for it was known that a firm and clear
stand would be taken by Nkrumah. He himself was
the personification of the African Personality about
which he spoke and wrote on so many occasions.

For Nkrumah, the African Personality which had
been temporarily submerged during the colonial period, was ripe for revival in the new environment of
post-colonial Africa. It was the spirit of the African
people, aware of their great heritage, and confident in
their immense potentiality: 'It is a concept of the African nation, and is not associated with a particular state,
language, religion, political system, or colour of the
skin. For those who project it, it expresses identification

not only with Africa's historical past, but with the struggle of the African people in the African Revolution to liberate and unify the continent and to build a just society.'[1]

In December 1962, there took place in Accra the first Africanist Conference ever to be held. In summoning eminent Africanist scholars to meet in Accra, Nkrumah wished to set them to work on planning a comprehensive programme of research into all aspects of Africa's history, culture, thought and human and material resources. He was deeply conscious of the fact that there was widespread ignorance of Africa's historical past and of her true economic dimensions. It was not an emotional or sentimental concept of the African Personality, but a rational, realistic assessment of facts. Africans must know themselves and their continent in order to adopt the correct strategy to solve their problems. With this in mind, Nkrumah established an Institute of African Studies at the University of Ghana.

In his speech at the opening of the Conference of Africanists, on 12 December 1962, Nkrumah spoke of the work being done in the Ghanaian Institute, where already scholars had discovered chronicles relating to the early history of northern Ghana. Africanists in other African learned centres were researching other aspects of African pre-colonial history. He mentioned work being done at the University of Dakar where documentary material had been collected on the history of Western Sudan. The Museum of Bamako in Mali had also gathered a great number of historical documents. In Nigeria, a study was being made of relations between the Delta States and Europe in the nineteenth century. In Guinea, also, the history of the contact between Europe and Africa was being written 'as an African experience and not as a European adventure.'[2] Nkrumah went on to speak of similar research into Africa's past being undertaken in Sudan, Ethiopia, Somalia, Kenya, Uganda and other African countries: 'There is a purposeful effort to bring to light those means which alone will enable us to present our history as the history of our actions and of the ideology and principles behind them, the history of our sufferings and our triumphs.'[3] There was a wealth of source material in African languages to draw on, documents in Hausa, Fufuldi, Kanuri, Nupe and Dagbani to name a few.

---

1. *Revolutionary Path*, p. 206.
2. Speech at the Congress of Africanists, 12 December 1962. *Revolutionary Path*, p. 210.
3. Ibid.

These reflected a tradition of learning going back to medieval times. In addition, there were the well-preserved, authentic records of oral tradition, the poetry, stories, legends, praise-songs and the chronicles of states, rulers and dynasties.

Nkrumah spoke at length of the many powerful African kingdoms which existed long before European penetration of the continent. There were, for example, the kingdoms of Ghana, Songhay, Sala, Berissa and the empires of Bornu, Wangara and Melli. Contrary to widely-held beliefs these kingdoms and empires were maintained with a high degree of efficiency and administrative competence. Africa had developed within its borders the instruments of civilisation and art. It had a culture and society of which it could be proud. 'Between ancient times and the sixteenth century, some European scholars forgot what their predecessors in African studies had known. This amnesia, this regrettable loss of interest in the power of the African mind, deepened with growth of interest in the economic exploitation of Africa.'[1] It served the purpose of those who wished to exploit the human and material resources of Africa to disseminate distorted and often completely false accounts of Africa's past 'to justify colonialism as a duty of civilisation'[2] and to spread the myth of racial inferiority and superiority. It was to deny that Africans are an historic people with their own unique forms of languages, culture and society, and imply that Africa's history was but an extension of European history. Nkrumah was convinced that knowledge of Africa's past, and of the continent's resources and peoples, would stimulate the demand for total liberation and unification, and for a restructuring of society more in tune with Africa's communistic and egalitarian traditions. It was the purpose, therefore, of those who met at the first Africanist Conference to prepare the groundwork for a comprehensive study to be made of all aspects of Africa's resources. But more than this the scholars were to make known the facts by publishing the results of their research in an *Encyclopaedia Africana*. Two eminent scholars, who had been living in the USA, Dr W.E.B. DuBois and Dr W. Alphaeus Hunton, were invited to live in Ghana to work on the project, and to organise the research of a team of specialists recruited to assist. The coup of 24 February 1966, however, occurred before the first volumes could be published, and like so many of Nkrumah's PanAfrican

---

1. Speech at the Congress of Africanists, 12 December 1962. *Revolutionary Path*, p. 208.
2. Ibid., p. 209.

projects work on the *Encyclopaedia Africana* was suspended. Dr DuBois had died sometime before the coup, and Alphaeus Hunton was compelled to leave Ghana and to abandon the vitally important work on which he was engaged.

While it was necessary to revive Africa's personality by encouraging cultural activities, it was to augment and enrich political endeavour and not to be a substitute for it. Nkrumah had no time for the negritude philosophy of Leopold Senghor and his friends which he regarded as dishonest, backward-looking and racialist.

> 'When I speak of the African genius, I mean something different from Negritude, something not apologetic, but dynamic. Negritude consists in a mere literary affectation and style which piles word upon word and image upon image with occasional reference to Africa and things African. I do not mean a vague brotherhood based on a criterion of colour, or on the idea that Africans have no reasoning but only a sensitivity. By African genius, I mean something positive, our socialist conception of society, the efficiency and validity of our traditional statecraft, our highly developed code of morals, our hospitality and our purposeful energy.'[1]

Nor did he support the holding of purely cultural festivals which might serve to divert attention from political realities. These he regarded as 'red herrings', attracting energies away from more serious matters, and involving time and expense which could be better employed, for example, in supporting the liberation movement. Once Africa was liberated and an All-African Union Government has been formed, then there would be the conditions under which purely cultural pursuits could flourish. Meantime, every effort should be directed to creating the necessary framework within which the talents of African people could find full expression. 'The spirit of a people can only flourish in freedom.'[2]

Within a year of the holding of the Conference of Africanists, Nkrumah officially opened the Institute of African Studies as part of the University of Ghana on 25 October 1963. By then, the Institute had a staff of seventeen Fellows and forty post-graduate students of which about one third were Ghanaians, and two-thirds were from other African states and countries as diverse as the USA, China, Japan and the Soviet Union.

---

1. Speech at the opening of the Institute of African Studies, Legon, 25 October 1963.
2. *Revolutionary Path*, p. 206.

Staff and students were engaged in a re-interpretation and a new assessment of the factors making up Africa's past, and of the origins and culture of people of African descent in the Americas and the Caribbean. As Nkrumah remarked in his opening speech: 'We have to recognise frankly that African Studies, in the form in which they have been developed in the universities and centres of learning in the west, have been largely influenced by the concepts of the old style "colonial studies", and still to some extent remain under the shadow of colonial ideologies and mentality.'[1] Ghana, through the work of the Institute, was to contribute to the advancement of knowledge about the peoples and culture of Africa through past history and through contemporary problems.

It was to be an institution which would attract scholars from all over the world who had an interest in African studies. But it was not to be an isolated, purely academic institution divorced from the political realities of the African situation. Like schools and universities it must identify with the aspirations of the people of Ghana and of Africa. Furthermore, close working relationships were to be maintained with scholars engaged on similar studies all over the world, 'so that there may be cross-fertilisation between Africa and those who have their roots in the African past.'[2]

Nkrumah insisted that staff and students of all places of learning and research should keep in close touch with the life of the people. There should be constant contacts between them and the public in the form of open lectures, discussions and other joint activities. The making of new knowledge available to the people as a whole was just as important as the acquisition of it. 'The demands are essentially interdependent. And in Ghana the fact that we are committed to the construction of a socialist society makes it especially necessary that the Institute of African Studies should work closely with the people-and should be constantly improving upon its methods for serving the needs of the people-of Ghana, of Africa and of the world.'[3]

Attached to the Institute was the School of Performing Arts which was to put into practice the research findings of the Institute, while a Ghana Dance Ensemble developed the work of the Institute in relation to dance. A further project to promote The African Personality was the

1. Speech at the opening of the Institute of African Studies, Legon, 25 October 1963.
2. Ibid.
3.   "

foundation of an orchestra, the music and instruments of which were, like other cultural developments founded by Nkrumah, designed to express the traditional and modern culture of not only Ghana, but other parts of Africa. They saw themselves as 'torchbearers in Africa', as Nkrumah wanted them to be.

From time to time Nkrumah found it necessary to remind university staff and students in Ghana of their responsibilities to the society which supported them. He was determined that they should not become a privileged, pampered elite, isolated from the community. He wanted students of the University of Ghana to be encouraged to find lodgings in Accra so that they would not be physically cut off from society in their halls of residence at Legon. He initiated action to cut down on extra-vagant living and the rigmarole of ceremonial dress and customs which the University had borrowed from Oxbridge. Such measures to bring the University into line with the life of the rest of country were fiercely resisted by some of the top administrators, who stood to lose most by them. He had plans also for students to work in agriculture, industry or the social services as part of their university training and to step up the extra-mural work of the University.

In a speech made at the University of Ghana on 24 February 1963, Nkrumah defined the role of the university. It was 'to become the academic focus of national life, reflecting the social, economic, cultural and political aspirations of the people … A university does not exist in a vacuum or in outer space. It exists in the context of a society … and without the sustenance which it receives from society it will cease to exist.'

Nkrumah detested intellectual arrogance and what he described as 'dishonest intellectuals.' He could understand ignorance and made allowances for it, and he could show the most remarkable patience in trying to explain a difficult point to someone, but intellectual dishonesty was something he would not tolerate. He saw it as a gross abuse of privilege and a betrayal of society. Dishonest academics served selfish interests and merited no place in a society pursuing a socialist path of development. Nkrumah did not hesitate to dismiss such people, and they would usually respond with the cry that academic freedom had been violated. It was a cry which found support among like-minded circles in the institutions of Western countries but which carried no weight among people in other parts of the world who were likewise intent on the work of social reconstruction. Nkrumah, a scholar himself, supported the freedom of scholars to pursue the truth and to publish the results of their researches without fear. But there was often abuse of academic freedom. This was the case when it became 'a dangerous cloak for activities outside the academic interests and preoccupations of the community or of the university. Where this has happened a grave disservice is done to everything for which knowledge and truth really stand. True academic freedom — the intellectual freedom of the university — is everywhere fully compatible with service to the community, for the university is, and must always remain, a living, thinking and serving part of the community to which it belongs ... We must not only feel the pulse and intensity of the great African revolution taking place in our time, but we must also make a contribution to its realisation progress and development.'[1]

The high standard of education in the schools, colleges and institutes of Ghana attracted staff and students from other African countries and from many parts of the world. There was a particularly large influx of peoples from the USA and the Caribbean, but by no means all were of African descent. Entry to Ghana was granted not on racial grounds, but strictly on merit and political acceptability. There were Ghanaians who resented the presence of so many whom they regarded as 'foreigners', and some of his party colleagues became jealous when a 'foreigner' appeared to get too close to Nkrumah. At these times he would become impatient, particularly if attempts were made to discredit them on the grounds of race or nationality.

Doubtless, Nkrumah 's first-hand experience of the conditions under which peoples of African descent lived in the USA made him especially receptive to African-Americans. He understood their special problems and saw their struggle to obtain basic human rights in the USA as part of the wider African and world human rights struggle. While he held the view that large-scale immigration of African-Americans and West Indians into Africa could only be planned and carried out within the context of a unified continent, he welcomed to Ghana any whom he considered had special skills. It was soon after Ghana's independence that Dr DuBois was invited to live in Ghana and to work on the compilation of the *Encyclopaedia Africana*. Among other distinguished visitors to Ghana were the African-American novelist Richard Wright and George Padmore.

---

1. Speech at the University of Ghana, 24 February 1963.

Nkrumah later parted company with Padmore politically. He was particularly disappointed in the views expressed by Padmore in his book *Pan-Africanism or Communism* in which he attacked communism implying the two ideologies were incompatible. Padmore wrote in the chapter 'Communism and Black Nationalism' as follows:

> Negroes are keenly aware that they are the most racially oppressed and economically exploited people in the world. They are also very much alive to the fact, demonstrated by the opportunistic and cynical behaviour of the Communists, that the latter's interest in them is dictated by the ever-changing tactics of Soviet foreign policy rather than by altruistic motives. Their politically minded intellectuals know that the oppressed Negro workers and peasants are regarded by the Communists as 'revolutionary expendables' in the global struggle of Communism against Western Capitalism. They know that Africans and peoples of African descent are courted primarily to tag on to the white proletariat, and thus to swell the 'revolutionary ranks' against the imperialist enemies of the 'Soviet Fatherland.' This attitude towards the Negroes is fundamentally part and parcel of the Communist philosophy relating to racial minorities and dependent peoples.

Padmore, like other African-Americans among Nkrumah's friends, had become disillusioned with what were perceived to be racist attitudes among members of the US Communist Party. They considered it a 'white man's party.' While Nkrumah considered class struggle to be at the core of problems facing those suffering oppression and injustice, it seemed to him that Padmore and others who thought like him, were primarily concerned with black nationalism. It was the issue of racism, a concept which Nkrumah detested, which lay at the root of some of the political rifts which occurred between Nkrumah and several of his African-American friends.

Nkrumah considered the African liberation movement, PanAfricanism and the pursuit of socialist goals were inextricably linked. 'These objectives are closely inter-related and one cannot be achieved fully without the other.'[1]

---

1. *Handbook of Revolutionary Warfare*, p. 24.

As far as Padmore was concerned, Nkrumah never forgot his friend's contribution to PanAfricanism and the liberation movement. When Padmore died in England where he was receiving medical treatment, Nkrumah arranged for his casket to be conveyed to Ghana where it was placed with due honour in Christiansborg Castle in Accra. In 1961, when the new research library of African Affairs was opened in Accra, Nkrumah named it The George Padmore Memorial Library. This library was to be a centre for research into the life of the peoples of the African continent. In common with most of the new amenities provided during Nkrumah's time, the library was, in his words, to know 'no national frontiers: for here shall be stored the cumulative experience, the collective wisdom and knowledge about the entire continent of Africa, and the assessment, re-evaluation and studies of observers from all over the world.... May it be an instrument of scholarship for the study of the African peoples, and an inspiration for those who work towards African freedom and unity.'[1]

Padmore's widow, Dorothy, continued to live in the family bungalow in Accra, maintaining the close personal friendship with Nkrumah. At the time of her death she was researching material for Nkrumah's book *Neo-colonialism: The Last Stage of Imperialism*, and also assembling material for a biography of her husband which she intended to write. The Padmore bungalow was later to become Nkrumah's research office.

In 1964, Malcolm X visited Ghana which he described as 'the very fountain-head of PanAfricanism.'[2] It was a time when racial tensions in the USA were erupting in urban riots in spite of the conscience-salving Civil Rights Bill. Writing of the time he spent in Ghana, Malcolm X said: 'I can only wish that every American black man could have shared my ears, my eyes, and my emotions throughout the round of engagements which had been made for me in Ghana. And my point of saying this is not the reception that I personally received as an individual of whom they had heard, but it was the reception tendered to me as the symbol of the militant American black, as I had the honour to be regarded.'[3] He regarded his meeting with Nkrumah as the highlight of his whole African tour:

1. Speech at the Opening of the George Padmore Memorial Library, Accra, 30 June 1961.
2. *Autobiography of Malcolm X*, Grove Press, 1966, p. 352.
3. Ibid., pp. 353–354.

'As I entered Dr Nkrumah's long office, he came out from behind his desk at the far end. Dr Nkrumah wore ordinary dress, his hand was extended and a smile was on his sensitive face. I pumped his hand. We sat on a couch and talked. I knew that he was particularly well informed on the Afro-American's plight, as for years he had lived and studied in America. We discussed the unity of Africans and peoples of African descent. We agreed that PanAfricanism was the key also to the problems of those of African heritage. I could feel the warm, likeable, and very down-to-earth qualities of Dr Nkrumah. My time with him was up all too soon. I promised faithfully that when I returned to the United States, I would relay to Afro-Americans his personal warm regards.'[1]

Not long after his return to the United States, Malcolm X was assassinated, in January 1965. He died convinced — greatly as a direct result of his African tour and his important meeting with Nkrumah — that the struggle for human rights in the USA must develop 'a working unity in the framework of PanAfricanism', and that 'philosophically and culturally we Afro-Americans badly needed to "return" to Africa.'[2] Like Nkrumah he was thinking of the 80 million or so people of African descent in South, Central and North America, and of the 300 million people of Africa. 'The world's course will change the day the African heritage peoples come together as brothers.'[3]

During Nkrumah's visit to the USA and Canada in 1958 he visited Harlem. The people there remembered how he had lived among them when he was studying in America. Ralphe J. Bunche, in a speech of welcome to Nkrumah expressed the feelings of the people of Harlem:

'We salute you, Kwame Nkrumah, not only because you are the Prime Minister of Ghana, although this is cause enough. We salute you because you are a true and living representation of our hopes and ideals, of the determination we have to be accepted fully as equal beings, of the pride we have held and nurtured in our African origin, of the achievement of which we know we are capable, of the freedom in which we believe, of the dignity imperative to our stature as men.'

---

1. *Autobiography of Malcolm X*, Grove Press, 1966, p. 356–357.
2. Ibid., p. 350.
3. "   p. 352.

It was a time of considerable world tension, and one of the main reasons for Nkrumah's visit to the USA and Canada was to discuss common problems and to explain to the governments of the USA and Canada the significance of Ghana's independence, the Accra Conference of April 1958, and the emergence of a distinctive African Personality. He had made it clear that African states in pursuing a policy of non-alignment did not intend to become silent spectators in world affairs:

> 'In asserting our African Personality we shall be free to act in our individual and collective interest at any particular time. We shall be able to exert our influence on the side of peace and to uphold the rights of all people to decide for themselves their own forms of government, as well as the right of all people regardless of race, colour or creed to lead their own life in freedom and without fear.'[1]

Ghana and the African countries which obtained independence soon after, emerged on the world political scene when the Cold War between the USSR and USA dominated international affairs. In the climate of the Cold War newly-independent states in Africa and Asia, and countries which came within the broad category of states with less-developed economies, considered their best interest lay in adopting a non-aligned stand. For one thing, they could not afford to be drawn into great power politics. Their economic conditions necessitated the maintenance of reasonably good relations with both sides. Furthermore, it seemed sensible for smaller nations, mainly the former colonial peoples of the world with similar economic problems, to band together so that their corporate voice might carry some weight internationally. Among the most notable supporters of the non-aligned movement (NAM) were Kwame Nkrumah, Jawaharlal Nehru of India, Abdel Nasser of Egypt, President Tito of Yugoslavia, and President Sukarno of Indonesia.

As far as Nkrumah was concerned, non-alignment did not imply a negative attitude towards international affairs. He preferred to refer to the policy of non-alignment as 'positive neutrality.' As a group, the non-aligned states had a chance of making their voices heard. As small, separate and relatively weak powers they were dangerously exposed. In a major speech on foreign policy in the National Assembly in Accra

---

1. *I Speak of Freedom*, pp. 128–129.

The leaders of the Non-Aligned Movement (NAM). [L to R] Nehru (India), Nkrumah (Ghana), Nasser (Egypt), Sukarno (Indonesia), Tito (Yugoslavia) — Bandung, 1955

on 3 September 1958, Nkrumah declared his government's adherence to the policy of non-alignment: 'This policy of non-alignment we have interpreted to imply that the government would act as it sees best on any issue in the light of the country's obligation to the United Nations Charter, our position in relation to the African continent and the Commonwealth, our adherence to the principles enunciated at the Bandung and the Accra conferences and our determination to safeguard our independence and sovereignty.' History was made at the Bandung Conference in 1955 when for the first time the peoples of Africa and Asia, and representatives of liberation movements met to discuss common problems. The programme and strategy to end colonialism was worked out at this conference, and bonds of friendship and solidarity formed.

Subsequently, Nkrumah attended the 1961 Belgrade Conference where twenty-five countries and three observer countries were represented; and the Cairo Conference of 1964 when forty-six countries and ten observer countries were represented, twenty-nine of them African. Although the non-aligned states at these conferences shared no common ideology it did not mean there was any lack of commitment. In their many resolutions and declarations a definite political line is apparent, although it did not crystallise until the Algiers Conference of 1973, attended by sixty-nine countries and eight observers. At that conference the two important issues which dominated proceedings, and which had figured prominently in earlier conferences, particularly at the Lusaka Conference in 1970, were the liberation movement and problems of economic development. On both of these questions, the non-aligned had become aligned. They were determined to end colonialism and neocolonialism in all its forms. As most of the non-aligned states were African or Asian, these were still the burning issues of the day.

It is pointless to speculate on whether Nkrumah would have attended the Non-Aligned Conference of 1970 in Lusaka had the coup not taken place in Ghana in 1966. But in view of his writings in Conakry between 1966 and 1971 it seems unlikely. In an article he wrote in 1968 entitled *The Myth of the Third World*, he said that he considered it impossible, either in terms of ideology or practical politics, in the ever-sharpening conflict between the progressive and reactionary forces in the world, to adopt a position of neutrality or non-alignment. As he put it: 'The world struggle, and the cause of world tension, has to be seen not in the old political context of the Cold War, that is of national states and power blocs, but in terms of revolutionary and counter-revolutionary peoples.'[1]

The expression Third World had come to be widely used during the time of the first two Conferences of Non-Aligned States. The Cold War and the nuclear arms race were then at their height. The world seemed poised on the brink of nuclear war. Nkrumah and his colleagues in the non-aligned movement then thought the holding of the balance of power by some third force might prevent either of the two opposing power blocs of east and west from starting a major war. After the first conference, Nkrumah and Nehru visited Moscow on behalf of the non-aligned states, while President Modibo Keita of Mali and President Sukarno went to Washington DC. No sudden lessening of world tension resulted, though the threat of nuclear war was to some extent lessened.

However, when Nkrumah wrote *The Myth of the 'Third World'* in 1968, he referred to non-alignment as 'an anachronism ... a form of political escapism ... reluctance to face the stark realities of the present situation.'[2] Nkrumah did not deny the existence of what Frantz Fanon termed 'the wretched of the earth', but maintained they did not exist in isolation as a Third World. They were an integral part of the peoples of the world committed to progressive policies to end the exploitation of man by man.[3]

By 1968, when Nkrumah exposed the myth of the Third World, most of the founder members of the non-aligned movement were either dead or had been removed from power. The death of Nehru was a particular blow to Nkrumah since the two leaders had much in common and a firm friendship had developed between them as a result of Nkrumah's visit to India in December 1958. Nkrumah went to India at the invitation of Nehru. He wanted to see at first hand how India had tackled economic and political problems during the eleven years of her independence, and at the same time to explain his policy for Ghana and his belief in the total liberation and unification of the African continent. Ghana and India had both suffered from colonialism and were both exposed to neocolonialism. They had similar economic problems and could learn from each other's experience. Then there was the additional link provided by their joint membership of the non-aligned movement.

---

1. *The Myth of the 'Third World'*, Kwame Nkrumah. First published in the *Labour Monthly*, October 1968. Full text in *The Struggle Continues*, Panaf 1973, pp. 74–77.
2. Ibid.
3.   "   .

For both Nkrumah and Nehru, Afro-Asian solidarity was much more than a political expression. It implied the solidarity of peoples rather than of governments. In the spirit of Bandung, Afro-Asian co-operation meant the development of a common political and economic strategy, and the organizing of associations, the exchange of students and other ways of strengthening the bonds of friendship between the peoples of Africa and Asia.

As on all visits abroad, Nkrumah was welcomed throughout India as the embodiment of resurgent Africa. Significantly, shortly before he left India, he was presented with a bronze sculpture entitled 'The Voice of Africa.'

Nearly seven years later, in May 1965, Nkrumah was host to the fourth Afro-Asian Solidarity Conference held in Winneba, Ghana. It met at a time when the Vietnam war was still raging; when there was wide-spread fighting in the Congo; and when the peoples of South Africa, Rhodesia (Zimbabwe), South West Africa (Namibia), Angola, and Mozambique were rising against their rulers.

In his opening Address to the conference, on 10 May 1965, Nkrumah said that economic exploitation, 'The heart of imperialism', was at the root of the problems of Afro-Asian nations. He called for solidarity and unity and warned:

> 'Let no-one mistake this as a racial alignment. We are neither racists nor racialists although we happen to be non-white in over-whelming numbers on these two continents. We are not here be-cause we come from Africa and Asia, but because we belong to that part of the human race whose lands have been colonised and whose freedom was taken away by the imperialists .... We are here because we are resolved that any system or regime which owes its existence to the exploitation of man by man, and the degradation of man by man, cannot and must not be permitted to continue its existence in the world.'

He went on to call for maximum support to be given to the liberation movements of Africa and Asia, and emphasised how much more effec-tive Africa's human and material resources would be when mobilised under a continental Union Government.

Nkrumah became one of the architects of an even wider grouping of peoples with the founding of OSPAAAL, the Organization of Solidarity of the Peoples of Africa, Asia and Latin America, with its headquarters in Cuba. This organization, strongly supported by Fidel Castro, Ben Bella, Nkrumah and others, did much to strengthen the ties between the peoples of Africa, Asia and Latin America. Although Nkrumah never visited Cuba, he was very interested in the Cuban revolution, and on the few occasions when he met Fidel Castro, questioned him closely about it. In Cuba's colonial background heavy dependence on a single commodity, sugar, he saw a parallel to Ghana's problem of the single crop economy, cocoa, a legacy of the colonial period. Cuba and Ghana were both pursuing a socialist path of development, and had many similar problems. The personal friendship between Castro and Nkrumah was strong and based on great respect for each other's achievements. Castro was one of the first to get in touch with Nkrumah after the 1966 coup in Ghana, and throughout the six years which Nkrumah spent in Guinea, Castro arranged from time to time for supplies of Cuban foods to be sent to him.

The emergence of an African voice in the largest of all international bodies, the United Nations Organization, may be traced to the Nkrumah era. On Ghana's independence, there were only eight independent African states, and their presence within the UN was scarcely noticed. They shared no common policy, and as small and relatively weak states, were considered of little account. Within a few years, however, with the gaining of independence of the African colonial territories of Britain, France and Belgium, African membership of the UN increased dramatically, and there began to develop within the UN an 'African lobby.' Before important debates in the General Assembly and in the Security Council, particularly when the subject for discussion was of vital concern to Africa, members of African delegations would meet and if possible agree on a common line. This development was due in no small measure to the initiative of the Ghanaian delegation acting on specific instructions from Nkrumah. However, such fragile unity of purpose, when it could be achieved, was no substitute for an African voice representing a politically united continent. As Nkrumah pointed out: 'It is an illusion to suppose that because Africa as a whole can cast thirty-six votes in the General Assembly of the United Nations this makes us powerful. Even when we have voted as a united group on such issues as South Africa and Southern Rhodesia, what has it availed us? In practice — nothing ... pious resolutions are no substitute for positive action.'[1] A single African vote in the

---

1. Address in the National Assembly, Accra, 3 September 1965.

Nkrumah welcoming Mrs. V.L. Pandit (née Swarup Kumari Nehru), sister of Nehru, first Prime Minister of India, in Accra

Nkrumah in discussion with President Nasser — Cairo, 1964

UN would be more powerful than any number of votes from separate African states, if that vote came from a delegation representing the African people as a whole through a Union Government of Africa. Nkrumah declared support for the United Nations as a useful instrument for harmonizing the policies of states and for the promotion of peace and mutual understanding among the nations of the world. But while Africa remained Balkanised he had no illusions about the strength of the African people's voice in the UN.

The failure of the UN intervention in the Congo between 1960 and 1964 was of particular concern to Nkrumah since Ghana had from the start been closely involved in the operation. When, within two weeks of the Congo's independence on 30 June 1960, Moise Tshombe announced the secession of Katanga, and Patrice Lumumba appealed to the UN for military assistance, Nkrumah immediately offered Ghanaian troops. In a message to Lumumba, dated 13 July 1960, Nkrumah said that he was prepared to send a battalion since he considered the problem was capable of solution through the effort of troops primarily from independent states. Lumumba at once called on Ghana for military aid, and two days later, Ghanaian soldiers arrived in the Congo as part of an advance UN force which also included Tunisian troops.

In his book *Challenge of the Congo*, Nkrumah published the documents relating to this period, and the subtitle of the book, 'A case study of foreign pressures in an independent state', indicates his viewpoint. He exposes the ways in which Lumumba's government was sabotaged from the start by the agents of neocolonialism; the forces behind Tshombe; the failure of the UN intervention and the reasons for it. Of particular interest are the full texts of messages which passed between Nkrumah and Lumumba, and Nkrumah and the Ghanaian ambassador, in Leopoldville. Here the dilemma of the Ghanaian government is revealed. Having supported the UN intervention called for by the legitimate government of the Congo, Ghanaian troops found themselves as part of the UN military force engaged in operations which resulted in the fall and consequent murder of Lumumba, the leader of the very government which had sought their support. The Ghanaian ambassador in the Congo, A.Y.K. Djin, in a dispatch dated 13 September 1960, reported that the prestige of Ghana 'had been run down to its lowest ebb by General Alexander's intrigues.'[1]

1. *Challenge of the Congo*, Kwame Nkrumah. First published in 1967, Panaf edition 1969 p. 47.

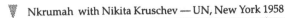 Nkrumah with Nikita Kruschev — UN, New York 1958

Nkrumah
with Canadian
Prime Minister,
John Diefenbaker
— UN, New York
1958

General Alexander, the commander of the Ghanaian UN contingent, had permitted Ghanaian troops to be used to prevent Lumumba from using his own radio station to broadcast to the Congolese people.

Nkrumah, who kept closely in touch with the day-to-day events of the developing Congo crisis, became increasingly exasperated both at the way the UN operation was being conducted and the duties which Ghanaian troops were being called upon to perform. As Nkrumah said in a note to Lumumba: 'I entirely appreciate your point of view and understand the difficult position in which you find yourself *vis-à-vis* the Ghana troops in Léopoldville. I also find myself in an embarrassing and invidious position in respect of the way in which my Ghana troops are being used in the Congo, though I have been fighting like mad day and night on your behalf ... I have already taken steps to deal with the situation.'[1] The nature of the 'steps' taken by Nkrumah were revealed in a note sent to Dag Hammarskjöld, UN Secretary-General, on 12 September in which he declared that if Lumumba was not allowed to use his own radio station, then the Ghanaian troops in the Congo would be placed 'entirely at the disposal of the legitimate Lumumba Government of the Congo Republic.'[2] The placing of Ghanaian troops under the command of the Congolese government would have been conditional on the making public of the secret Agreement for the Ghana-Congo union agreed between Nkrumah and Lumumba in August 1960. Only then could Ghanaian troops have operated legitimately with Congolese forces. However, the step was never taken. Lumumba was arrested on 12 September on the orders of the Army Chief of Staff. Joseph Ileo formed a new government; and so began the chain of events which led inevitably to the coups of Joseph Kasavubu and Mobutu and the tragic murder of Lumumba.

Lumumba had invited UN troops to the Congo in the belief that they would be under the command of his government and would bring about the end of the secession of Katanga. In fact, they had failed to dislodge Tshombe's regime in Katanga. A particularly distasteful aspect of the situation was the use which had been made of African and Asian troops serving under UN command. These had been called upon to perform duties which had positively assisted in the breakdown of Lumumba's government.

---

1. *Challenge of the Congo*, pp. 41–42.
2. Ibid., p. 42.

Following Lumumba's visit to Accra in August 1960, and the signing of the secret agreement to form a Ghana-Congo Union, there had developed a close bond of friendship between Nkrumah and Lumumba. They thought alike on the basic issues of continental liberation and unification. Both in turn were betrayed. Two of the Ghanaian army officers who served in the Congo, Ankrah and Otu, were among the leaders of the coup who seized power in Ghana on 24 February 1966. These men had already stabbed Lumumba in the back, and then betrayed Nkrumah and the people of Africa.

Nkrumah said he had received a note personally signed by King Baudouin of Belgium in August 1960 in which the King offered a large sum of money if Nkrumah would arrange, on Lumumba's visit to Ghana, for him not to leave the country alive.[1] This was on the occasion of Lumumba's visit to Accra, when the Ghana-Congo Union agreement was signed. Nkrumah's reaction to the note can well be imagined. It was his intention to publish a copy of it in his book, *Challenge of the Congo*, but just over five years later when *Challenge of the Congo* was nearing completion, and Nkrumah called his secretary to bring the note it could not be found. Nkrumah had the offices of Flagstaff House virtually turned upside down, and the few who had seen and handled the 'Baudouin letter', notably Michael Dei-Anang, were closely questioned. But to no avail. In the circumstances, Nkrumah decided not to include mention of it in *Challenge of the Congo* without proof in the form of a photograph of the actual letter bearing King Baudouin's signature.

One of the last letters Lumumba was able to write before his arrest and subsequent murder was to Nkrumah. He wrote:

> 'Mr President and dear Friend, it is with very real pleasure that I received your several messages, and I thank you most heartily. I have taken into consideration all the advice you have given me and have spoken about it with Mr Djin, the Ambassador ... I should like to ask you to send me military reinforcements at Stanleyville. Congo and Ghana must fight together until final victory is achieved ...

---

1. Nkrumah told me this in 1965 in Flagstaff House when we were working on the manuscript of *Challenge of the Congo*. Member of the Cabinet, Michael Dei-Anang, confirmed that the 'Baudouin letter' had been received, and said he would let me see it before I left Accra, so that I could include the text in the book. In spite of my several reminders he did not produce it.

The United Nations, as a result of their mischievous action in the Congo, wished to sow the seeds of discord between the Congo and Ghana. The situation has just been clarified and our ties are now stronger than ever. Consequently, there is no further disagreement between us.

You can rely on me and I on you. Today we are one and our countries are one.

P. S Parliament has given me full powers and I have the law behind me.'[1]

Within a few months, Lumumba was dead. He had been murdered because the United Nations, which Lumumba had invited to the Congo to preserve law and order, had not only failed to do so, but had also denied the legal government of the Congo all means of self-protection. Nkrumah, in a broadcast to the Ghanaian people on 16 February 1961, recounted the sequence of events which had led to the murder of Lumumba and of his comrades, Maurice Mpolo and Joseph Okito. He exposed the role of Union Miniére in the secession of Katanga and the large financial stakes which the great powers generally had in the Congo. 'Patrice Lumumba, Maurice Mpolo and Joseph Okito have died because they put their faith in the United Nations, and because they refused to allow themselves to be used as stooges or puppets for external interests.'[2]

Lumumba's death was felt in a very keen and personal way by Nkrumah. He had regarded him as a son and freedom-fighter, and had recognised in him exceptional ability which could be harnessed to the African revolutionary struggle. Nkrumah suffered much personal grief during his lifetime when comrades in the struggle were either killed, died or were removed from power. Lumumba was one of the first to go. There followed Frantz Fanon, Ben Barka, Felix Moumie', Modibo Keita, Eduardo Mondlane, Malcolm X, and many others whose names are not so well known, but whose loss was a great blow to Nkrumah.

In the case of the Congo, Nkrumah continued to do all in his power to see that Lumumba's work was successfully completed. As the situation in the Congo deteriorated, and as one regime followed another, each one seeming to increase the sufferings of the Congolese people,

---

1. *Challenge of the Congo*, pp. 61–63.
2. Ibid., p. 132.

Nkrumah was constantly in touch with the UN Secretary-General, and with the governments of the independent African states to bring about an African solution. The climax to his efforts came in September 1963 when he instructed the Ghanaian delegation at the United Nations led by Kojo Botsio, to 'take immediate steps to discuss with the Africa Group the plan which I have already put to the Secretary-General and Premier Adoula for an All-African Brigade in the Congo in the event of the UN Military Mission being withdrawn at the end of this year.'[1] There were reports that the USA, Britain and Belgium intended to keep a small mobile UN force in the Congo, and if this happened, Nkrumah considered that 'the Western powers would retain undue political influence in the Congo, to the detriment of the sovereignty and independence not only of the Congo but of Africa as a whole.'[2] Right from the start of the Congo crisis, Nkrumah had held the view that the problem concerned not the Congolese people alone, but the African people as a whole, since none could escape the consequences of strongly-entrenched neocolonialism in the Congo. In a despatch to the UN Secretary-General dated 13 December 1963 Nkrumah wrote:

> 'Is there any need to stress to you what independence of the Congo must mean to every African leader who regards the freedom and prosperity of the whole African continent as indivisible? ... Geographically, strategically and politically, the Congo is the most vital region of Africa ... Foreign powers which have concerned themselves with what they like to call 'the defence of Africa' — by which they mean the defence, on the African continent, of interests which are mainly contrary to those of the African people — clearly regard the Congo as the key to the military control of Africa ... Thus the degree of the Congo's independence will substantially determine the ultimate fate of the whole continent of Africa.'[3]

Nkrumah went on to say that 'nothing and nobody can help the Congolese people to free themselves unless the African nations come to their help in unity and in accordance with the spirit of Addis Ababa.'[4]

---

1. *Challenge of the Congo*, pp. 229.
2. Ibid.
3.   "   pp. 235–237.
4.   "   p. 239.

The African nations must insist that the UN force in the Congo be an All-African one, under African command. It should be this force, and not NATO, which should be in charge of the retraining programme for the Congolese army. Unless an All-African force took over the task of freeing the Congolese people, then the dominant interests in the Congo would continue to be those of a group of Western powers, which would operate through puppet governments under such men as Mobutu and Tshombe.

There followed the return of Tshombe, foreign military intervention at Stanleyville, and ultimately Mobutu's coup d'état of November 1965. In the final chapter of *Challenge of the Congo*, which Nkrumah wrote shortly afterwards, he described Mobutu, whom he considered as guilty of the murder of Lumumba, as having 'special leanings towards the Western powers.'[1]

---

1. *Challenge of the Congo*, pp. 288.

11

The Gathering Storm

In 1965, the year before the coup which ended the CPP government, storm clouds were gathering on three fronts. First, there was the problem of Rhodesia and the Unilateral Declaration of Independence declared by the Ian Smith government on 11 November 1965. Events leading up to this raised urgently the whole question of settler minority rule in southern Africa. Nkrumah considered this to be a PanAfrican matter which closely involved the Ghanaian government.

Second, the policies of the CPP were attracting increasingly hostile attention from Western governments and media. It was the time of the Cold War. Ghana, regarded as a pace-setter in Africa, was being seen as a threat to Western political and economic interests. Although a founder member of the non-aligned movement, Nkrumah was considered to be far from neutral in the Cold War. His domestic and PanAfrican objectives indicated a clear commitment to 'Eastern Bloc ideology.' The final straw as far as the USA was concerned was the publication in 1965 of Nkrumah's book *Neo-colonialism: The Last Stage of Imperialism* which exposed the workings of international monopoly finance in Africa. The US government regarded the book as a hostile, dangerous statement which justified instant retaliation. There were angry diplomatic exchanges and US 'aid' to Ghana was suspended.

Third, those opposed to CPP policies combined to cause domestic discontent. Old opposition elements led basically by those in the professions, the bureaucracy and the business community who stood to lose by the building of a socialist society, capitalized on difficulties arising during the implementation of Development Plans. Furthermore, there was some resentment over Nkrumah's concentration on PanAfrican matters which involved Ghana in the problems of non-Ghanaians, sometimes at considerable expense.

The conditions under which the African people of Rhodesia lived concerned Nkrumah just as much as those of the Ghanaian people. He could neither relax nor concentrate on domestic issues while Africans remained unfree in Rhodesia, Mozambique, South Africa, Angola, so-called Portuguese Guinea, South West Africa and elsewhere. As he said: 'Brothers, we know your needs and will not forget them. You are entitled to your freedom at any cost, and if you are only able to gain your freedom by an armed struggle, we will not only consider your wars against the foreign oppressor as just and holy, but we will be prepared to help you as if these were our own wars for our own liberation.'[1] He was similarly prepared to support freedom-fighters struggling against neocolonialist puppet governments in what he called the 'contested zones' of Africa. As a Nigerian journalist wrote: 'Nkrumah saw himself first and foremost as an African, in the widest continental sense. He thought African, lived African and died African ... He regarded the whole continent as his country; Ghana was only his constituency.'[2]

It was to some extent the failure of the OAU Liberation Committee to provide adequate support and training facilities for liberation movements that led Nkrumah to sanction the setting up of freedom-fighter training camps in Ghana. Members of the PanAfrican National Congress (PAC), the African National Congress (ANC), the Zimbabwe African National Union (ZANU), the Zimbabwe African People's Union (ZAPU), the Popular Movement for Liberation of Angola (MPLA), the South West African Peoples' Organisation (SWAPO), the Front for the Liberation of Mozambique (FRELIMO), to name a few, received aid and training in Ghana. So-called refugees from reactionary regimes in the 'contested zones' of Africa were given the same measure of assistance and facilities to organise. They came from states where independence was a sham, and often where there had already begun a

1. True Freedom for All, Speech by Nkrumah at the Fourth Afro-Asian Solidarity Conference in Ghana, 10 May 1965.
2. Sam Uba, *A Personal View of Nkrumah.* Article in *Africa Features*, LN 292, p. 2.

people's war in the form of a guerrilla struggle to bring down the puppet government.

In 1959, an African Affairs Centre was opened in Accra to house freedom-fighters from all over Africa. The following year the Bureau of African Affairs was founded to be a centre for study of developments in all parts of Africa, and to further the activities of all organisations working for the freedom and unity of Africa. The Bureau as part of its work of disseminating information about the PanAfrican struggle published the periodicals *The Spark, L'Etincelle, Voice of Africa, Freedom Fighters' Weekly, PanAfricanist Review*, African Chronicle and the *Bulletin on African Affairs*.

Although no liberation movement was denied recognition in Ghana, and all freedom-fighters were allowed to organise and to train there, Nkrumah constantly sought to get them to combine their organizations and where possible to plan united strategy and tactics. He would personally discuss problems with them, and was often criticised by colleagues and members of his staff for spending too much time with them and for being too generous in the help he authorized. Among the organizations he tried to unify were ZANU and ZAPU, the nationalist movements of Zimbabwe, for he recognised no basic difference between the aims of both which should prevent them from combining to bring about majority rule in their country. If they disagreed on long-term issues concerning the nature of the state of Zimbabwe once the racist settler government had been destroyed, this must not be allowed to jeopardise the nationalist phase of the struggle. Long-term disagreements could be sorted out once independence had been achieved, and when the people of Zimbabwe were free to express their opinions on how their country should be governed.

Nkrumah had already written about most of Africa's problems, but had not written specifically on the question of settlers and settler rule. As the Rhodesian crisis developed, he was determined to fill the gap. He organised a collection to be made of papers and diplomatic documents relating to the subject. The 1966 coup in Ghana interrupted the work, and many of the documents which Nkrumah wanted to publish were not available to him in Guinea. But he intended, nevertheless, to write the book, to draw on all the material he could gather there, and to rely on memory for the rest.

He had in Guinea a file which contained a synopsis of the intended book, and quite a large collection of papers which he had managed to accumulate, some of them from the archives of the Ghanaian embassy in Conakry, closed down by Sékou Touré after the 1966 coup in Ghana. But he considered that other books which he felt compelled to write, such as *Dark Days in Ghana, Class Struggle in Africa*, the *Handbook of Revolutionary Warfare*, and *Revolutionary Path* took priority, and tragically for posterity he became seriously ill before he was able to get down to writing the book which he intended to publish under the title, *Rhodesia File: A Case Study of Settler Politics*. Instead, it was left to Panaf Books in 1976 to bring out a collection of his papers under the title *Rhodesia File*.

It had become clear by the beginning of January 1964 that Rhodesia was moving towards a unilateral declaration of independence. In a statement to the Rhodesian Parliament in February 1964, the Prime Minister, Winston Field, said: 'The only thing holding independence up is a desire to appease certain members of the Commonwealth.' African nationalist leaders Joshua Nkomo and Ndabaningi Sithole denounced Winston Field's statement. It was clear even then to those in the best position to judge that UDI could be declared without serious risk of British military intervention, and without more than verbal protests from African independent states. The latter, although the OAU had been formed, lacked unity and strength since no political or military machinery had been set up to give authority and teeth to the organisation.

On the resignation of Winston Field on 13 April 1964, Ian Smith became Prime Minister of Rhodesia. He was determined to achieve independence at all costs, regardless of African or world opinion, and was not invited to the June 1964 Commonwealth Prime Ministers' Conference. The British Secretary for Commonwealth Affairs, Duncan Sandys, declared that the British government would not accept any UDI. Independence for Rhodesia would only be granted when Britain was satisfied that it was the wish of all the people of Rhodesia expressed in a representative government based on a 'reasonably wide' franchise.

Nkrumah's presence at the 1964 Commonwealth Conference in London was keenly felt. At informal discussions with the heads of other African states, and in the conference chamber, he strongly opposed independence for Rhodesia before majority rule. The official communiqué, issued at the end of the conference on 15 July, as it related to Rhodesia was in large measure the result of the intensive work put in by Nkrumah. According to the communiqué, conference members would not recognize any UDI by the Rhodesia government, and it was the responsibility of Britain to decide when the independence of Rhodesia should be proclaimed. Furthermore, the African prime ministers managed to get the British government to agree to arrange a conference of all political parties in Rhodesia to work out a constitution based on majority rule, and called for the release of all political prisoners in Rhodesia.

There followed in September 1964 the visit of Ian Smith to London for talks with the British Prime Minister, Alec Douglas Home. It was a pointless exercise. Ian Smith was informed of the views expressed at the Commonwealth Prime Ministers' Conference, and Ian Smith, for his part, said that he was confident that he would be able to get the British government to grant Rhodesia independence since he would be able to show that he had the support of the Rhodesian people as a whole.

Nkrumah hoped that with the Labour Party victory in Britain there might be a more resolute stand taken by the British government on the Rhodesian issue. In a statement issued on 27 October 1964, Harold Wilson warned of serious consequences to any unilateral declaration of independence. 'A mere declaration of independence would have no constitutional effect. The only way Southern Rhodesia could become a sovereign, independent state was by an Act of the British Parliament. A declaration of independence would be an open act of defiance and rebellion and it would be treasonable to take steps to give effect to it; all financial and trade relations with Rhodesia would be jeopardised, and Rhodesia would find herself virtually friendless in a largely hostile continent.' Ian Smith's reaction was to call the statements of the Wilson government flagrant interference in Rhodesia's internal affairs; and step-by-step the situation moved towards UDI. In a referendum held in Rhodesia in November 1964, voters were asked if they were in favour of Southern Rhodesia obtaining independence on the basis of the Constitution of 1961. Some 58,176 voted 'yes' and 6,101 voted 'no.' There was a boycott of the referendum by most B-Roll voters, mainly Africans. In February 1965 a UK delegation headed by Commonwealth Secretary Arthur Bottomley, visited Rhodesia on a fact-finding mission. Little came of it. But Wilson still appeared confident that Ian Smith would not dare to declare UDI and so defy Britain, the Commonwealth, most of Africa and the United Nations. It was in this atmosphere that the June 1965 Commonwealth Prime Ministers' Conference was held in London.

As soon as he arrived in London, Nkrumah began calling on the delegations of African and Asian countries to organise a united front on the Rhodesian issue. Supported by the representatives of Kenya and

Sierra Leone, Nkrumah pressed Harold Wilson to set a specific date and a time limit of three months for holding a constitutional conference in Rhodesia. The Prime Minister of Gambia, Dr Jawara, agreed but suggested a six month time limit. African leaders also sought a declaration by Britain that its aim was to bring majority rule to Rhodesia. They demanded the release of all political detainees in Rhodesia; the suspension of the existing constitution if they were not released, and the formation of an interim government to repeal repressive laws and to prepare for elections on the basis of one man, one vote. Nkrumah emphasised that basically the problem facing the world was the division of mankind into the 'haves' and 'have nots', and the question of Rhodesia was a microcosm of that problem. He viewed the situation in Rhodesia as part of the wider problem of southern Africa as a whole, and called for the setting up of a permanent Commonwealth Secretariat responsible to the Commonwealth as a whole. Such a body could prepare plans for trade, aid and development, and could circulate information and ideas to all members of the Commonwealth. This idea was subsequently acted upon and a Commonwealth Secretariat was established.

Nkrumah proposed that the conference should authorize the issue of a communiqué indicating the position from which they should unanimously approach the Rhodesian question. In the final communiqué issued on 25 June, it was stated that the Prime Ministers welcomed the British Government's statement that the principle of one man one vote was regarded as the very basis of democracy and should be applied to Rhodesia; and that there should be unimpeded progress towards majority rule. The other main topic at the 1965 Commonwealth Prime Ministers' Conference was the war in Vietnam, and it was at this conference that a decision was made to send a Commonwealth peace mission to Hanoi. Nkrumah was an obvious choice to lead such a delegation, and the only leader acceptable to Hanoi. When, therefore, Wilson assumed leadership of the Commonwealth peace mission, the whole project became unrealistic and never in fact materialised.

Nkrumah's stature in Africa, in the Afro-Asian solidarity movement and in the non-aligned movement throughout the world, had risen to a high level. His reputation was further enhanced when, largely owing to his efforts, South Africa was forced to leave the Commonwealth. He had made it clear to the British government that it had to choose between South Africa and Ghana, since Ghana could not remain a member of an organisation containing the racialist, minority government of South

Africa. It was well known that many African states would follow the lead of Nkrumah in taking their countries out of the Commonwealth, and so South Africa was expelled.

While in London, Nkrumah was persuaded to have a medical checkup at University College Hospital. The incredible pace at which he worked worried some of his friends, and they were relieved when doctors found him basically a very fit man, but suggested a daily short rest in the middle of the day in order to preserve his health. One of the doctors expressed the view that Nkrumah had packed into a few years a degree of effort and achievement which the vast majority of people did not achieve in a lifetime and warned him of possible effects on his health unless he slowed up a little. Apart from a short rest of ten minutes or so when possible during the day, Nkrumah carried on as before. He did not ignore medical advice, but considered he knew his own strength, and once assured that there was nothing medically wrong, he thought he was the best judge of what he could or could not do. Throughout his life he persistently overworked. His pace and the high standard of work and commitment he expected of those around him, became proverbial. He exhausted many a secretary, party colleague and cabinet minister, and the pace set by Nkrumah seemed to penetrate every corner of Ghana. As one tired secretary who worked in his office in Flagstaff House remarked with relief when Nkrumah had left Ghana for a few days: 'When the President is away, the whole of Ghana rests on its oars.'

As soon as the Commonwealth Conference ended, Nkrumah faced problems involved in arranging the OAU Summit meeting scheduled to take place in Accra in October 1965. Some of the francophone states threatened not to attend in order to sabotage the Conference. It proved to be impossible for Nkrumah to succeed in getting sufficient votes in favour of his proposals for an Executive Council and an African High Command designed to transform the OAU into an organization with the necessary machinery to act swiftly and effectively to solve African problems. On 31 October 1965, within a few days of the ending of the OAU Summit in Accra, the British prime minister paid a fleeting visit to Accra where he had talks with Nkrumah on the Rhodesian question. Nkrumah made it clear that the Ghanaian government stood firmly by the OAU resolutions on Rhodesia. He warned that if Britain failed in her duty, then the African states would have no alternative but to take whatever steps would be necessary in support of the four million Africans who formed the majority in Rhodesia. He followed up the warning with

▲ Disappointment at failure to get the necessary number of votes for African unity — OAU Summit, Accra 1965 [L to R] Foreground — Sékou Touré, Nkrumah, Kwesi Armah

a message to Harold Wilson dated 2 November 1965, in which he declared that if it became necessary to use force against the settler government in Rhodesia, then it was Britain's clear responsibility to use it. Nine days later, on 11 November 1965, Ian Smith's government illegally declared UDI.

The response from Accra was immediate and strong. Nkrumah in an official statement issued the very same day as UDI, called for 'appropriate and speedy action' to be taken at once to end the Smith rebellion. While he approved the decision of the British government to refer the Rhodesian issue to the Security Council, he had no confidence in the effectiveness of economic sanctions, and called on Britain to revoke forthwith the 1961 Constitution and to call a constitutional conference. In the words of Nkrumah: 'My firm conviction is that the only way to deal with the treasonable seizure of power by the racialists of Southern Rhodesia is to use force against them immediately, and before the situation escalates. We must eradicate at once this illegal regime, root and branch, and for all time.'[1] Ghana was prepared, he said, to place troops at the disposal of the UN, the OAU, or Britain, for service in support of the people of Rhodesia. Furthermore, he proposed an immediate meeting of the Defence Ministers of African states to prepare joint action.

On 19 November, he sent notes to the Heads of State of the Congo, Sudan, Uganda, Tanzania, Zambia and Guinea, which showed that he considered an African solution was the only one likely to be effective in the case of Rhodesia. He called for the urgent formation of an African force capable of being deployed against the 'illegal' government of Rhodesia. He went on to propose the signing of a Treaty of Mutual Defence and Security between as many African states as possible in order to deal with the possibility of hostilities breaking out between any of the states subscribing to the Treaty. At the same time he called for a meeting of the Defence Ministers of the Treaty states to be held in Accra, and to be attended also by military advisers and Chiefs of Staff.

Nkrumah once again, as during the Congo crisis, tried to get the African states to act together to solve an African problem. It is significant that the call was made directly to the governments of states rather than to the OAU. The machinery of the OAU worked too slowly, and in any case, Nkrumah had been disappointed in its performance at the

---

1. Message to the Prime Minister of Singapore, 12 November 1965.

previous month's Summit Conference in Accra when it had failed to form an Executive Council or an African High Command.

Meantime, on 25 November, Nkrumah placed before the National Assembly in Accra a Bill to give his government general powers to make all laws necessary for mobilzation, the requisition of aircraft and ships, and the power to close airports, seaports, and roads in order to facilitate troop movements. Ghana was to be militarily prepared to assist in the overthrow of the Smith regime, or to go to help of any African state attacked or threatened by it. As Nkrumah pointed out to the Assembly members: 'Any war against the rebels would not be like a normal war. For every racialist in Southern Rhodesia there are sixteen Africans. Once arms have been put in their hands the war is as good as over. As I see it, if African armed forces are compelled to put down the Smith regime by force then this will not be done by means of conventional warfare but by organising a rising in mass by the people.'[1]

But Nkrumah stood, as he so often did, virtually alone as the only African leader prepared to take positive action when it came to the test. Again and again throughout his life he was disappointed at the apparent short-sightedness, and even blindness, of so many of his brother Heads of State to the realities of a situation when it seemed to be staring them in the face. He understood the pressures under which many of them worked but he always hoped that, if only in the interest of their own survival, they would surely see the wisdom of unity.

If the Rhodesian problem had not been tied up so closely with the whole situation in southern Africa it might have been less difficult to solve. But the settler government in Rhodesia could not be seen in isolation from the Portuguese colonial governments in Mozambique and Angola, and the governments of South Africa and South West Africa (Namibia). While African states were continuing in disunity, South Africa, Portugal and Rhodesia were drawing closer together militarily and in their political and economic policies. They exchanged information about guerrilla activities and gave each other assistance in various other ways, allowing overflights and landings of military aircraft in each other's countries; and in the case of South Africa, supplying armed forces and police to help the Portuguese and Smith governments to fight off freedom fighter attacks. In addition, Nkrumah was later informed of

---

1. *Call for Action on Southern Rhodesia*. Address by Nkrumah in the National Assembly, Accra, 25 November 1965.

the existence of a 'Council of Three' said to meet regularly in Pretoria, Salisbury (Harare), Lourenço Marques (Maputo) or Luanda, to prepare joint action. It was well known that the South African government was building a huge airbase in the Caprivi Strip in Namibia, only ten miles from the Zambian border.

Apart from the military threat to independent Africa posed by minority governments of southern Africa, there were the more insidious workings of neocolonialism to combat. As Nkrumah said in the Ghana National Assembly on 30 May 1961, 'Portugal can count on heavy backing from vested financial interests throughout the world.' Portuguese colonialism was, in addition, immensely strengthened by her membership of the North Atlantic Treaty Organisation (NATO).

Nkrumah maintained that Africans must create their own political, economic and military organisations and not support or become members of organisations whose loyalties were beyond Africa. In the face of collective imperialism, the African situation demanded 'immediate and drastic remedy. We must throw the full weight of a united revolutionary Africa into the struggle. Each day that we delay, we fail our gallant freedom fighters and destroy our people.'[1]

Nkrumah had for some time been considering taking Ghana out of the Commonwealth, and had been prepared to do so immediately on the formation of an All-African Union Government, or even if it was decided to establish the necessary preliminary political machinery. In Ghana's Republican Constitution of 1960, provision had been made for the surrender of Ghana's sovereignty in the event of a political union of African states; and Ghana's withdrawal from the Commonwealth would have taken place at the same time. Nkrumah had kept Ghana in the Commonwealth because he considered it could serve the purposes of Ghana and Africa as a whole. At the time, there were obvious political and economic advantages in being a member of an organisation of such size and influence. At Commonwealth Conferences it was possible to achieve some measure of success in discussion and debate, and some at least of the resolutions passed were put into effect. In the case of South Africa, Nkrumah had been able to make very effective use of Ghana's membership of the Commonwealth simply by threatening to withdraw. It was this which had precipitated the expulsion of South Africa. But as the years passed, and the Commonwealth began to decline sharply as

---

1. Africa Day Special Message, Kwame Nkrumah. *The Struggle Continues*, p. 15.

an organisation of weight in world affairs, the advantages of remaining a member seemed less and less worthwhile.

Ghana's continued membership of the Commonwealth became impossible with Britain's inadequate handling of the Rhodesian crisis. 'The conception of the Commonwealth', Nkrumah said, 'was built upon the idea that it provided a bridge between peoples of all races and of all stages of development. The manner in which events in Southern Rhodesia have been handled by the United Kingdom Government has undermined and destroyed this conception. In these circumstances, and in order to preserve African unity so as to facilitate the earliest formation of a Union Government for Africa, the Government of Ghana must consider withdrawing from the Commonwealth.'[1] In a letter to June Milne dated 1 December 1965, he wrote: 'As to the Rhodesia question I am fighting like mad. Wilson is hopeless. It is damned unfortunate that he plays internal politics with the Rhodesian crisis. We are standing adamant. We are sending a strong delegation to Addis Ababa. OAU must react very strongly.'

He intended placing before the next OAU Summit Conference a resolution calling upon all member states to sever links with former colonial powers which stood in the way of a Union Government of Africa. In his opinion there should be no political or economic re-grouping or blocs in Africa in alliance with an ex-colonial power, or with any foreign power. He called for African states to create a Common Monetary Authority, an All-African Common Market, an African High Command, and an Executive to co-ordinate efforts on an All-African basis.

Both Ghana and Zambia offered Britain the use of their territories for any purpose connected with the suppression of the rebel regime in Salisbury (Harare). But the offer was not taken up, and as the weeks went by it became obvious that there was no question of force being employed by the British to bring down the Smith government. The weapons to be used were simply those of economic sanctions. From the very beginning of the Rhodesian crisis, Nkrumah had made it clear he considered it would be necessary to use force to quell the rebellion. Economic sanctions and a blockade of Rhodesia to be effective would require the co-operation of not only Britain, but of South Africa, Zambia and Portugal, all of which controlled territory adjoining Rhodesia. In addition, the

---

1. Address by Kwame Nkrumah in the National Assembly, Accra, 16 December 1965.

economy of Zambia would be seriously damaged, since all essential imports required by Zambia were supplied through a railway system which passed through Rhodesia. In view of this, and the fact that there was no way of ensuring that economic sanctions were applied by all nations against Rhodesia, Nkrumah declared the proposals 'unrealistic' and called for military action against the rebels. What Nkrumah had in mind was for the UN to authorise military intervention by African states, and to guarantee such states from attack by Portugal and South Africa.

On 15 December 1965, Ghana broke off diplomatic relations with Britain, thus honouring a unanimous decision reached by the OAU Council of Ministers which had met a short time previously in Addis Ababa. It was agreed there that all member states of the OAU would sever relations with Britain if, by 15 December, Britain had failed to suppress the Smith rebellion. Some of the African states followed Ghana's lead and broke off relations with Britain, but by no means all of them. It was at this point that Nkrumah decided to take Ghana out of the Commonwealth, and to press other African states to sever any links with former colonial powers.

When Ghanaian government archives are examined for this period there should be discovered a copy of a note dated 11 December 1965 sent by Nkrumah to Harold Wilson in which he stated that Ghana would end diplomatic relations with Britain if the Smith rebellion was not suppressed by 15 December 1965, adding: 'In the opinion of the government of Ghana severance of diplomatic relations with Britain would mean Ghana's withdrawal from the Commonwealth.' Between 11 and 15 December 1965 notes were sent to African governments informing them of the Ghana Government's decision to leave the Commonwealth. When the Commonwealth Conference took place in Lagos in January 1966, Ghana did not participate. Nkrumah wrote to June Milne on 5 January : 'I am not, repeat not, attending the Lagos conference. I think Wilson is trying to use Balewa, who does not understand anything. I have written Balewa a diplomatic stinker.'

The Ghanaian government drew up proposals for joint action by the African states. These were to be placed before the OAU Council of Ministers due to meet in Addis Ababa on 27 February. They were never presented. The coup took place in Ghana on 24 February, and Quaison Sackey who was with Nkrumah on the Hanoi mission, and was sent by him to represent the legal government of Ghana at the OAU Addis Ababa meeting, went instead to Accra.

The relief in rebel government circles in Salisbury (Harare) at the coup in Ghana was expressed in the two-word newspaper headline: 'Salisbury jubilant.' Without Nkrumah, not only was it almost certain that an African solution would not be imposed in the Rhodesian crisis in the foreseeable future; but more than that, the prospect receded of an All-African Union Government and an African High Command being formed. Nkrumah's voice had not been silenced, but he was no longer in power in Ghana. It was less than three months since UDI had been declared in Rhodesia; and only a few weeks since Balewa's government in Nigeria had been toppled by a military coup, yet here was another example of what appeared to be an increasing trend towards military intervention in the political affairs of African independent states.

In a major speech in the Ghana National Assembly on 1 February 1966, Nkrumah had warned that there would be no political or economic stability in Africa until a continental union government was formed. Reactionary military coups were expressions of neocolonialism, and as such could be expected to continue as long as Africa remained divided. He went on to declare that it was 'not the duty of the army to rule or govern, because it has no political mandate.... If the national interest compels the armed forces to intervene, then immediately after the intervention the army must hand over to a new civil government elected by the people and enjoying the people's mandate under a constitution accepted by them.'[1] If the army failed to do this, it betrayed the people and the national interest.

In the same speech, Nkrumah defended the adoption of a one-party system in Ghana and other African states. The multi-party system existing in Western countries, he said, reflected social and class cleavages, and where introduced into Africa perpetuates feudalism, tribalism and regionalism. There was no place for it in a country such as Ghana, where a people's state was in process of construction. However, he emphasised that a one-party system of government was an effective and safe instrument only if operated in a socialist society.

The 'crime' of adopting a one-party system was a key criticism in the mounting Western media campaign to discredit Nkrumah and CPP government, which reached a climax in 1965/6. The system was equated with dictatorship and oppression, the argument being that

---

1. *Revolutionary Path*, pp. 370–371.

without an Opposition, preferably Westminster style, there can be no democracy. However, as other newly independent African states also adopted one-party rule, the British two-party system being deemed unsuitable for Africa, single party rule became the widely accepted norm for developing countries where national unity was essential for nation-building and to combat tribalism. There was, for example, no hysterical press campaign against the one-party rule of Julius Nyerere in Tanzania. In countries with one-party systems, differences could be tolerated within the ruling party, but the notion of a paid Opposition, representing a small minority of the population, whose purpose was simply to oppose, was deemed an expensive, negative and unnecessary brake to impose on a developing country's progress.

Nkrumah's friend and fellow PanAfricanist Sékou Touré put the case for one-party rule somewhat differently, though making the same point about national unity:

'We have chosen the freedom, the right, the power, the sovereignty of the people, and not of the individual. Before this people, you should have no individual personality. Our personality becomes part of the personality of the nation.

Tribalism was about the only 'crime' of which Nkrumah was not accused during the growing foreign media campaign. For any attempt to charge him with tribalism would have been laughable, even among those Ghanaians the most critical of him. During the period of CPP government, all regions of Ghana were developed without any consideration of tribal affiliations. The same non-tribal policies applied to the appointment of government and other officials. In Nkrumah's cabinet were always members from many different backgrounds. Suitability and support for CPP policies were the only qualifications for office. Nkrumah detested tribalism as much as racism. It was never part of his, or the CPP, political agenda. Those visiting Ghana in CPP times seldom heard the word mentioned.

A further problem for the Ghana Government at this time was economic pressure brought about by the foreign manipulation of cocoa prices. In 1965, the price of cocoa in the world-market fell to the unprecedented low figure of £87.50 per ton, and this jeopardised Ghana's Seven Year Development Plan. The income which Ghana derived from cocoa depended primarily not on the amount of cocoa produced, but on the price which powerful world forces determined.

As Nkrumah saw it, the problem was a political one first and fore-most. It could be solved by the cocoa-producing states of Africa if they were united in a Union government which had effective, economic overall planning powers. A realistic price could then also be obtained for other primary commodities produced in Africa such as groundnuts, coffee and sisal. But until a political solution was found, the separate African states would continue to be at the mercy of world-market manipulations over which they had no control. The year 1966 would be for Ghana a year of stocktaking but not of stagnation. The bulk of the investment needed for the industrialisation programme of the Seven Year Development Plan would have to come from a vigorous savings campaign. Imports of non-essential goods would have to be severely curtailed, and more of Ghana's resources devoted to productive invest-ments in agriculture, mining and industry to reach the planned growth rate of 5.5% per annum. In addition, it would be necessary to replace some development projects, in order to make available the necessary funds for public services and state enterprises. It was the purpose of the 1966 budget to make Ghana as self-sufficient as possible and thereby to make maximum use of her own material and human resources.

Already, great strides had been made. The Volta River Project had been completed one year ahead of schedule, and the official inaugura-tion ceremony took place on 23 January 1966. On that day, at Akosombo, one of Nkrumah's greatest dreams came true. With the 'electrification' of Ghana would come the breakthrough into a new era of economic and social progress. Ghana was poised for a breakthrough into economic independence.

In addition, the Volta Lake, some 250 miles long and with a shoreline of 4,500 miles, would provide facilities for a freshwater fishing industry. A number of ports and villages were developing round the lakeside. These were benefiting from the new cheap means of transport from the north to the south of Ghana, and would in due course profit from a lake holiday and tourist trade. Furthermore, the vast reservoir of water pro-vided by the lake made possible the improvement of water supplies not only for industry but for domestic use and for agriculture.

In his speech at the inauguration of the dam, Nkrumah said: 'As far as I am concerned, this project is not for Ghana alone. Indeed, I have already offered to share our power resources with our sister African states.' He referred to Togo, Dahomey, Ivory Coast and Upper Volta (now Burkina Fasso).

At that time, building was about to start on a large subsidiary dam at Bui. Plans were also well-advanced for the construction of an alumina plant, which would have given Ghanaians control of the whole process of aluminium production. The industrialisation of Ghana, a priority of the CPP government after independence, was on schedule.

Already, there were fifty-two state enterprises in operation, including twenty-five manufacturing and industrial enterprises. Among recently commissioned enterprises were the Glass Manufacturing Corporation at Aboso, the Cement Works and the Government Electronics Industry at Tema, the Cocoa-Processing Factories at Takoradi and Tema, the Publishing Corporation at Tema which printed school textbooks, and the Textile Corporation producing locally-designed cloths and prints. A corned-beef factory at Bolgatanga, a sugar factory at Akuse, and a factory to produce pre-fabricated houses were soon to begin production. There were further factories at Asamankese, Nkawkaw, Enyiresi, Oppon Valley, Asanwiso, and Bobikumadua to go into production within the year. And within the five years, from 1966/71, there were to be a thousand rural industrial projects established throughout the country. Already the agricultural programme of the Seven Year Development Plan had begun to bring results and Ghana was producing more of the food she needed. The people of Ghana were benefiting from the improved quality of meat and dairy products. The reorganisation and development of the co-operative movement which had resulted in the establishment of strong network of consumer co-operatives throughout the country had brought about a big improvement in distribution.

It was an impressive record, and even more so because it had been accomplished in spite of the sabotaging of many of the government's economic measures by a comparatively small but powerful section of the population. These were the people who engaged in all kinds of trade malpractices, tax evasion, profiteering, hoarding and so on. In some cases, dishonest traders were aided and abetted by government officials, especially those concerned with the issue of import licences. Such problems were not peculiar to Ghana. They occur in practically every part of the world in greater or lesser degree. But in 1965 in Ghana, the activities of this minority, coinciding with the problems brought about by the collapse of cocoa prices, and the resulting necessity for the government to cut down on the imports of non-essential consumer goods, caused acute shortages and difficulties in the consumer market which required immediate investigation.

Accordingly, a Commission of Inquiry was set up on 20 April 1965 to look into the whole supply and distibutive systems and to make recommendations. The Abrahams Commission, as it came to be called, after W. E. Abrahams, the Chairman, began its sitting six days later, on 26 April 1965. Its terms of reference were very wide involving a detailed and comprehensive examination of the whole pattern of Ghana's internal trade, and the determining of the causes and the nature of trade malpractices. It was to find out 'how the avoidable difficulties and misery in the purchase of essential commodities, recently experienced by the people of Ghana, might be prevented in the future.'[1] In all, there were twenty-seven formal sittings of the Commission, fourteen of which were held in Accra, five in Kumasi, four in Sekondi, two in Cape Coast and one each in Tamale and Tema. There were, in addition, many informal sessions. Some 300 witnesses were called, and discussions were held with as many people as possible throughout the country. Shops, factories, and business premises of all kinds were visited and staffs questioned. It was a thorough and detailed investigation carried out at high speed in view of the urgency of the situation and the need to ensure the most equitable distribution of essential commodities to consumers.

The report was published in August 1965, and throws light on many of the difficulties Nkrumah was up against in his economic and social policies. The report describes a large number of malpractices which had slowed down the rate of progress in Ghana. In the words of the Commissioners: 'We are satisfied that the irregularity is not a reflection on the competency and efficiency of the people of Ghana, but a grim testimony to the rascality, corruption, lack of integrity and honesty on the part of small-minded individuals, who have found themselves in positions of responsibility. The dishonesty of one individual in a position of responsibility stirs ripples over a wide area.'[2]

For example, it was found that there was a certain amount of illicit trafficking in imported goods, appreciable quantities of which were being re-exported by private persons to neighbouring countries. Where goods were under-imported or imports mistimed, shortages were heightened by the practice of hoarding on the part of firms and petty traders, and the practice of unfair and irregular distribution on the part of district managers, wholesale managers, storekeepers and retailers. The monopoly over the importation of essential goods

---

1. *Report of the Commission of Enquiry into Trade Malpractices in Ghana*, p. 1.
2. Ibid., p. 2.

accorded to the Ghana National Trading Corporation (GNTC) had also caused problems, due to lack of expertise, and in some cases the dishonesty of employees.

Although the government had reduced imports of non-essential consumer goods in order to save foreign exchange for the import of machines, equipment and supplies of all kinds for Ghana's factories, imports of essential consumer goods were kept at the same level, and in the case of some goods actually increased above the 1964 level. Yet largely for the reason given in the Abrahams Report the people of Ghana were experiencing shortages and rising prices. The report contains the names of many men and women indulging in trade malpractices at the time, and states the nature of their activities. As a result of their findings many of them were dismissed and/or prosecuted.

It was a bold Report, sparing no one, however influential, and doubt-less produced a hard-core of disgruntled people who were delighted to see the removal of the CPP government in February 1966. But more important, the report made some forty three recommendations which, if there had been time to implement them, would have gone a long way to eliminating practices which jeopardised Ghana's economic develop-ment. The coup occurred before most of them could be carried out.

While a large number of the offenders listed in the Abrahams Report were small-scale, traders or shopkeepers in some of the more remote areas of Ghana, there were others who held key positions, some of them the managers of important GNTC branches. In the Report there is no hint that there was any motive other than self-interest behind their illegal activities, but it is likely that some at least were linked with Opposition elements which, ever since the CPP was formed, had tried to undermine it. By sabotaging the government's economic plans these dishonest trad-ers played a political role in causing confusion and discontent, thereby helping to create the conditions in which a reactionary coup could take place. They were the natural allies of Opposition elements which had formed the backbone of the UGCC, and later the NLM and the United Party (UP).

These elements had consistently resorted to subversion and violence in order to destroy the CPP, and had been involved in several attempts on Nkrumah's life.

The first attempt was on 10 November 1955, when a bomb was placed against Nkrumah's house in Accra. Although the colonial police made no arrests in connection with the bomb explosion, it was generally accepted that the attack was the work of NLM supporters, and formed part of their general campaign to spread disorder and confusion.

The second major occasion on which Opposition members were directly involved in violence occurred some three years later, in 1958. Having been rejected by the Ghanaian electorate, in the general elections of 1951, 1954 and 1956, Opposition members seemed finally to have abandoned all hope of ever winning victory at the polls. They therefore tried to divide Ghana by whipping up tribal and regional animosities, and carried out a vicious press campaign to try to discredit the CPP and Nkrumah personally. When this failed, they resorted to plotting to overthrow the government by force. Their plan, according to evidence given at the court martial of Major Benjamin Awhaitey which opened in Accra on 21 January 1959, was for a military coup to take place on 20 December. Nkrumah, who was due to leave for a state visit to India that day, was to be assassinated at the airport when he was about to board the aircraft. Organizing the coup were two leading Opposition members of Parliament, Reginald Reynolds Amponsah, General Secretary of the UP, and Modesto Apaloo, Deputy Leader of the Opposition and spokesman on military matters. Fortunately for Nkrumah and his government, the plot was revealed to military intelligence by a loyal officer, Lieutenant Amenyah, in whom Awhaitey had confided. Awhaitey, Amponsah and Apaloo were arrested on 19 December, the day before the coup was to have occurred. Awhaitey, after trial by court martial, was dismissed from the army. Amponsah and Apaloo were detained under the Preventive Detention Act, after a full-scale quasi-judicial investigation of the whole affair had been carried out by a Tribunal set up under the chairmanship of an English QC, Gilbert Granville Sharp.

The Attorney General at that time, Geoffrey Bing, who had strongly opposed the introduction of a Preventive Detention Act into Ghana, became convinced of its necessity as a result of the Tribunals findings. 'It seemed indeed that the only positive achievement of the Commission was to vindicate preventive detention. No government could be expected to release individuals whom a majority of a quasi-Judicial Tribunal had found were engaged in a plot to murder the Head of Government ... the only logical answer was that Amponsah, Apaloo and Awhaitey should be detained under the Preventive Detention Act and that such legislation was necessary.'[1]

The Act itself, and the use made of it, have been criticised by some in order to try to discredit Nkrumah and the CPP government. For this reason, it is necessary to state the facts and the circumstances which made its introduction necessary. The Act provided for detention of up to five years, and a detainee had to be served within five days with a detailed, written statement giving the reason for his detention. He had the right of appeal to the Cabinet, or could bring his case to court through habeas corpus proceedings. By the end of 1960, some 318 detention orders had been made. Of these, 255 were made in 1960, after the Act had been extended at the request of the police to cover cases which could not be adequately dealt with through normal court procedure. Most of those detained were criminals and not political opponents of the CPP.

The Preventive Detention Act had been passed in July 1958 as a precautionary measure, after it had been discovered that Amponsah had been buying military equipment, and when a secret Ga organization known as the Ga Shifimo Kpee — 'The Ga Standfast Organization' — had been formed. The latter was a conspiratorial organisation, advocating violence, designed to preserve the dominant position of Ga in their own community which they considered threatened by the influx of people of other tribes into the area as a result of the growth of Accra and the new port of Tema. There was oath-taking, and a Direct Action Group was formed to carry out acts of violence against non-Gas. The police were apprehensive of a complete breakdown of law and order if the organisation was not suppressed, and some forty-three members of the Direct Action Group were arrested under the Prevention Detention Act.

The number of political detainees held under the Act was very small considering there had been by then three attempts made to assassinate the President, and a series of bomb explosions in Accra, the work of terrorists supporting the Opposition. Their activities had resulted in the deaths of thirty men, women and children, and more than three

---

1. *Reap the Whirlwind*, p. 265. In this book, Bing gives a full account of the Tribunal's findings. It seems that other leading members of the Opposition, such as J.B. Danquah, Joe Appiah, Kofi Busia and Victor Owusu may well have known of the coup plot, and even have been involved in planning it. The entire Opposition leadership were found by the police at 1 a.m. gathered in Amponsah's house on the morning of his arrest. Every single person in the room that night was later to be appointed by the National Liberation Council (NLC) to draw up a new constitution for Ghana after the overthrow of the CPP government on 24 February 1966.

hundred had been wounded. In the words of Nkrumah: 'We could not allow a small minority of unprincipled men to continue to stir up disunity and confusion with the objective of overthrowing the government, which had the support of the overwhelming majority of the people of Ghana, support shown decisively in the general election before independence and in the 1964 referendum which established the CPP as the national party of Ghana. Maximum unity and effort was vital if my government was successfully to carry out its mandate of reconstruction and development.'[1]

Most governments in times of crisis resort to preventive detention or internment, when it is considered that the national interest demands its introduction. It has been used, for example, in Northern Ireland, India, Malaya, Kenya at the time of Mau Mau emergency, and in many other countries, often with far less reason than in Ghana, and much more extensively.

Nor can the reports spread by Opposition elements, and the Western press, of ill-treatment of prisoners under the CPP government be substantiated. The names most often mentioned in this connection are those of J. B. Danquah and Obetsebi Lamptey, both of whom died while under detention. In the case of the former, there is no evidence to suggest that he was ill-treated in prison, or that he died from anything but natural causes. He was an elderly man and had suffered for some time from high blood pressure. After the 24 February 1966 coup, prison officers at Ussher Fort when questioned about Danquah's death would have felt quite free to say if there had been any ill-treatment, but not one of them suggested anything of the kind. As far as Obetsebi Lamptey was concerned, he was suffering from an advanced stage of cancer of the liver at the time of his arrest, and until he died was in a private ward in the best equipped civilian hospital in Accra where he had expert medical attention, and was visited by relatives.

During the whole period of Nkrumah's rule not one political execution took place. Such a record seems all the more remarkable today when there is scarcely a government, particularly in the coup areas of the world which has not allowed the execution, often in public, of people whose only 'crime' has been their political beliefs. During Nkrumah's rule in Ghana there were no military tribunals, no torturing of prisoners, and no firing squads.

---

1. *Dark Days in Ghana*, p. 64.

Indeed, what stands out is the moderation and humanity of CPP rule in Ghana in the face of periodic extreme provocation. There were two further attempts on the life of Nkrumah after the Awhaitey plot. Both of them the work of a small minority of Opposition elements. On 1 August 1962, a grenade was thrown at Nkrumah as he stopped to speak to a group of children at Kulungugu in northern Ghana. He was returning from a visit to Upper Volta and had made an unscheduled stop at the village, when a grenade landed a short distance from him. Pieces of shrapnel penetrated his back, and several people including a child were killed. It was considered that someone from among Nkrumah's immediate entourage was implicated since only a small number of close associates could have known of the switch of plans which resulted in a brief stop at the village of Kulungugu. Suspicion rested on Tawia Adamafio. He was arrested and tried, acquitted then tried again and sentenced to death. Nkrumah, however, commuted the death sentence and Adamafio remained in detention until his release by the NLC in 1966.

On 1 January 1964 another attempt was made on the life of Nkrumah, and this time it was a policeman who actually made the attempt. The policeman, who was on guard duty in the garden of Nkrumah's residence, Flagstaff House, fired at him as he walked from his office. Four shots were fired almost a point blank range, but all missed. Instead, a loyal security officer, Salifu Dagarti was killed. Nkrumah, after chasing the assassin, was able to throw him to the ground and to hold him until help arrived. The policeman was later executed for the murder of Dagarti. In the investigation which followed it was revealed that the police assassin, who was not normally a guard at Flagstaff House, had been driven there in 1 January by a senior police officer, whose home he had visited on many occasions.

At about the same time, police involvement in a further assassination plot was revealed when two bandsmen in the police band reported that they had been asked to shoot Nkrumah when he went to congratulate the band on their performance at an official function at Flagstaff House. As a result of the ensuing investigation, the bandmaster together with the Commissioner for Police, Eric Madjitey, and his Deputy, Amaning, were arrested. It was then that J. W. K. Harlley became Commissioner of Police, and A. K. Deku, Head of the Criminal Investigation Department. What was not known at the time was that they themselves were involved in dubious dealings concerned with diamond smuggling.

In view of the role they both played in the coup of 24 February 1966, they were most likely even then closely in touch with Opposition minority groups, and with subversive army officers planning to overthrow the CPP government of Ghana. Both Harlley and Deku were to become members of the National Liberation Council set up as a result of the coup. Harlley and Deku were among the small party of officials and service chiefs which gathered at Accra airport on 21 February 1966 to see Nkrumah board the aircraft which was to take him to Hanoi on the invitation of Ho Chi Minh, who hoped Nkrumah would be able to bring about a peace settlement to end the war in Vietnam. Nkrumah, in his book *Dark Days in Ghana*, has described the occasion, the handshakes and the expressions of good wishes from Harlley and Deku. 'These men, smiling and ingratiating, had all the time treason and treachery in their minds. They had even planned my assassination on that day, though later abandoned the idea.'[1]

In Conakry, Nkrumah said that he believed the English Prime Minister, Harold Wilson, was in favour of him being killed at Accra airport. But the Americans were against the idea, it being too risky.

Ever since the London 1965 Commonwealth Prime Ministers' Conference, when the decision was made to send a peace mission to Vietnam, Nkrumah had been making preparations to lead such a mission. Nkrumah was ready to go to Vietnam with peace proposals in July. But the visit was postponed because Ho Chi Minh informed him that for security reasons he could not invite him unless the Americans stopped the bombing. On my visit to Ghana in August 1965 to work on the page proofs of *Neo-colonialism* and the draft of *Challenge of the Congo*, I expressed fears for his safety if he went to Hanoi while the Americans were still bombing. His plane could be shot down 'by accident.' He remarked, 'I know many people would like to see me dead.'

That same month, in August, Nkrumah instructed his Foreign Minister, Quaison Sackey, to ask President Johnson to suspend the bombing in Vietnam to allow the peace mission to proceed. If this approach failed, Nkrumah considered proposing that peace talks might take place in Accra.

On 10 August, Quaison Sackey returned from the USA with a message from Johnson that Nkrumah could go to Hanoi 'in perfect safety.' He reported that Johnson had said that 'Ho Chi Minh was only making

---

1. *Dark Days in Ghana*, p. 20.

excuses when he declared that he could not provide for Nkrumah's safety in Hanoi.' 'Who's kidding who?' he asked Quaison Sackey.

It was not until nearly the end of January 1966 that Nkrumah was able to make definite plans to go ahead with the peace mission. He expected to leave within about three weeks. President Johnson had sent an emissary, Menon Williams, to Accra to encourage Nkrumah to go. The CIA plans for the coup depended on Nkrumah being out of Ghana at the time.

I was in Accra in January 1966 to attend the inauguration of the Volta Dam. I had taken with me the draft of *Challenge of the Congo*, and also a card index box containing key excerpts from Nkrumah's speeches and writings which were to form the basis of a collection to be published under the title *Axioms of Kwame Nkrumah*.

In spite of his heavy work schedule Nkrumah set aside time each day to work on the Congo book. It was important to get every word right. The draft, which I had taken from a UK publisher for Nkrumah's final check, was thoroughly scrutinised and several alterations made. As with all his books, Nkrumah was never satisfied until he had gone over what he had written time and time again. He would ask me about a word which he was not quite sure of, 'It is your language, not mine.' I found it embarrassing sometimes when waiting to see him in his office at Flagstaff House. There would often be an important visitor with me in the waiting room adjoining his office. I would frequently be called in ahead of him. Nkrumah always gave top priority to his books.

He decided that the Congo book should have a sub-title, *A Case Study of Imperialism in an Independent State*, though he subsequently substituted 'foreign pressures' instead of the word ' Imperialism.' In view of the November 1965 coup in the Congo which brought Mobutu to power, he added a final chapter and reshaped two other chapters, cutting out two references to American interference. 'I have hit them hard in *Neocolonialism*.' For diplomatic reasons, Ghana had reluctantly to recognise the Mobutu government. Mobutu had given an undertaking to put the interests of Africa first in all its dealings. Mobutu had sent a special envoy to Accra, Marcel Lengema, to reassure Nkrumah. As a result, Nkrumah in a written message to Mobutu said that he believed that the 'Congo can never have peace and stability unless all foreign intervention is removed.' Because of its geographical position in the heart of Africa and its vast natural resources, the Congo had become an important centre of attraction for foreign powers. Nkrumah added that he hoped that the

Congo would identify itself with the African Revolution 'and maintain a vigorous position in the ranks of the progressive African states in order to assist effectively in the crusade for the total liberation and unity of Africa.'

Significantly, he ended the final chapter of *Challenge of the Congo*, with the following prophetic words:

'The people of the Republic of the Congo will undoubtedly decide their own future free from foreign interference. Difficulties and uncertainties will have to be faced. But of one thing I am sure. The victors in the final battle for the Congo's emancipation will spring from the blood of Lumumba.'

In view of the 1997 ending of Mobutu's rule by the forces of Laurent Kabila, representing the Lumumba political heritage, it was a remarkable prophesy.

Nkrumah had wanted me to stay on for a few weeks holiday while he was away on the Vietnam peace mission. It was fortunate that I declined the invitation. For if I had been in Accra at the time of the 24 February 1966 coup, all the papers in my possession, notably the corrected proofs of *Challenge of the Congo*, would certainly have been seized, and probably destroyed.

12

24 February 1966 Coup d'état

The coup in Ghana began early in the morning of Wednesday 23 February 1966, when some 600 soldiers of the Kumasi garrison were ordered to move southwards towards Accra. En route, the convoy was stopped by Colonel E. K. Kotoka, Commander of the Second Infantry Brigade Group and Major A.A. Afrifa of the Second Brigade. Afrifa took over command of the men while Kotoka went to Accra to report progress to chief of police Harlley. The troops were told that Nkrumah had left Ghana for good, taking with him £8 million, and that as Ghana was without a government it was the duty of the army to assume control to maintain law and order. Furthermore, the troops were informed that Russian planes were landing at a secret airstrip in northern Ghana and that for days Russian soldiers had been secretly entering Flagstaff House through a tunnel from Accra airport. It had been Nkrumah's intention, so the traitors said, to send Ghanaian troops to fight in Rhodesia where they would face certain death. In addition, his formation of a people's militia threatened the very existence of a professional army. If they wished, therefore, to save both themselves and Ghana, they must seize Flagstaff House.

In the early morning of 24 February, Brigadier Hasan, the Head of Military Intelligence was arrested. But Colonel Zanerigu, the Commander of the Presidential Guard Regiment escaped arrest and was able to drive to Flagstaff House to warn the garrison. Major-General Barwah, Deputy Chief of Defence Staff,

President Nkrumah
waving to crowds at Accra
airport before he flew to
Hanoi at invitation of
President Ho Chi Minh —
February 21, 1966

Nkrumah at Flagstaff
House, Accra with his
son Gamal and
daughter Samia, 1965

who was in command of the army while the Chief of Defence Staff, General Aferi, was abroad, was woken from his sleep by the arrival at his house of Kotoka and some twenty-five soldiers. He was invited to join the traitors; when he refused he was shot dead in front of his wife and children. In the meantime, Harlley had arranged for the arrest of most of Nkrumah's ministers and leading CPP officials. By 6 a.m., with the help of troops under the command of A.K. Ocran, the airport, cable office and radio station had been seized. Kotoka broadcast that the army and police had taken over the government of Ghana. But fighting was still going on at Flagstaff House where the Presidential Guard Regiment resisted fiercely. This continued for several hours, until Kotoka was able to order from the combined Army/Police HQ which he had set up at Police Headquarters, the intervention of the Second Battalion. However, the defenders of Flagstaff House, although fighting against overwhelming odds, refused to surrender until the rebels threatened to blow up the house in which Nkrumah's elderly mother and his wife and three young children lived. Rebel troops ransacked Flagstaff House, 'smashing windows and furniture, ripping telephones from desks, and destroying anything they could lay their hands on.'[1] Nkrumah's own office was singled out for special treatment, and the large collection of books and manuscripts which he kept there was destroyed. Madam Fathia, Nkrumah's Egyptian-born wife, had fled with her three children to the Egyptian Embassy, and a few days later they were put on a flight for Cairo. His mother was told to go 'where you belong' and was taken by some friends to the village of Nkroful where Nkrumah was born.

Nkrumah's elder son, Gamal, was only seven years' old at the time of the coup. It was a traumatic experience for him and for his younger brother, Sékou and sister, Samia. Before the gun battle began at Flagstaff House, the children had been awakened by the unusual roaring of unfed lions in the zoo a short distance from the house. Soon, the sound of gunfire was heard coming from the direction of the airport. By then, the whole household was awake. Over the radio they heard the broadcast by coup leader Colonel E.T. Kotoka, announcing the coup. Fathia at once phoned the Egyptian embassy telling them to contact President Nasser to send an aircraft immediately to Ghana to rescue them. She had barely finished speaking when the telephone was cut off. Fathia and the children only just managed to reach the nearby Egyptian embassy.

---

1. *Dark Days in Ghana*, p. 25.

As soon as it became clear that the coup had been successful, Nasser sent an aircraft to convey Nkrumah's wife and children to Cairo. En route to the airport their car was stopped by tanks and troops at an army roadblock. Fathia and the children were ordered out of the car at gunpoint, while the officer in charge, taken by surprise at confronting Nkrumah's family, radioed for instructions. Eventually, they were allowed to proceed to the airport to board the Egyptian aircraft which was to fly them to safety in Cairo. They were never to see Nkrumah again.

There was much brutality and suffering in Accra as troops and police rounded up hundreds of key CPP personnel and flung them into prison. Practically the entire CPP leadership throughout the country was arrested in the days which followed the coup. This included all cabinet ministers, members of Parliament, officials of the CPP and all its subsidiary and associate organizations, including trade union leaders. In the course of the operation, many people were beaten up and their houses looted. Among them were Professor W.E. Abraham, Acting Vice-Chancellor of the University of Ghana, who was beaten unconscious and then flung into a police van; and N.A. Welbeck, Minister of Education and Party Propaganda who had several teeth knocked out and who died later, mainly from the effects of the brutal treatment he received at the time of the coup and in prison afterwards. Attorney-General Geoffrey Bing was arrested and kept in prison for a month while he was interrogated about the investigation he had been carrying out into diamond smuggling.

Exactly, how many casualties occurred in the fighting and its aftermath is not known for certain, but Nkrumah was informed that the total was probably in the region of 1600 dead and many more injured. Whatever the exact figure, it was far from the 'bloodless coup' reported in the British press.

There was gross exaggeration of the size and strength of 'favourable' reaction in Ghana. Obviously, there were some who welcomed the change, namely Opposition elements hostile to the CPP. Then there were relatives and friends of those released from prison, political and criminal detainees. Maximum publicity was given to their demonstrations of joy, and to the pulling down of Nkrumah's statue outside the Parliament building in Accra. In addition, there was a section of market traders who had suffered as a result of the Abrahams report, which had exposed malpractices. There were opportunists and the genuinely misled who thought the coup would usher in a new era devoid of shortages of consumer goods and other problems associated with the implementation of CPP development plans, coupled with the disastrous fall in the world price of cocoa.

But there was no popular participation on the coup. The ordinary people in Ghana were initially stunned by the military/police seizure of power, and were powerless to stop it. With Nkrumah out of the country, with all key points seized, with almost the entire leadership of the CPP arrested overnight, and without guns, effective resistance was out of the question. Yet the heroic stand of the Presidential Guard Regiment at Flagstaff House, and the acts of personal courage by Ghanaians in resisting the take-over are not forgotten. For there was resistance right from the start, typified by the heroic stand of Major General Barwah. It continued long afterwards, as evidenced by the determination of succeeding generations of Nkrumaists to restore Nkrumaism to Ghana.

Since the 1966 Ghana coup there have been many military coups throughout the world which have overthrown elected civilian governments. A notable example, resembling the Ghanaian experience, was the 1973 coup in Chile when the Marxist government of President Allende was overthrown. In Chile, as in Ghana, a socialist society was in process of construction which had attracted much the same kind of opposition both domestic and international as in the case of Ghana. Furthermore, Chile, like Ghana under the CPP government, had become a haven for freedom fighters from other countries where there were oppressive regimes. Just as the fall of the Nkrumah government set back the African revolution, so the coup in Chile and the death of Allende struck a formidable blow at progressive forces throughout the South American continent.

In his book *Dark Days in Ghana*, written in Guinea, Nkrumah reflected on the causes of the coup and its consequences for Ghana and the rest of Africa. He saw the coup as a severe setback, though not an unmitigated disaster. Lessons could be learned from it During the first few years in Guinea he was confident that he would return to Ghana, welcomed back by the Ghanaian people, to continue with his work. For he could not believe that Ghanaians would tolerate the 'dark days' for long. 'It pays no-one to tamper with Ghanaian freedom and dignity. Ghana is out of the gambling house of colonialism, and will never return to it.'[1]

---

1. *Dark Days in Ghana*, p. 29.

It is now generally accepted that the USA Central Intelligence Agency (CIA) was involved in planning the coup. This involvement has been confirmed in a book *In Search of Enemies* written by a former CIA officer, John Stockwell, published in 1978. He disclosed that the CIA station in Accra 'was given a generous budget and maintained intimate contact with the plotters as a coup was hatched ... Inside CIA headquarters, the Accra station was given full, if unofficial credit for the eventual coup.' The CIA station chief in Accra, Howard T. Bane, was rewarded with promotion to a senior position in the Agency. Nkrumah, certainly, was in no doubt about foreign involvement. In a message sent to Sékou Touré on 25 February 1966, the day after the coup, he wrote: 'This incident in Ghana is a plot by the imperialists, neo-colonialists and their agents in Africa ... We must strengthen our resolution and fight for the dignity of our people to the last man, and for the unity of Africa.' He was convinced the embassies of the USA, Britain and West Germany were all implicated in the plot to overthrow the CPP government. He considered that the Afro-American US ambassador in Accra at that time, Franklin Williams, was closely involved. For it would have been extremely unlikely he did not know what was going on in the embassy with CIA officers operating from there.

Nkrumah thought that the military/police regime would fail through lack of experience and that the restoration of constitutional government was only a matter of time. This view was strengthened by the reports Nkrumah received in Guinea from Ghanaians and others who visited him in Conakry to give him first hand accounts of what they had seen. He was contemptuous of the National Liberation Council (NLC) which was set up after the coup to govern Ghana. He named the eight-member NLC the 'Notorious Liars Council.' It was composed of four members of the army: J.A. Ankrah (Chairman), E.K. Kotoka, AK. Ocran and A.A. Afrifa; and four police officers: J.W. Harlley, B.A. Yakubu, J.E. Nunoo and A.K. Deku.

Nkrumah was sure that it was Harlley and his close associates 'inspired and aided by disgruntled former opposition party members and neo-colonialists, who were the real initiators. They alone possessed the necessary vital information needed for its success.'[1] Ankrah had been dismissed from the army in 1965 for incompetence. Kotoka, who commanded the military operations on 24 February 1966, was trained in

1. *Dark Days in Ghana*, p. 44.

Britain. In fact, all members of the NLC were trained in Britain. The four policemen were at the police Metropolitan Training College in Hendon, while the four soldiers attended various army training centres, though only Afrifa went to Sandhurst. Not one of them had any political training or experience. 'If it were not for the great harm these traitors have done to our beloved Ghana, we could laugh at them ... How could men such as these imagine for one moment that they had any hope of successfully administering the country?'[1] In Nkrumah's view, it was Harlley and his associates who subverted army officers to carry out the coup. Harlley knew and trusted Kotoka. They were both Ewes born in the Volta Region. They had even attended the same school. Kotoka then approached other officers, notably Afrifa, an Ashanti. 'There has always been a close link between the Ewes and Ashanti reactionary elements, and Kotoka judged rightly that Afrifa would be likely to respond favourably. So it went on, until a sufficient number of officers had been roped in.'[2] However, as Nkrumah reflected, only a relatively few officers were subverted. The majority were taken completely by surprise and were faced with a *fait accompli*.

When the coup took place, Nkrumah was well on his way to Hanoi at the invitation of President Ho Chi Minh, with proposals for ending the war in Vietnam. For some time he had been prepared to go to Hanoi with peace proposals, though many of his colleagues feared for his safety. They were reassured, however, after the Americans sent a message a few days before his planned departure, saying they would suspend the bombing of Hanoi to allow the aircraft carrying Nkrumah to land safely.

Nkrumah was informed of the coup soon after his arrival in Peking. He had been greeted at the airport by Prime -Minister Chou En-Lai and Liu Shao-Chi, together with other officials including the Chinese Ambassador in Accra who had gone on ahead to Peking to be there to meet him. It was the ambassador who broke the news to Nkrumah, after the airport welcome and when he had reached the privacy of the government guest house where he was to stay: 'Mr President, I have bad news. There has been a coup d'état in Ghana.'[3]

Nkrumah was taking a brief rest after the long flight from Rangoon. For a moment he thought he might have misheard the ambassador. His first reaction was to return immediately to Ghana. He would have done

---

1. *Dark Days in Ghana*, p. 36.
2. Ibid., p. 44.
3.   "   p. 9.

Nkrumah with Chinese Premier Chou En-Lai — Accra, January 1964

so if the VC10 of Ghana Airways in which he had travelled as far as Rangoon had been available. But the aircraft had been left behind in Rangoon, the Chinese government having sent a plane to bring him from Burma to China. The VC10 was already on its way back to Africa.

In the circumstances, there was no question of proceeding to Hanoi. Nkrumah decided to make an immediate statement to the Ghanaian people, and to return to Africa as soon as transport could be arranged. His statement was brief, urging the people 'to remain calm, but firm in determination and resistance.' Officers and men of the armed forces were ordered to return to their barracks to await his return. 'I am returning to Ghana soon.'[1]

Nkrumah's entourage included some twenty-two officials of the government, among them A. Quaison Sackey (Foreign Minister), Kwesi Armah (Minister of Trade), M.F. Dei-Anang (Ambassador Extra-ordinary, in charge of the African Affairs Secretariat, J. E. Bossman (Ambassador to the UK) and F. Arkhurst (Ghana's Permanent Repre-sentative at the United Nations). There were sixty-six other personnel, security officers and members of Nkrumah's personal secretariat. Their reaction to news of the coup was in marked contrast to the defeatist attitude of the government officials. 'These were men. Compared with them, the politicians were old women.'[2]

However, the full extent of their defeatism did not become apparent until later, after they had left Peking. For a few days they managed to dis-guise their true feelings and to discuss with Nkrumah the next moves. It was decided that Nkrumah should carry out official engagements in Peking as planned. Prime Minister Chou En-Lai was particularly sup-portive of his guest. Having long experience of political struggle, he re-garded the Ghana coup as no more than a temporary setback. 'You are a young man', he told Nkrumah, 'you have another forty years ahead of you.'

Nkrumah attended a banquet held in his honour on 24 February at which he spoke of Afro-Asian solidarity, condemning US policy in Vietnam and calling for the complete withdrawal of their forces so that peace negotiations could begin. President Ho Chi Minh, disappointed at the cancellation of Nkrumah 's peace mission, declared that he would be welcome in Hanoi at a future date.

---

1. *Dark Days in Ghana*, pp. 10–11.
2. Ibid., p. 11.

Messages of support for Nkrumah poured into Peking from all over the world.[1] President Sékou Touré of Guinea, President Nasser of Egypt, President Nyerere of Tanzania, and President Modibo Keita of Mali each offered hospitality. Deeply touched by their expressions of solidarity Nkrumah after much thought decided to accept the invitation from Sékou Touré. Apart from the strong bond of friendship and political rapport between the two leaders, Nkrumah wanted to go to a country as near to Ghana as possible.

On 25 February he replied to Sékou Touré's invitation:

> My dear Brother and President, I have been deeply touched by your message of solidarity and support I have received today. It is true, as you say, that this incident in Ghana is a plot by the imperialists, neo-colonialists and their agents in Africa. As these imperialist forces grow more militant and insidious, using traitors to the African cause against the freedom and independence of our people, we must strengthen our resolution and fight for the dignity of our people to the last man, and for the unity of Africa. It is heartening to know that in this struggle we can count on the support and understanding of Africa's well-tried leaders like yourself.
>
> I know that our cause will triumph and that we can look forward to the day when Africa shall be really united and free from foreign interference.

Shortly afterwards, Sékou Touré sent a further message to Nkrumah:

> 'The political Bureau and the Government after thorough analysis of the African situation following the seizure of power by the instruments of imperialism have decided:
>
> 1.   To organize a national day of solidarity with the Ghanaian people next Sunday. Throughout the length and breadth of the country there will take place popular demonstrations on the theme of anti-imperialism.
>
> 2.   To call on all progressive African countries to hold a special conference and take all adequate measures. We think that the time factor is vital here, since it is important to make a riposte without delay, by every means. Your immediate presence would

---

1. For the text of some of them, see *Dark Days in Ghana*, pp. 14–16.

be very opportune it seems to us, and we are therefore impatiently waiting for you.'

Arrangements were made for all except Quaison Sackey and Bossman to travel to Guinea via Moscow. Quaison Sackey was instructed to go to the OAU Council of Ministers meeting in Addis Ababa to represent the CPP government. Instead, he went to Accra to offer his services to the NLC. Bossman went to London where he declared support for the NLC. By then, Kwesi Armah and others had left Moscow 'to deal', they said, with 'urgent private matters.' The plan was for them to return to Moscow to join up again with Nkrumah and his entourage so that all could travel together to Guinea. In fact they did not return. When Nkrumah heard of the defections, he decided to wait no longer in Moscow but to travel to Guinea with his personal entourage, accompanied by Ghanaians who had been studying in the Soviet Union and who wished to join him.

Nkrumah left Peking on 28 February in an aircraft provided by the Soviet Union. It landed near Moscow at dawn on 1 March after a brief stop at Irkutsk in Siberia. At midnight on the same day Nkrumah and his entourage re-embarked for the flight to Guinea. After brief stop-overs in Yugoslavia and Algeria, they reached Conakry, during the afternoon of Wednesday 2 March. For Nkrumah 'it was wonderful to be on African soil again.'[1] President Sékou Touré, members of the Parti Démocratique de Guinée, and a large crowd were at the airport to welcome him. A twenty one gun salute was fired, signalling to the world that Guinea still recognised Nkrumah as Ghana's Head of State.

At a mass rally the following day Sékou Touré declared that Nkrumah had been appointed Secretary-General of the PDG and Head of State of Guinea. 'The Ghanaian traitors', he said, 'have been mistaken in thinking that Nkrumah is simply a Ghanaian.... He is a universal man.'[2] Sékou Touré spoke in French, and at the time, Nkrumah's knowledge of French was sketchy. He thought that to judge by the cheering crowds, Sékou Touré had made a rousing speech of welcome, but had no idea that he had been named President of Guinea. When afterwards he was told of the extraordinary and unprecedented expression of practical PanAfricanism, he declined the honour, agreeing only to become co-President. So began one of the most constructive periods of

---

1. *Dark Days in Ghana*, p. 18.
2. Ibid.

Nkrumah's life, the years from 1966 to 1971 which he spent in Guinea. The coup, far from eliminating Nkrumah from the Ghanaian and PanAfrican scene, had freed him from the day-to-day work of government, enabling him to pursue with greatest vigour the objectives to which he had dedicated his life. In his words: 'One step backwards has been taken. We shall take two forward.'

PART TWO

The Conakry Years

Foreword

The primary source material which follows in Part Two supplements that published in my book, *Kwame Nkrumah: The Conakry Years*, published in 1990, which was based largely on the hundreds of letters which Nkrumah wrote to me from Guinea; on the forty-three files of correspondence which I retrieved from his residence, Villa Syli, in 1986; and on the notebooks which I compiled during my sixteen visits to Conakry and three to Bucharest where Nkrumah went in 1971 for medical treatment.

In Guinea, I stayed weeks at a time in a bungalow adjoining Villa Syli, and worked close to Nkrumah at a desk in his office. I experienced the same conditions, met his visitors, got to know members of his entourage. But more important, I spent many hours working and relaxing with him in the shade of mango trees in the villa garden, or in my adjacent bungalow which he named Villa June. He would talk of the ups and downs of his life, reminiscing, planning the future, discussing his books, and what was happening in Ghana, Africa and the world in general.

13

Villa Syli

For the first few weeks in Guinea, Nkrumah and his entourage lived in Belle Vue, a government guest compound on the coast near to the centre of Conakry. Then they were accommodated in Villa Syli, an old French colonial-style residence on the seashore about a mile from the town centre. It was a long, low white concrete building, constructed on two levels, parts of which jutted on to the beach. Smaller buildings to the side and back of the villa housed the Ghanaian entourage and Guinean army and security personnel.

To the rear of the main building was a large garden courtyard with a driveway in the centre leading to the inner entrance to the villa. There were orange and mango trees, flowering shrubs and other plants. During the hottest months, Nkrumah would sit in the shade of the trees and do his work there. Occasionally, the gates would be flung open to allow a car to pass through, but this was rare. The only visitors allowed were those permitted by Nkrumah and the Guinean government. At the gates in sentry boxes outside stood Guinean soldiers, red capes slung over their uniforms, bayonets fixed. The gates were not locked, but kept closed by a piece of wood jammed underneath where they met at the centre. As soon as a car had been admitted or allowed to depart, the gates would be quickly closed again. The visitors would be driven up to the office area of the villa, and would pass straight into a small waiting room, consisting of a table and some four or five armchairs. For a time, Camara Sana the Guinean

Protocol Officer had a desk there. He was a career diplomat appointed by Sékou Touré to act as interpreter and to liaise with the Guinean government. From this room the visitor could glimpse the long verandah, and beyond the sea.

In large concrete pots all along the verandah were rose plants. During the dry season, these were placed at the edge of the verandah, by the sea. At the start of the rains they were moved back under the shelter of the roof. Usually every day Nkrumah would take the secateurs from his desk and cut off any dead flowers. The rose plants were sent to him by Hanna Reitsch, the flying ace who had established a flying school in Ghana at Afienya. Knowing how he enjoyed his rose garden at Flagstaff House, she sent the rose plants to Nkrumah in Conakry soon after his arrival.

At the end of the verandah was a recessed, square room where Nkrumah sat at his desk, out of sight of the main part of the verandah. There was a door, concealed by curtains behind the desk, which he used when going to, and returning from, his private quarters down some steps to the lower level of the villa.

His private area consisted of a bedroom and a large sitting room facing the sea. Next to his bedroom was a room occupied by Nyamikeh, Nkrumah's personal attendant and nephew, and by A.K. Buah, a senior member of Nkrumah's bodyguard. A dining table stood at one end of the sitting room near to a Philips record player obtained from the diplomatic store. Nearby, was a table on which were a draughts board and a box of dominoes. During the first year of Nkrumah's stay in the villa, Sékou Touré and his wife used to visit Nkrumah every evening after dinner. They would sit and talk, and often play draughts. On these occasions, Sékou Touré would drive up to the villa in his black Citroen, the windows wound down and himself at the wheel.

Nkrumah's bedroom was a large square room with two shuttered windows which opened on to the stoep outside overlooking the sea. Hard against the wall between the windows stood a large four-poster bed with a mosquito net above. At each side of the bed was a small table on which were books, papers and little personal things, a clock, photo, pen and so on. All along the wall to the left of the bed were fitted cupboards. On the other wall there was a bookcase and a small refrigerator in which Nkrumah kept biscuits, water, chocolate and any other items of food from parcels which I regularly sent to him. The dressing table was in a dark part of the bedroom leading to the bathroom. Alongside the dressing table there was always a neat row of sandals and shoes, polished by Nkrumah himself.

The bedroom, tiled in black marble, had once been smart, but was no longer in good shape. The black, low bath was fitted with a shower attachment which was not very efficient. The plumbing in Villa Syli was generally poor. It was necessary to stand well back when turning on the taps in the basin to avoid the initial spurting out of reddish water. The lavatory cistern seldom functioned smoothly. At times it was necessary to pour water into the toilet bowl from a pail filled from the bath tap.

The bookcase in his bedroom contained a variety of books most of them posted to him or taken by myself. There were books on military tactics, guerrilla warfare, biographies, reference books, the standard works of Marxism, Maoism, a Pears medical encyclopaedia, philosophical texts, and books on other mainly political topics. Fiction did not interest him. He was a voracious reader, almost tearing a new book apart as he sought the key passages, flipping through the chapters, marking them freely, and always ticking a chapter as he ended it. A few he would read through word for word. Although he valued his books highly, he would never hesitate to lend them. He lost many books in this way as he made no note of who had borrowed them. Frequently, he would find a book missing when he went to fetch it to lend to another person. He would then rack his brains trying to remember who had borrowed it, and would send a member of his entourage to try to find it.

When President Siaka Stevens fled to Guinea after the coup against him in Sierra Leone, the first thing Nkrumah did was to lend him some of his books. Stevens was very depressed and Nkrumah spent much time encouraging him. It was a disappointment, when after a counter-coup soon restored Stevens to power in Freetown, he appeared to forget the moral support Nkrumah had given him in Guinea. He never sent so much as new typewriter or food or medical supplies to the villa when he knew these were badly needed. I could not help thinking how different would have been Nkrumah's treatment of an old friend if he had returned to power in Accra. I am reminded of a remark made by Nkrumah some time afterwards, on the subject of certain other African leaders. 'When I see some of them I feel sorry for their people.'

Within weeks of his arrival in Villa Syli, Nkrumah had turned the higher part of the villa into an office area. Sékou Touré had closed the Ghana embassy in Conakry immediately after the 24 February 1966 coup, making all property on the premises, including the ambassador's car, available to Nkrumah. Desks, books, typewriters, stationery and so on were taken to the villa. An office routine was quickly established. In addition, an electric generator and radio station were installed.

The seventy-nine Ghanaians who had accompanied Nkrumah to Guinea were assigned duties in accordance with their training and skills. Those with secretarial and clerical experience were employed in the work of Nkrumah's office dealing with the enormous quantity of cables, letters and messages of support which poured in from all parts of the world. Each morning, members of the entourage would go to the main Conakry post office to collect and dispatch mail and cables.

Right from the start there were problems of security, letters which had clearly been scrutinized, envelopes opened and resealed, inexplicable delays. Camara went frequently to the post office to try to determine whether interference with correspondence occurred in the Conakry post office, or in the country of origin. It was impossible to be sure. Nkrumah and I used red or green wax to seal our letters. I possessed two silver rings decoratively engraved. We each used one to stamp the wax. I addressed envelopes to 'Camara Sana, P. O Box 834, Conakry'. Nkrumah used various pseudonyms, 'Saidou', 'Amadou', and 'Diallo' when he was in Bucharest. In cabling me, Nkrumah signed 'Sana' if he wanted a reply, 'Sophie' the name of Camara's wife, if no answer was required. Simple codes, often publishing terms, were also employed in attempts to achieve confidentiality.

A regular correspondent was Shirley DuBois, widow of the African-American campaigner W.E.B. DuBois. She visited Nkrumah in Conakry several times before he was able to arrange for her to work in Peking with the Afro-Asian Writers' Bureau. Another correspondent was Pat Sloan, until the coup a British senior lecturer in Political Science at the Ideological Institute in Winneba. Pat Sloan wrote a lengthy account of what happened at the Institute at the time of the coup, describing the confusion of the students. During the course of a long correspondence, Sloan suggested changes which should be made in the curriculum at Winneba. He advised Nkrumah not to attempt an early return to Ghana: 'My own estimate is that within two years you may well be invited back.'[1]

---

1. *Kwame Nkrumah: The Conakry Years. His Life and Letters,* June Milne, Panaf, an imprint of Zed Books, London, 1990, p. 26.

Nkrumah with Mrs. Shirley DuBois — Villa Syli, 1967

Nkrumah and the author
in the office —
Villa Syli, 1967

Gamal Nkrumah,
Nkrumah's elder son,
with the author —
Cairo, April 1997

Madame Fathia,
Nkrumah's widow,
with the author —
Cairo, April 1997

Geoffrey Bing, Ghana's Attorney-General before the coup, also corresponded frequently with Nkrumah. He wrote first on 15 June 1966 describing what happened to him and his wife (Teddy) when the coup occurred. Bing was maltreated and imprisoned for a month in Ussher Fort, along with most of the Cabinet ministers. Everything in Bing's office in Flagstaff House was destroyed, including papers relating to an investigation being made into diamond smuggling, in which a leading police officer, A.K. Deku was implicated. On returning to England, Bing gave a press conference, and appeared on both the BBC and ITV. 'I have been doing what I could to put our case across.'[1] Bing tried on several occasions during the Conakry period to persuade Nkrumah to agree to interviews by the British press and TV. But Nkrumah consistently refused.

Bing, like many others who supported Nkrumah, was infuriated by the vicious misrepresentation of Nkrumah's political record by the Western media, and wanted to see action taken to put the record straight. Having failed to persuade Nkrumah to be interviewed, Bing began to work on a book setting out the truth about Nkrumah and the CPP government. This was published in 1968 under the title *Reap the Whirlwind: An Account of Kwame Nkrumah's Ghana 1950–1966*. Nkrumah, however, was not very impressed by it. In a letter dated 1 July 1968 to Pat Sloan, he wrote: 'I have read Geoffrey Bing's book.... Bing did well, but here and there I do not like the apologetic tone. We make no apologies.... Apologies are an attitude characteristic of British liberalism.'[2]

Nkrumah only kept up a sustained correspondence with those who had been specially close to him when he was in Ghana. For the rest, he considered those who sincerely wanted to know his views and to study his policies could read his books, particularly the new ones written in Conakry. The only exception he made as regards media interviews in Guinea was in the case of Douglas Rogers, editor of the magazine *Africa and the World*, who visited him in Villa Syli on several occasions; and the very occasional representative from Chinese or Cuban news agencies. The well-known author on African affairs, Basil Davidson, was disappointed when Nkrumah refused to see him. Davidson had written an article in the magazine *West Africa* which at that time was printing

---

1. *The Conakry Years*, p. 47.
2. Ibid., p. 245.

hostile material. In a letter to Pat Sloan of 6 November 1967, Nkrumah wrote: 'I think I am right not to have seen Basil Davidson ... As you know, *West Africa* is one of our greatest detractors.'[1]

Hundreds of Africans, people of African descent and others from countries world-wide who shared Nkrumah's political philosophy, wrote to him. A prolific writer, for example, was Reba Lewis, an American who had lived in Ghana before the coup, and had left immediately afterwards. She never met Nkrumah, but had great admiration for him. Her letters, written from her new home in Geneva, were full of informed political comment and encouragement.

Among others were James and Grace Boggs, civil rights activists living in Detroit, USA. They kept Nkrumah informed of the progress of the Black Power movement in America and the Caribbean. They visited Nkrumah in Conakry in 1968. Throughout the Conakry period, they posted newspaper articles, books and pamphlets to Nkrumah. This material, together with letters and articles written by the eminent African-American columnist Charles Howard, kept Nkrumah up-to-date with the theory and strategy of the Black Power movement.

One of the books I gave to Nkrumah during his first year in Conakry was *Sahara Conquest* by St. Barbe Barker, founding member and Director of Sahara Reclamation Studies. The author had visited Nkrumah in Ghana to discuss both the possibility of reclaiming the desert so that its enormous economic potential could be developed; and the need to maintain a defensive barrier of trees to prevent the desert advancing further. Nkrumah had always believed that 'the Sahara could be made to bloom', but maintained that the strength for the task required Pan-African unity and cooperation.

St. Barbe Barker kept in touch with Nkrumah after the coup, in 1967 asking him to become President of the Sahara Reclamation Commission. Nkrumah replied on 28 September 1967 accepting the position on condition that St. Barbe Barker continued as General Secretary and chief organizer. 'It seems to me', he wrote, 'that as part of the renaissance of our continent we have a duty to tackle this immense problem.'[2] Nkrumah's great interest in the future of the Sahara Desert was key to the robust and successful campaign he waged nearly ten years earlier to halt the French testing of nuclear bombs there.

---

1. *The Conakry Years*, p. 193.
2. Ibid., p. 183.

In Guinea, Nkrumah corresponded with other campaigners engaged in struggles with which he identified. As part of his policy of promoting world peace, he had established, in Ghana, The Accra Assembly: The World without the Bomb. Julie Medlock, director of the organization, was compelled to leave Ghana after the coup. After trying unsuccessfully to find another home in Africa for the organisation, she eventually carried on the work of the Accra Assembly in India, as international director of the Conference for the Public Interest. Nkrumah and Julie Medlock wrote often to each other during the Conakry period. As late as 22 April 1971 Julie Medlock wrote: 'The Accra Assembly is still alive'.[1]

The eminent peace campaigner Bertrand Russell was also in touch with Nkrumah before and after the coup. Nkrumah had identified with Bertrand Russell's 'Ban the Bomb' campaign. In a letter to me dated 5 April 1967, Nkrumah asked me to send him Bertrand Russell's newly published *Autobiography*. Two days later, Bertrand Russell wrote to Nkrumah asking him if he would join with him in launching the World Vietnam Committee in support of the people of Vietnam. He told Nkrumah that the initiative had begun with the full support of Prime Minister Fidel Castro, President Ho Chi Minh and Ernest Ché Guevara: 'We begin', he said 'with those whose record in opposing aggression and exploitation is unequivocal and clear.'[2] There is no record, in the Conakry files of correspondences which I retrieved from Villa Syli after Nkrumah's death, of how Nkrumah replied. But after the 1966 coup in Ghana, as Nkrumah became convinced of the need for armed struggle in African liberation and unification processes, he lost sympathy with Bertrand Russell's pacifism. However, after hearing on 3 February 1970 of Bertrand Russell's death at the age of 87, Nkrumah wrote to me: 'I don't think he has much to worry about beyond the grave. He had a really full life — knowledge, love and adventure.' He added a postscript: 'I dropped a rose petal into the sea for Bertrand Russell, in his memory, and for his search for knowledge and his pity for suffering mankind.'[3]

But the letters which Nkrumah treasured most were those which poured in from countless ordinary folk who just wanted him to know that they were thinking of him, and appreciated what he had done for them. Many African students wrote from countries both within and

---

1. *The Conakry Years*, p. 397.
2. Ibid., p. 134.
3.   "   p. 365.

outside Africa, offering their services in any capacity. A typical letter is one dated 9 March 1966 from Lusaka. It began: 'You receive this letter from a person you do not know, nor expect to know neither. But the fundamental reason for writing to you is this: that the Ghana problem is of growing concern in the hearts of Africanists ... Whatever may be said about and against you, your presence on Africa's political scene means a lot. Should you go forever, true to say, Africa will be the most doomed continent on our planet.... Should the Ghana problem not be solved, no African state will ever feel safe.... Kwame, fulfil your long and old-standing plans to build the Africa of your dreams. I pray that you will regard my little note as both a consoling and encouragement-giving letter.'[1]

Another supporter, an African-American, wrote: 'It saddens my heart to receive news that my one great hero has been betrayed by a bunch of misled fools.... It's so sad that our people are so blind that they couldn't see what you were doing for them ... I only wish it was possible to get out of this devil country and join ranks with you, and die for a just cause.'[2]

Demonstrations and rallies were held in many parts of the world in support of Nkrumah. These were attended by Africans from every part of the continent, and included many Ghanaians, particularly students. One of them, writing in October 1966, said that he had not been able to get a good night's sleep 'since those traitors betrayed us. Sometimes I feel like weeping because our only hope of survival is you'.[3] Letters such as these deeply touched Nkrumah. All were carefully filed, and a large number were published in his book *Dark Days in Ghana*, in which in an Author's Note he wrote: 'I have written, in Conakry, about Ghana's "dark days" in the hope that publication of the facts may help to expose similar set backs in other progressive African states.'

Nkrumah's secretarial staff in Villa Syli were kept busy dealing with the massive mail and with the work of typing the texts of broadcasts to the people of Ghana, and the manuscripts of books and pamphlets which Nkrumah began to work on within a few weeks of his arrival in Guinea. Assisting in the office work for the first few months or so was Julia Wright, daughter of the well-known African-American author Richard Wright. French-speaking, her knowledge of the language was

1. *Dark Days in Ghana*, pp. 174–175.
2. Ibid., p. 181.
3.   "   p. 206.

invaluable when it came to translating letters and messages in French. Each day, she would go through Guinean newspapers, making notes in English of material which she thought would interest Nkrumah. Julia was reluctant to leave Guinea when towards the end of 1966, Nkrumah arranged for her return to Paris.[1] By that time, Nkrumah had began French lessons, and was becoming quite proficient in the language. A teacher from Conakry, Madame Batchily, visited the villa regularly, the lessons being supplemented by listening to Linguaphone records. Three notebooks filled with handwritten exercises in French were among Nkrumah's papers at Villa Syli when he died. They reveal a strong political content to the vocabulary he was interested in learning, as well as his determination to master French grammar. It was Madame Batchily who gave Nkrumah the small bamboo bookcase which he kept in his bedroom.

Members of the entourage with security or police training joined the Guinean security forces in protecting Villa Syli, screening visitors and generally carrying out the duties they were accustomed to in Ghana. Others, who were members of Nkrumah's personal household attended to the day-to-day work of running the villa. Nkrumah saw to it that the men were kept fully occupied. Some were assigned the task of monitoring news broadcasts from Ghana, and of compiling daily reports for him. All at one time or another had to attend political discussion groups, and to undergo courses of military training. It was Nkrumah's purpose to organize the life of Villa Syli into a highly-disciplined, constructive unit, with each member equipping himself ideologically and physically for the return to Ghana and the arduous struggle which lay ahead. Nkrumah himself underwent a course of military training, and frequently took part in meetings of the Political Committee formed by members of the entourage as part of the politicization programme.

One of the first tasks of the thirteen man Political Committee was to examine and discuss the coup in Ghana. The findings, which were typed and bound, were presented to Nkrumah on 30 July 1966, with the

---

1. Nkrumah had lost confidence in Julia's (then) husband Henri Hervé, suspecting that he was involved with French Intelligence. While completely confident of Julia's integrity, he did not feel able to allow her to remain in Guinea while banning her husband. At the time, Nkrumah did not tell Julia the true reason for her departure from Guinea. He told her that it was her duty to return to Paris where her young daughter and mother lived. Subsequently, when Julia herself began to suspect Henri, she divorced him.

signatures of all the Committee members, except for that of Boye Moses who had by then been taken prisoner by the NLC.

Nkrumah at the time was working on *Dark Days in Ghana*, his own analysis of the coup and its aftermath. So he was particularly interested in the Political Committee's first topic of discussion, 'The coup in Ghana: who planned it?,' and the Committee's 'Task: first, to find out the external factors to the coup; second, to find out the internal factors both objective and subjective; third, to make recommendations where necessary.'

They came to the conclusion that the main external forces 'from our point of view are mainly the intelligence forces of the imperialist countries of USA, Britain, and West Germany. African countries of Togo and Ivory Coast are also counted with the external forces'. The report went on to state that the efforts of these external forces might have been futile had there been no internal forces to carry out the intentions of the former. In addition to the police and army who visibly carried out the coup, there were 'certain deficiencies in the party, its integral wings', and in the Civil Service and the state corporations and enterprises.

The reasons for disaffection within the army and police are examined in the Report. But perhaps the most interesting section is that headed: 'The Party and its integral wings'. Mention is made of the failure of 'party high-ups and MPs' to go to their constituencies to explain government policies and socialist ideology to the people. In addition, 'Some of the party officials did not take seriously the Dawn Broadcast because it threatened their capitalist interests and this brought dissensions within the Party.' When Bills were introduced involving economic issues, the sacrifices involved were not fully explained to the people. 'But rather messages of support are sent and published creating the impression that the masses are satisfied.' Efficient administration was lacking. The National Executive of the Party had agreed that Osagyefo the President should visit party HQ each week 'to see to things', but for one reason or another this was not done. 'As a precautionary measure, we suggest that this decision be implemented.'

The work of the Trade Union Congress is criticized. The TUC 'failed to work in the interest of the workers', and misused funds. There was mismanagement of state farms. waste of equipment and lack of technical advice. The Farmers' Council, the Women's Council, the Civil Service, Young Pioneers, Workers' Brigade all came in for criticism for their inefficiency and lack of political orientation. Failures in the Security Services were noted, and these Nkrumah marked on his copy of the Report.

In Appendices One and Two, detailed recommendations were made to be implemented on the Party's return to power in Ghana. Fundamental improvements were suggested in party organisation and discipline. The armed forces and intelligence services should be politicized in order to ensure their loyalty and to tighten security. Underlying most of the recommendations was the need to stress the importance of educating the masses to understand the policies and methods necessary for the building of a society based on socialist principles.

Two weeks after Nkrumah's arrival in Guinea, a rally was held in Conakry at which Sékou Touré announced his determination to send troops to Ghana to restore Nkrumah's government. But Houphouet-Boigny quickly moved troops to the Ivory Coast border and declared that they would block any attempt by Guinean forces to pass through Ivory Coast territory. Nkrumah, not wishing to be the cause of a war between Guinea and Ivory Coast, urged Sékou Touré to be patient, and gradually the tension relaxed. With the reports he was receiving from Ghana, Nkrumah thought that the NLC would not be able to continue in power for long, and that the Ghanaian people themselves would restore legal government. Meantime, he would organise and prepare for his return.

For the first six months Nkrumah was in Guinea, he broadcast regularly to the people of Ghana on Radio Guinea's Voice of the Revolution. In his words: 'Their purpose was first, to expose the true nature of the so-called coup carried out on 24 February by traitors among the army and police ... and secondly, to encourage resistance.'[1] The first broadcast was made on 6 March 1966, the ninth anniversary of Ghana's Independence Day. The sixth of March is the date which more than any other is associated with the name of Kwame Nkrumah and the Convention People's Party. On 6 March 1966, however, the NLC forbade any celebrations of meetings, and the usual public holiday was cancelled. It was less than two weeks since the coup had taken place, and the NLC had embarked on a senseless campaign to try to obliterate all memory of the achievements of the Nkrumah period.

In his broadcast, Nkrumah spoke of the independence struggle, the socialist gains of the CPP, and of the need to organize, to resist the traitors who were attempting to destroy 'what we have taken years to build'.[2] It was a message to inform the people that he was safe and well, and was

1. *Voice from Conakry*, Kwame Nkrumah, Panaf 1967, Introduction.
2. Ibid., p. 3.

continuing the struggle from Guinea. 'What has happened is only a phase of our struggle and it shall pass.'[1] He ended with the familiar party slogans: Forward Ever, Backward Never. There is Victory for us.

Between March and December 1966, Nkrumah broadcast fifteen times to the Ghanaian people, the final broadcast being made on 22 December. It was a short message, summed up in the words: 'Stand firm and organise. Continue your resistance wherever you are. I have faith in you.'[2] A few weeks before, the NLC had declared that Nkrumah had resigned as President of the Republic of Ghana, and Nkrumah had immediately replied on radio Guinea's Voice of the Revolution. 'You have been told that I have resigned my constitutional position as President of the Republic of Ghana. THIS IS NOT TRUE. Let me repeat, THIS IS NOT TRUE. It is a calculated lie deliberately invented by the NLC, that Notorious Liars' Council, to deceive my unfailing supporters, the chiefs and people of Ghana.'[3]

The NLC made it a criminal offence to listen to any of Nkrumah's broadcasts, but to judge from the many messages Nkrumah received from Ghanaians who heard them, it seems that the NLC prohibition was not very effective. However, the possession of radio sets was by no means general, and the majority of Ghanaians heard of them indirectly, and later read them in the Panaf book, *Voice from Conakry*.

The decision to make no further broadcasts to the Ghanaian people after 22 December 1966, was taken by Nkrumah primarily because he considered they had served their purpose. The Ghanaian people knew he was in Guinea and that he was actively continuing the struggle. Furthermore, he had decided to concentrate on writing as a more effective weapon. Within months of his arrival in Guinea he was at work on *Dark Days in Ghana*,[4] a detailed examination of the causes and effects of the coup on Ghana and the progress of the African Revolution. He followed up this book with other books and pamphlets outlining strategy and tactics for the tasks ahead.

Together with Sékou Touré he tried to organise a conference of militant states of the OAU to meet in Bamako, Mali on 29 May 1966, but apparently without success. However, Sékou Touré, Modibo Keita and Nkrumah kept in touch and met frequently during those early months.

---

1. *Voice from Conakry*, p. 3.
2. Ibid., p. 72.
3.   "   p. 70.
4. Published by Panaf in 1968.

There was a time when Nkrumah thought of moving to Bamako because of its proximity to Upper Volta (now Burkina Fasso), and the latter's common frontier with northern Ghana. The coup of 19 November 1968 which overthrew the Modibo Keita government ended any chance of such a move.

It was during the first few weeks that Flight Captain Hanna Reitsch arrived unexpectedly in Guinea. She had been in Afienya at the time of the coup, and had left Ghana as soon as she could. Travelling incognito, with her hair dyed, she flew into Conakry to give Nkrumah an eye-witness account of what she had seen in Ghana, and to offer any help he might need. She warned him against trying to return too soon, describing scenes of celebration and general chaos in Accra. Her courage and loyalty were proverbial. However, during those early weeks in Conakry, when Nkrumah and his entourage were adjusting to their new situation, Hanna's lurid, superficial descriptions were tactless. She seemed to imply that because she had seen some people applauding the soldiers in Accra, that the Ghanaian people as a whole had turned against Nkrumah, when in fact there been no popular participation in the coup.

Hanna remained in Guinea only a few days. Nkrumah arranged for her to leave after assuring her that she would be contacted if she could be of help. She continued to keep in touch with Nkrumah, writing to him often and sending parcels containing chocolates and health foods. But she never saw him again.

Nkrumah allowed no member of his family to visit him in Guinea though he kept in touch with them by letters transmitted by the Egyptian Ambassador in Conakry. His life was ascetic, a disciplined routine of work and exercise. During his entire stay in Guinea he always wore white, a simple, 'political', short-sleeved suit. Though he did ask me to get him some navy and dark grey material to be made into suits by a Guinean tailor, these were to be kept for his return to Ghana. I got the impression that he wore white as a symbol of mourning for Ghana. In Guinea, white is worn at funerals.

Nkrumah's average day would begin early when he would spend an hour or so doing yoga-type exercises in his room. Breakfast consisted of grapefruit and perhaps a little cereal and honey, or occasionally an egg. He would usually be at his office desk by 9 a.m. and would often work through until about 2 p.m with only a fruit drink to sustain him, or a cup of herbal tea. There would sometimes follow a game of chess with Leonard Blay, a member of his entourage. Blay knew how to play well, so he usually had an early lunch to be ready to play chess with Nkrumah when called. The Russians had given Nkrumah the chess set. It was nothing special, just a plain wooden board with orthodox pieces. If I had finished my work, I used to watch. To start with, Nkrumah would look the picture of concentration, but it usually did not last long. He would pick up the pieces with great speed and bang them down. The slower and more anxious Blay became, the faster Nkrumah would move. He once turned to me, a mischievous smile on his face: 'You see? I am too fast for him.'

He played chess as one would play draughts. He would take slightly longer to move if Blay looked like winning, but this did not happen often. If Blay delayed too long, Nkrumah would hurry him up, asking if he hadn't seen his 'plan?' Nkrumah did not like to lose. He seemed to regard each game as a test of his skill as a strategist and tactician, thinking of the game as a battle. If Blay won, he would sometimes say: 'Blay has eaten', as if that explained the victory. When, as was much more usually the case, he won, then he would remark that although he had not eaten, his mind was 'so sharp!'. Either way, Blay would feel the loser.

After chess would come the main meal of the day, eaten sometimes as late at 3 p.m.. It was a simple two-course meal of meat or fish, followed always by fruit salad. His favourite food was the traditional stew and fou-fou of Ghana. In Conakry, this was cooked for him on certain days of the week by members of his entourage. Frequently, Madame Sékou Touré sent ready-cooked meals to the villa, stews and other foods in large, covered, tureens. After lunch, if there were not more visitors to see or any more office work to attend to, he would retire to his bedroom for a short rest. He would read, and sometimes sleep for a little while, but often his rest was interrupted by the arrival of one of his office staff with a cable, letters or a message. The evening meal was little more than a snack, and afterwards Nkrumah would talk with Sékou Touré or his ministers, or with some other visitor to the villa.

During my visits to Conakry, Nkrumah came to my bungalow every evening, to keep me company, unless there was a film show at the villa. He would be accompanied by Camara and some Ghanaians on the short walk through the villa back garden, briefly into the road outside, and then into my bungalow. Camara would leave us to return to his home on the other side of Conakry, while the Ghanaians positioned themselves around the bungalow. I would see the little procession as it approached.

Nkrumah would sometimes walk a little ahead. But usually, he would be chatting with Camara, Buah, Yankey or one of the others. I remember a time when he almost danced up the steps to the bungalow, doing a 'high life' along the verandah. 'Hello, how are you?' he said, as if he had not seen me for weeks.

He liked to inspect the inside of the old refrigerator in my kitchen. There was never anything much in it, just a few bottles of the local squash, some oranges, perhaps a bar of chocolate, and old squash bottles filled with boiled water. The fridge was rusty and noisy, shaking with age each time the motor started up. To keep the door shut it was necessary to wedge a piece of wood under it.

In some respects, Nkrumah's life in Villa Syli appeared like that of a man under house arrest. Strictly guarded, he seldom left the compound, and when he did it was only for a short time. For the first year or so he made a point of being driven to see Sékou Touré and his wife on Sunday mornings. He would hardly ever stay with them for more than an hour. Sometimes, he would return holding a small white flower which Madame Sékou Touré had picked for him. It was the sweetly-scented white jasmine. Though the tiniest of flowers it has a scent as strong as a carnation. It was one of Nkrumah's favourite flowers in Conakry, second only to his roses on the villa verandah, a constant reminder of his garden at Flagstaff House.

Other days, Nkrumah would occasionally go for a walk in the grounds of Belle Vue. It was there that he took driving lessons from a Guinean army instructor. Nkrumah never looked really at home in the driving seat of the old Peugeot, but he was determined to learn. Seeing him struggling with the gears one day, I asked if it was not possible for him to learn on an automatic car. He liked the idea, but this was yet another matter which would have to await his return to Ghana.

Members of the various political organizations of Guinea were frequent visitors to Villa Syli, as were the representatives of socialist embassies in Conakry. Then there were the visits from members of liberation movements. As in Ghana, Nkrumah always found time to see freedom fighters.

Probably the most frequent visitor from the liberation movements was Amilcar Cabral, president of PAIGC (African Party for the Independence of Guinea and the Cape Verde Islands). He would be driven into the villa compound by a uniformed member of the PAIGC, and was usually accompanied by one or more soldiers wearing khaki battle dress

The President and Co-President of Guinea. Sékou Touré and Kwame Nkrumah — Conakry Stadium, 1966

Nkrumah pruning his roses — Villa Syli, 1968

Nkrumah walking to his office — Villa Syli, 1967

marked with the zigzag camouflage of the guerrilla fighter. Cabral himself was usually dressed in a plain white 'political' suit. He and Nkrumah would sit and talk privately together, sometimes for as long as an hour or so. But often the meetings would be short, because Cabral was either about to leave for a visit to PAIGC forces in Guinea Bissau, or had returned from there or from a mission abroad. For Cabral made a point of calling to see Nkrumah before and after each visit. He would report on the progress made, and would bring Nkrumah the latest PAIGC bulletins, and Nkrumah would give him copies of his new books as they were published. Nkrumah was uneasy at Cabral's frequent visits to Western countries, both in the interests of his personal safety, and because he thought he should depend wholly on support from socialist states. On one occasion, I heard him warn Cabral of bourgeois elements in the national liberation movement and of their Western class allies, specially when they appeared 'bearing gifts'. Cabral laughed, and replied that he took every precaution, but that the PAIGC needed every bit of help it could obtain no matter from what source.

Before retiring for the night, Nkrumah would take his final exercise. This was usually a walk round and round the compound, sometimes ten times, at a blistering speed which often left anyone accompanying him breathless trying to keep up. He would finally go to his room and would sleep at most between four to six hours.

On some evenings there would be a documentary film shown on the office verandah, arranged by the Guinean Minister of Information or by the North Korean or Vietnamese embassies in Conakry. In June 1967 for example, I heard Cabral who was sitting on Nkrumah's right, translate from the French commentary of a film showing various aspects of the PAIGC liberation war in Portuguese Guinea. Shots of villages bombed by Portuguese aircraft, moving episodes of doctors attending the wounded in village dispensaries. Of particular interest to Nkrumah was the footage showing the work of administering the areas liberated by the PAIGC. Nkrumah spoke to Cabral of the importance of the organization of political structures from the people's struggle which would form the basis for the future administration of the country when military victory had been won, and colonial rule ended.

The North Koreans frequently had film shows in their embassy grounds adjoining my bungalow. I was sometimes able to watch them standing on a stool on the verandah and looking over the wall. These films, showing mainly industrial and agricultural projects and state ceremonial occasions, I would often see again, sitting beside Nkrumah on the verandah of Villa Syli, when the Korean Charge d'Affaires would translate the commentary.

The Vietnamese also showed films. These were of the war, the American bombing, the speedy repair of damage to roads and bridges, scenes illustrating the indomitable spirit of the Vietnamese people, totally committed to achieving victory. After one such film, the Vietnamese diplomat presented Nkrumah and myself with rings made from the metal of destroyed US aircraft. Each ring was stamped with a number denoting the total of American aircraft shot down at the time the ring was made.

Often after a film ended, Nkrumah would discuss it with the members of his entourage who, together with Guinean staff of the villa, had watched it with him. He always related what he had seen to the situation in Ghana and Africa as a whole, drawing attention to what lessons could be learned from the experience of other people intent on liberating and developing their countries.

Nkrumah took care always to give the impression that he was absolutely confident of a return to Ghana, and that it was only a question of time. It was important never to stop working and organizing to that end. Physical fitness was a priority. When he arrived in Guinea he was in excellent health. He weighed about eleven stone and had the blood pressure of a young man. He did not drink alcohol or smoke, or indulge in heavy meals or rich food. He took various vitamin pills, but only 'natural' ones from health food stores. I used to buy these for him from the health food shop in Baker Street, London, along with other items such as honey, wheat germ, 'healthy life' biscuits and so on.

For the first six months, Nkrumah's food was prepared by Amoah, a Ghanaian ex-army cook who had been in charge of his food long before the coup, and who had accompanied him to Hanoi. He was an oldish man, tall and thin, obviously devoted to Nkrumah. Nkrumah's food was safe in his hands. Amoah seemed to be very fit when I first saw him in Conakry in June 1966. Not long afterwards, however, he began to suffer from nausea, and vomiting. Nkrumah arranged for a Russian doctor in Conakry to examine him. After tests, the doctor diagnosed cancer of the liver. He said that it was useless sending him to the USSR for treatment as he was terminally ill. It would be kindest to let him die in hospital in Guinea where his friends could visit him. Amoah spent months in a Conakry hospital, visited frequently by Nkrumah. He died on 20 July

1967. His death affected Nkrumah deeply. Sékou Touré, aware of this, called at Villa Syli specially to offer his condolences.

After Amoah's death, a succession of Guinean cooks prepared Nkrumah's food. It was impossible to check on them, or on the many others employed in the kitchen of Villa Syli. Every time I went to Guinea there seemed to be changes of kitchen staff, all of whom lived in Conakry, travelling daily to and from the villa. Apart from the few meals prepared by Nyamikeh, a trusted relative of Nkrumah, there was no way in which one could be sure that his food was safe. Nyamikeh or another member of the entourage usually cooked breakfast and meals on days when the Guinean cook was off-duty, and it was they who brought tea, soft drinks and occasional snacks.

During the first year, John Ketsowo Kosi, a senior (Ewe) security officer was in close attendance. He was subsequently arrested and imprisoned by Guinea police, accused of betraying Nkrumah by supplying information to the NLC in Ghana. He was said to have been paid US$ 300 a month for his reports. The American embassy in Conakry was suspected of being implicated. Kosi used to accompany Camara to Gbessia airport to meet and see me off when I visited Guinea. The last occasion he was there to see me off I said to him on leaving: 'Take good care of the President.' Kosi replied 'And of myself.' I was unhappy about his response, hardly appropriate for a senior security officer, and I considered mentioning it when I wrote to Nkrumah on my arrival in London. But then I thought I might be over-reacting, and decided instead to tell him on my next visit. By then, Kosi had been arrested, a Guinean girlfriend having reported to the police, who were already watching him, that Kosi had unaccountable dollars to spend.

At another time, the Guinean head of security at Villa Syli was found to be guilty of subversion, being closely involved with opposition elements, working to overthrow the government of Sékou Touré.

Being exposed to so many dangers was not a new experience for Nkrumah. In Guinea, however, he had less room for manoeuvre. Nor did he want to be the cause of further problems for Sékou Touré. He therefore concentrated on doing all he could to maintain his health, while at the same time working on his books and planning a speedy return to Ghana. He made a point of regular exercise, walking, doing daily yoga exercises, playing table tennis. He devised tests for himself, placing a leaf or small twig at a certain spot on the verandah, then going back some distance, closing his eyes and walking to stamp on the exact spot where he had placed it. Other times, he would walk along the low brick wall which edged the flower beds in the villa garden. The wall was narrow. He liked to see if he could walk quickly along it without losing his balance.

He was determined to fill each day with activities which he considered would make him fitter for the tasks ahead when he returned to Ghana. It was the time factor which troubled him most. If too much time elapsed before his return, the infrastructure which the CPP government had so carefully constructed, and which was necessary for the ongoing PanAfrican struggle, might be irreparably damaged. He longed to be back at the centre of African politics, in Ghana, where he could pursue his Ghanaian and PanAfrican goals.

He listened to all the main news bulletins he was able to pick up on his radio, the BBC World Service, Ghana radio and occasionally the Voice of America. Broadcasts from Ghana were often difficult to hear on his little portable radio. He had to concentrate hard to catch every word. The hurt of hearing the familiar voices, and particularly broadcasts in the vernacular, showed in his expression and in his eyes.

Nkrumah missed little of what went on in Ghana. He was kept well-informed by Ghanaians and others who remained loyal to him, both within Ghana and elsewhere. Newspapers and mail arrived from many sources. Members of the entourage who monitored official Ghana radio broadcasts were also able to pick up confidential messages between units of the army and police. These reports were typed and presented daily to Nkrumah.

He was determined at all times not to let anyone see that he was anything but in his usual good health and spirits. I recall a day when we were having lunch and the Guinean foreign minister called. Nkrumah invited him to join us at the table. The minister asked: 'And how are you Mr. President?' Nkrumah smiling broadly, made a fist and showed the muscle of his arm. 'Like a lion', he replied in his deepest voice. The minister always called at the villa before leaving Guinea on a mission, and reported when he returned. Nkrumah asked questions about his mission, though not with the same interest as I had observed in Ghana, when he spoke with those who were directly responsible to him, and were carrying out his instructions.

It was different too, when talking with someone like Amilcar Cabral. Freedom fighters he regarded as specially close. When they came he was at full concentration, listening, advising, encouraging. It was then that he felt the maximum frustration, at not being in a position to do more to help them. Several times he told me that the reason for his never-ceasing efforts to return to Accra was so that he could help Africa's freedom fighters. He said that he did not intend to live again in Flagstaff House or the Castle. He would live in largely underground headquarters in the hills around Aburi, on the lines of the 'cave' where he had visited Chairman Mao Tse-Tung in China. He would devote his time to organising the total liberation and unification of Africa, leaving the day to day administration of Ghana to the Party. Musing on the Aburi plan, he spoke of James Moxon, expressing disgust at the lack of solidarity he showed in his attitude to the coup and his acceptance of a chieftaincy. He was angered at passages in Moxon's book on the Volta Dam in which he claimed credit for negotiating the project, when in fact, Moxon's role was merely public relations (PR) — a role he had filled when working for the colonial government before independence. Nkrumah said that after his return to Ghana, there would be no place for Moxon in Aburi.

Nkrumah sketched a plan of his intended Aburi headquarters, and asked me to draw one too. He did not think much of my effort, deeming it more like a bungalow. He said that he would have a bungalow built for me, probably at the Volta Dam, so that I could stay in Ghana as and when I wished. It was usually after we had been working hard in his office, and had gone to relax for a time under the trees in the villa garden, that Nkrumah liked to talk about what he would do on his return to Ghana. Plans for the new Ghana were written down in a small, black leather notebook. During my visit in September 1966 he was drafting statements which he would broadcast when he returned to Accra. They concerned the announcement of emergency measures, and the long-term changes to be made under the heading: 'The Tasks Ahead'.

We spent hours discussing Nkrumaism. I hoped to write a book on the subject at some stage. Nkrumah encouraged the idea, which I had first mentioned to him in Ghana in 1965, when setting up the President's Research Office in Padmore's old bungalow. There was no time to start work on the book then. But in Conakry we were able to discuss it on many occasions.

It was decided that *Some Essential Features of Nkrumaism*, a book compiled and published in Accra in 1964 by editors of *The Spark* newspaper, should be updated by adding a Part Two to take account of the development of Nkrumah's political thought expressed in the books he wrote after that date. In view of the heavy schedule of work at Villa Syli, this would be the quickest and most practical ways to proceed to make known the full meaning of Nkrumaism.

Nkrumah maintained that his political philosophy was not a static, rigid ideology, but one which evolved progressively during a lifetime of study, political struggle and practical experience of government. Although tactics varied to meet changing circumstances and conditions, the broad strategy of Nkrumaism, embodying three objectives, remained consistent. First, political emancipation which Nkrumah considered to be the necessary pre-requisite for economic independence without which there could be no meaningful freedom. Second, the total liberation and unification of Africa. Third, the building of a just society. These objectives, to be pursued concurrently, are the consistent thread linking all his endeavours. They are the core ingredients of Nkrumaism.

The expanded edition of *Some Essential Features of Nkrumaism*, published by Panaf in 1975, three years after Nkrumah's death, was constructed from notes I assembled from our discussions in Villa Syli between 1966 and 1970. It was not possible to publish sooner because priority had to be given to *Dark Days in Ghana, The Handbook of Revolutionary Warfare, Class Struggle in Africa*, and the various pamphlets, broadcasts and speeches prepared by Nkrumah during the Conakry years. There was never a time when he was not engaged on some writing project, or when there was not some urgent matter occupying his attention. There was no slowing of the pace at which he worked.

In November 1966, the NLC detained in Accra a Guinean delegation en route to an OAU meeting in Addis Ababa. The Dutch KLM aircraft had intended a brief stopover in Abidjan, but 'because of bad weather' had diverted to Accra. The NLC declared that the delegation was being detained because Ghanaians of Nkrumah's entourage were being held in Guinea against their will. The OAU sent a mission to Conakry to find out if this was so. Each member of the entourage was interviewed separately, after which the OAU mission reported that there was no truth in the NLC allegation. The military regime in Accra was then compelled to release the Guineans.

Sékou Touré was convinced that the USA had masterminded the affair. The US ambassador in Conakry was put under house arrest until the Guinean delegation was released. All members of the Peace Corps were ordered to leave Guinea. In response, the American airline Pan Am, and later KLM, ended flights to Guinea.

The safety of Nkrumah, always of paramount importance to the Guinean government, necessitated the strictest security measures. Apart from guarding the villa, Guinean naval ships patrolled coastal waters around Conakry. On 29 November 1966, the Ghanaian Daily Graphic had printed on its front page the heading: NKRUMAH AND THREE OTHERS WANTED FOR MURDER. A reward of $10,000 was advertised for their return to Ghana 'dead or alive'. the three others were Ambrose Yankey, M. A. Mensah and Boye Moses. On more than one occasion, patrolling Guinean ships escorted Ghanaian 'fishing' vessels into Conakry for investigation. The threat of an attempt to kidnap Nkrumah was taken very seriously, specially after a Ghanaian boat was caught well inside Guinean waters, a short distance off-shore from Villa Syli. It was manned by Ewes, with criminal records, most of whom had been recently released from Ghanaian prisons. Clearly, the intention was to raid the villa under cover of darkness, and to kidnap or even kill Nkrumah.

It was discovered during interrogation that the bogus fishermen had detailed knowledge of the layout of Villa Syli. In a letter to me dated 4 December 1966, Nkrumah wrote of the NLC: 'What fools they are ... they are at their wits end and in such a panic.'

While consistently urging the people of Ghana to continue their resistance in the form of strikes, boycotts and non-co-operation, Nkrumah nevertheless was convinced by the end of 1966 that a counter-coup was needed to restore constitutional government. For this it was necessary for the ground to be prepared by Positive Action. 'Once the fire is lit the blaze will spread throughout the country.'[1] He was confident that increasing hardship and discontent would lead to a popular uprising in support of Positive Action. In a New Year letter to me he predicted that 1967 would be a year of 'success, health, happiness and victory'. His optimism was fuelled by reports reaching him from Ghana of plans being made for a counter-coup. Nkrumah himself was involved in planning. A senior member of his entourage, Boye Moses, travelled under a false name, visiting Sierra Leone, Togo, Dahomey and Nigeria, to link up with other supporters determined to overthrow the NLC. The Guinean government provided passports and other facilities, allowing their embassies to be used for the transmission of messages and weapons.

---

1. *Call to the Workers of Ghana*, Kwame Nkrumah. This was printed by Panaf in 1968 and distributed clandestinely in Ghana. Full text in *The Struggle Continues*, pp. 9–12.

By February 1967, however, a major setback occurred with the capture of Boye Moses in Dahomey by agents of the NLC. He was flown to Ghana and paraded through the streets of Accra in a cage. I was booked to travel to Conakry in early February. But after the arrest of Boye Moses, Nkrumah cabled me to postpone and to fly instead on 27 February. I stayed until 19 March working with Nkrumah on his books and correspondence.

As time went on, it became clear that security leaks were mainly responsible for the failure of plans for Nkrumah's return to Ghana. Apart from the impossibility of maintaining maximum security at Villa Syli, there was the constant possibility of leaks of information occurring in Guinea, Ghana and elsewhere resulting from the penetration of pro-Nkrumah forces by hostile agents and double agents. Nkrumah was faced not only with Ghanaian opposition elements, plus Western anti-Nkrumah pressure, but also with Guinean opposition forces bent on the overthrow of the Sékou Touré government. Suspicion arose as to the loyalty of certain Guinean diplomats manning Guinean-embassies, for example in Lagos, through which from time-to-time plans for Nkrumah's return to Ghana were processed.

Although well aware of this and other dangers, Nkrumah refrained from burdening Sékou Touré with problems which would add to his difficulties.

It was impossible for Nkrumah not to place trust in some of those who claimed to be working for his return, though maybe he was too trusting in some cases, being keen to believe their sometimes exaggerated reports of plans being made, the typical optimistic predictions of émigré politics. Nkrumah practised the 'need to know' principle, only the absolute minimum of persons being kept informed of his intentions. But then methods of communication provided other channels through which sensitive information could leak. For example, each day a member of the entourage would take mail and cables for dispatch to the central post office in Conakry where they were vulnerable to scrutiny.

There was a time when Protocol Officer, Camara Sana, suspected Nkrumah's most trusted secretary, W. Sarfoh of leaking sensitive information. He was certainly in a position to do so, being responsible for typing letters, messages and cables. Furthermore, his desk was on the verandah of the villa in a position from where he could see every visitor, and often hear conversations.

In the circumstances of Villa Syli, the possibility of security leaks could never be entirely plugged, even with the strictest vigilance.

At times the strain showed in notes Nkrumah wrote to me which were delivered by hand to Villa June, usually first thing in the morning. Shortly after the Ghanaian fishing vessel incident he wrote: 'I am well but I had a rough night. It was mental, thinking about so many different things. I had three hours sleep. I lay awake and kept on thinking. I get this way once in a while. So don't worry about me. It will pass off.' Another morning he wrote: 'After I left you last night I came back to my room.... I then remained awake. I couldn't sleep. I just lay there thinking. I thought and thought about my return to Ghana. The situation I find myself in is serious, but I must be master of it. To Ghana I must go. The African Revolution dictates that. But how? This is what I have been thinking about.... I am fine in spite of a sleepless night.'

In fact, at Villa Syli, everything was calculated with a return to Ghana in mind. It was a bitter disappointment when the counter-coup attempt led by Lieutenants Samuel Arthur, Moses Yeboah and Second Lieutenant Ebenezer Osei Poku failed. During the early hours of 17 April 1967, with 120 men of the Reconnaissance (Recce) Squadron, they captured the radio station and Flagstaff House, and fought their way into Christiansborg Castle. They broadcast that the NLC had been 'dissolved' and that a three-man military junta had seized power. Their success was short-lived. Within four hours, Lieutenant Arthur and his men were under arrest, their only satisfaction being the killing of Colonel E.K. Kotoka, leader of the 1966 coup. Lieutenants Arthur and Yeboah were executed in public by firing squad on 9 May. Second Lt Poku was sentenced to thirty years' imprisonment with hard labour.

News of the counter-coup attempt came as a complete surprise to Nkrumah. At no time did Lieutenant Arthur state that his intention was to restore the CPP government to power, though it was clear that his bold attempt to overthrow he NLC was linked to popular discontent with NLC rule. Nkrumah was horrified at the barbaric treatment of Arthur and Yeboah.

Nkrumah and his closest aides certainly thought that if the NLC had been overthrown in April 1967 his return to Accra would have followed. He dedicated *Dark Days in Ghana* to the two courageous lieutenants and to General Barwah, who like them had been killed 'resisting the traitors of the 24 February 1966'. Clearly, the 17 April attempt had been poorly

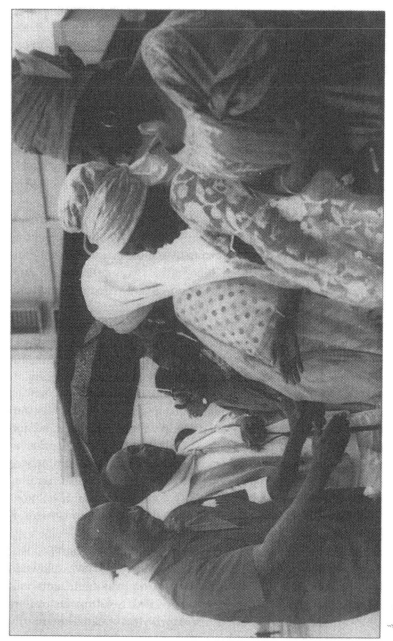

Guinean party militants greeting President Kenneth Kaunda (Zambia) and Nkrumah — Conakry airport, 1969

organised. But lessons could be learned from it. As Lieutenant Arthur himself remarked at his court martial, 'It set people thinking'.

During 1968, three statements to the people of Ghana were written by Nkrumah and published by Panaf. The first, *A Call for Positive Action and Armed Struggle* was addressed specifically to members of the CPP. It called on them to form secret cells throughout the country, to organise strikes and demonstrations and other methods of Positive Action. Ghana, he said, could not be saved by constitutional methods alone. With the CPP banned, its members disfranchised, any election would be bogus. 'No-one is taken in by the vague and foxy promises of a "return to civilian rule".... If they believe in free elections and are not afraid of the power of the CPP, why have they banned and disfranchised the CPP? Constitutions are powerless before guns.'[1]

The second statement entitled *Ghana: The Way Out*, contained an even clearer call for the use of force. The time for non-violent action has passed ... Ghana is no longer being run by an African government. It is being administered by a small clique of army and police officers, and behind the Ghanaian façade, the decisions are being made by foreign interests.'[2]

The third statement was made in July 1968. Its purpose was to expose the true nature of the NLC announcement of 22 May 1968 which outlined its programme for Ghana's return to civilian rule by 30 September 1969. The title, *Civilian Rule Fraud*[3] summed up Nkrumah's attitude to it. 'Let none be deceived for one moment by this bogus and dishonest gesture. The last thing the NLC and their neo-colonialist masters intend is to allow free and democratic elections.'[4] There was to be no lifting of the ban on political activity, and the Elections and Public Offices Disqualification Decree remained in force. Any election result unfavourable to a military regime was liable to be declared null and void.

All the statements made to the people of Ghana by Nkrumah during 1968 were published in *Africa and the World*, a London based monthly magazine founded in 1960 and sponsored by the CPP government. After the coup of 24 February 1966, the NLC brought pressure to bear on

---

1. *A Call for Positive Action and Armed Stuggle*, Kwame Nkrumah, Panaf 1968. Full text in *The Struggle Continues*, pp. 30–31.
2. *Ghana: The Way Out*, Kwame Nkrumah, Panaf 1968. Full text in *The Struggle Continues*, pp. 19–25.
3. Full text in *The Stuggle Continues*, pp. 26–29.
4. *The Stuggle Continues*, p. 26.

Douglas Rogers, the editor of *Africa and the World* to cease publication. But he steadfastly refused to be intimidated or to change the magazine's political orientation, and continued to publish the truth about Ghana and Africa. The magazine which had a world-wide readership and a high reputation for progressive and accurate reporting, was regularly published until mid-1971 when due to lack of funds it had to close. After the fall of Busia's government in January 1972, Rogers visited Ghana twice to try to persuade the National Redemption Council (NRC) to support the resumption of publication, either in Ghana or London, but he was unsuccessful. The magazine's office at 89 Fleet Street had to be closed finally in June 1972.

The office at 89 Fleet Street was also the original home of Panaf Books, the publishing company which Nkrumah asked me to set up in 1968 to publish the books he wrote in Conakry. It was necessary to form a publishing company since neither of his two previous publishers, Thomas Nelson & Sons and Heinemann Educational Books (HEB), were prepared to publish any more of his works after the 1966 coup. Neither were they interested in keeping in print Nkrumah's books which they had published before 1966, and there were plans to pulp the remaining stocks.

🔺 Nkrumah with staff of Heinemann Educational Books (HEB), his pre-1966 London publishers — London, 1964. (Extreme left, June and Van Milne)

The attitude of his previous publishers after the coup shocked Nkrumah, though it did not discourage him from writing more books. It was when the manuscript of *Dark Days in Ghana*, the first book to be compiled in Guinea, was completed that the question of a new publisher became urgent. I brought the MS back to London and tried to interest HEB in reconsidering their stand, but without success. Finally, I managed to get Maurice Cornforth, an old friend of Nkrumah's and founder of publishers Lawrence and Wishart, to produce a limited paperback edition. For reasons of economy, he said that the Appendix containing messages of support from Heads of State, and the large section of personal letters, would have to be omitted. Nkrumah reluctantly agreed to this condition. But he valued very highly the letters he had received from ordinary people all over the world, and was determined that the complete MS of *Dark Days in Ghana* should be published in a new edition as soon as possible. It was the apparent hopelessness of getting a publisher to do this that made him decide to set up his own book publishing company. He asked me to find out what was needed to register such a company. I remember his surprise at learning that only £100 was required once the necessary formalities had been completed. It was his idea to name the company, founded in 1968, Panaf Books. In the same year, Panaf published a new edition of *Dark Days in Ghana* which contained the full Appendix of the original MS. By then, the small Lawrence and Wishart edition was out of print.

Initially, I worked in the Fleet Street office of *Africa and the World*. The printer of the magazine, John Marshment, allowed me to use part of his desk until Douglas Rogers was able to make a table available for me in the large attic room where his secretary sat, and from where the magazine was packaged and dispatched. When in 1972 *Africa and the World* had to close, I rented a small room three mornings a week in an office building at 243 Regent Street. At no time was I in a position to employ any staff, so the question of accommodation was no problem.

A further inhabitant of the attic premises at 89 Fleet Street for a time was Ekow Eshun, secretary of the CPP Overseas, who, until the coup, worked in the Ghana High Commission in London. His loyalty, and the continuing dedication of the CPP Overseas have fulfilled an historic role. Through their meetings, demonstrations, political seminars, and their bulletin *The Dawn*, they continued to make nonsense of the NLC's claim to have abolished the CPP. A great historic Party cannot be destroyed simply by declaring that it no longer exists.

In a statement dated 24 February 1966, the very day that the coup took place in Ghana, the CPP Overseas issued a statement in London condemning the military action and declaring support of the constitutional government. Nkrumah particularly during the first few years of his stay in Conakry, was in close touch with the CPP Overseas. Eshun made several trips to Guinea, until he was betrayed and captured in Cotonou by agents of the NLC. In a letter to me dated 8 October 1967, Nkrumah wrote: 'There are other plans in the fire. I always plan with the consideration of a betrayal in mind.'

During the Conakry period there were many counter-coup plans presented to Nkrumah by Ghanaians and others who somehow managed to convince Guinea security officers and those of Nkrumah's entourage, that they were genuine. Each person who managed to see him had for days before been vigorously screened. Very occasionally, Nkrumah would see them in his office in Villa Syli, but usually he would be driven to either Belle Bue or some other rendezvous outside Conakry.

Nkrumah found it distasteful to have to meet with often dubious characters who claimed to be working for his return to Ghana. But deprived of the security procedures to which he was accustomed in Ghana, he had no alternative but to see such men. Otherwise, he ran the risk of letting slip perhaps the one realistic chance of a successful counter-coup. Sometimes, Nkrumah would be given a definite date when he could expect to hear good news. Other times, he would be promised action between certain dates. On one occasion, the Guinean government was so convinced of a date, that Nkrumah was invited to spend the night at Sékou Touré's residence so that he would be ready to make a broadcast and a quick return to Ghana. I was in Conakry at the time, and spent the night listening to the World Service of the BBC in the hope of hearing news of a pro-Nkrumah coup in Ghana. Nkrumah returned to Villa Syli during the morning, disappointed but philosophical, believing that something unforeseen must have occurred necessitating a delay.

Among those who visited Conakry was Captain (rtd) Kojo Tsikata. He arrived there with plans for a counter-coup. He was interviewed by Ambrose Yankey and two other members of the entourage. Nkrumah adamantly refused to see him. I understood from Nkrumah that he believed Tsikata to have been implicated in an anti-CPP coup plot before 1966, and he did not trust him. Neither did the Guinean authorities. Tsikata was arrested and imprisoned for a time by the Guinean police.

Apparently, Tsikata said he wanted Nkrumah's approval of his coup plans and the arrangements which were to follow after the NLC had been overthrown. Having been trained at Sandhurst, and with first-hand knowledge of the Ghanaian army, Tsikata it seems had worked out detailed plans for the coup. As subsequent events showed, what was planned was almost exactly what did actually happen on 4 June 1979 when Flight Lieutenant Jerry Rawlings, on trial on a charge of mutiny, was rescued from prison by soldiers from Burma Camp, and pro-claimed Head of State as Chairman of the Armed Forces Revolutionary Council (AFRC).

More often than not, visitors to Conakry with plans for coups would ask for cash to pay for 'travel expenses' and to buy 'equipment'. Sooner or later I would hear Nkrumah call to Nyamikeh to bring 'the key'. This was the key of his bedroom where cash was kept in a tin box. Nkrumah would disappear for a few minutes, then emerge carrying a brown envelope, or sometimes a small packet wrapped in newspaper.

For a time it was not difficult for Nkrumah to supply cash. He had arrived in Conakry with funds provided by the Russians when he passed through Moscow en route from Hanoi to Conakry. Later, the Chinese gave him some. Then Presidents Milton Obote of Uganda and Julius Nyerere of Tanzania sent envoys carrying diplomatic bags containing cash. Both wanted to see Nkrumah back in Accra, and were realistic enough to know that this was unlikely to be achieved without money.

Nkrumah had no funds in foreign bank accounts, and his account in Barclays Bank in Accra into which his presidential salary had been paid, was frozen by the NLC. He was therefore entirely dependent on the generosity of political friends. The provision of cash was welcome because it meant that he could, at least for a time, be spared financial worry. He kept a careful account of funds given to him, intending to repay the donors in full on his return to power in Ghana.

Apart from those who asked for money to carry out plans to restore constitutional government in Ghana, money was needed to finance *Africa and the World*. Until 1966, the magazine had been financed by the Ghana government through the Bureau of African Affairs in Accra. After the coup, the NLC stopped the funding of the magazine and froze its account with the Ghana Commercial Bank in London. Quick action by Douglas Rogers and the accountant 'Roley' Randall succeeded in switching funds to another bank, and the magazine continued pub-lishing regularly, assisted by funds from Nkrumah.

In addition, Nkrumah faced considerable expense in providing for the needs of his entourage. Board and lodging at Villa Syli was provided by the Guinean government. But Nkrumah paid the Ghanaians a weekly wage, half of what they had earned in Ghana, the understanding being that they would receive the other half of their pay, made-up in full, on their return to Ghana.

14

The Struggle Continues

Although most of Nkrumah's time in Conakry was devoted to the situation in Ghana and in Africa, he kept abreast of developments concerning peoples of African descent living in the USA, the Caribbean, Latin America and elsewhere. In October 1967 he was presented with the first annual Black Power Award, 'In memory of Marcus Garvey, Malcolm X, Patrice Lumumba and Harriet Tubman.' In the words of the citation, 'We offer this award as an onward expression of our gratitude to a man whose literary ability, as well as that of influencing people, has been a source of inspiration to all Black People.' Nkrumah hung the shield on a wall in his office.

It was a time when black Americans, demanding basic human rights, took part in riots, demonstrations, marches and boycotts. The year 1968 was probably the most violent in the United States civil rights campaign. Racial riots had become so widespread that an official report on the National Advisory Commission on Civil Disorders declared: 'Our nation is moving towards two societies, one black, one white, separate and unequal.'[1]

On 28 October 1968, Dr Martin Wachman, President of Lincoln University where Nkrumah had been a student, wrote to Nkrumah to say that many students at the university wished to keep in touch with him. Dr. Wachman arranged for copies of Alumni *Bulletins* to be

---

1. The Commission was set up in July 1967 after the Detroit riots. The report was published in 1968.

posted. Nkrumah, in a letter of acknowledgement dated 5 November 1968 thanked him, listing the new books he had written in Conakry, adding: 'I hope you have all my books at the Library.'[1]

In the following year, when James M. Nabrit, President of Howard University, Washington DC announced that he intended to retire, students who wanted his successor to be more in tune with Black Power philosophy suggested the appointment of Nkrumah as president. The editor and publisher of the *Chicago Daily Defender*, John H. Sengstacke, reported the matter stating that although the chance of Nkrumah being appointed was remote, nevertheless the suggestion carried with it a sense of history: 'KN is still a popular figure among American black men. There has been no diminution in his prestige. It was his tenacity, his courage and indefatigable labour that ushered in a new era of freedom and independence in Africa ... Nkrumah is the epitome of black pride. He would bring dignity and leadership to embattled Howard.'[2]

From time to time, African-Americans visited Guinea to see Nkrumah, one of the most frequent callers at Villa Syli being Stokeley Carmichael (later named Kwame Turé) of the Student Non-Violent Coordinating Committee (SNCC). Carmichael and his (then) wife, Miriam Makeba, lived for a time in Guinea, though Guinean security forces were never happy about Stokeley Carmichael's presence.

Nkrumah eventually tired of Carmichael, disappointed by his lack of personal discipline and having failed to rid him of his racialist views. He told him not to visit Villa Syli again unless he sent for him. Shortly before this, Nkrumah introduced Stokeley to me, bringing him to where I sat at my desk on the villa verandah. Nkrumah said, 'I want you to meet Stokeley Carmichael. He is not yet a man.' I was very embarrassed. I had never before heard Nkrumah deliberately humiliate anyone. Stokeley looked furious as we shook hands, but said nothing. Later when I spoke of the incident, Nkrumah told me that before he decided to introduce me, Stokeley had been talking his usual 'racial nonsense', so he said he would introduce him to a white woman who had come to Guinea at considerable personal risk to work on his books and his return to Ghana.

---

1. *The Conakry Years*, p. 268.
2. Ibid., p. 314–315. Nkrumah was moved by the report and told me of Howard University's pre-eminence in the field of African Studies. This was a major factor in my decision to donate the precious files of correspondence and other papers, which I retrieved from Villa Syli after Nkrumah's death, to the Moorland-Spingarn Research Center of Howard University where I knew they would be expertly and safely preserved.

It was to some extent the confused ideas of Carmichael which prompted Nkrumah in 1968 to write *The Spectre of Black Power*.[1] He wished to make clear his views on the whole question of Black Power. He dedicated the statement to:

Ernesto Ché Guevara
Ben Barka
Malcolm X

In the first edition, Nkrumah mentioned the visit of Stokeley Carmichael to Guinea. However, he deleted all reference to him when the pamphlet was reprinted in 1969. In essence, the message contained in *The Spectre of Black Power* is summed up in the brief conclusion:

'Racial discrimination is the product of an environment, an environment of a divided class society, and its solution is to change that environment. This presupposes the fact that it is only under socialism in the United States of America that the African-American can really be free in the land of his birth.'[2]

In the same year 1968 Nkrumah sent a *Message to the Black People of Britain* at the request of Obi Egbuna, a Nigerian writer, who paid a two week visit to Conakry to collect material for a play which he said he intended to write about Nkrumah. Egbuna was at the time prominent in the Black Panther movement in Britain, and he was anxious to return to the UK with a taped message from Nkrumah.

The *Message to the Black People of Britain* contains virtually the same definition of Black Power as that which appears in *The Spectre of Black Power*. Nkrumah subsequently ceased to communicate with Egbuna when he continued to write from a racialist standpoint.

Nkrumah was busy with his own books. First, he wrote an introduction to *Challenge of the Congo*. This book, for which a contract had been signed with Nelson's before 1966, was in page proof at the time of the coup. The Introduction, dated 22 June 1966, which is the only part of the book written after the coup in Ghana, begins: 'Since writing the final chapters of this book Ghana has temporarily fallen victim to the same external forces which have, for six years, tried to prevent progress

1. *The Spectre of Black Power*, Kwame Nkrumah. Full text in *The Struggle Continues*, pp. 36–43.
2. *The Struggle Continues*, pp. 13–14.

towards real independence in the Congo.'[1] He continues: 'The true nature of the struggle taking place in Africa and the world between the forces of progress and those of reaction ... in the final analysis is the fight of the common man against injustice and privilege. For we live in a world in which one quarter of the people are becoming richer, while the rest grow poorer and poorer.'[2] Three years later, in June 1969, when Panaf published a paperback edition of the book, Nkrumah added an Author's Note in which he emphasised the armed phase of the African revolutionary struggle.

Another work to be published during the Conakry period was a Freedom Fighters' edition of *Axioms*. It was a small, plastic-covered, pocket edition which differed in content from the previous *Axioms of Kwame Nkrumah* prepared before the 1966 coup in Ghana. The Freedom Fighters' edition contained extracts from *The Handbook of Revolutionary Warfare* and *Dark Days in Ghana*, books which Nkrumah began to compile within weeks of his arrival in Guinea. In addition, The Freedom Fighters' edition of *Axioms* differed from the original version in that extracts concerning non-alignment and co-existence were not included. They belonged to a period of Ghana's history which Nkrumah no longer considered relevant to the contemporary situation in Africa. 'There is such a thing as peaceful co-existence between states with different social systems; but as long as oppressive classes exist, there can be no such thing as peaceful co-existence between opposing ideologies.'[3]

This quotation, from the revised edition of *Consciencism*, published in 1970, indicated the emphasis which Nkrumah wished to give to class struggles. *Consciencism* had been first published in 1964, and Nkrumah was not entirely satisfied that it accurately expressed his political philosophy in light of the 'new phase' of the African Revolution:

> The succession of military coups which have in recent years taken place in Africa, have exposed the close links between the interests of neocolonialism and the indigenous bourgeoisie. These coups have brought into sharp relief the nature and the extent of the class struggle in Africa... It is in consideration of the new situation in Africa that some changes have become necessary in this edition.[4]

---

1. *Challenge of the Congo*, Preface, p. x.
2. Ibid., pp. x–xi.
3. *Axioms*, pp. 31–32.
4. *Consciencism*, Kwame Nkrumah, Panaf revised edition 1970. Author's note, p. vi.

The changes in *Consciencism* are in line with the theme of two articles published by Panaf in pamphlet form in 1968 under the title *Two Myths*. The first article, *The Myth of the Third World*, was first published in the October 1968 edition of *Labour Monthly*. In this article, Nkrumah posed the questions: 'First, does a Third World really exist? Secondly, is it possible, either in terms of ideology or practical politics, in the ever-sharpening conflict between revolutionary and counter-revolutionary forces in the world to adopt a position of neutrality or non-alignment?'[1] He had come to the conclusion that the Third World was a misused expression which has come to mean everything and nothing.[2] He continued:

> If we are to achieve revolutionary socialism then we must avoid any suggestion that will imply that there is any separation between the socialist world and a 'Third World.'
>
> I do not deny the existence of the struggling 'wretched of the earth', but maintain that they do not exist in isolation, as a 'Third World.' They are an integral part of the revolutionary world, and are committed to the hilt in the struggle against capitalism to end the exploitation of man by man.[3]

The second article was a reprint of an article which had been published in 1966 in *African Forum Vol. 1, No. 3*, under the title *African Socialism Revisited*. The purpose of this article was 'to show that there is no such thing as African Socialism.' The term had come to be employed as proof of the existence of brands of socialism peculiar to Africa, such as Arab socialism, pragmatic socialism, and this and that socialism, 'when in fact there is only one true socialism: scientific socialism.'[4] Nkrumah held that misused and misleading political terms should be abandoned or defined clearly, and in his own writing maintained the utmost clarity of political expression.

Nkrumah wrote for the ordinary reader, and not for elite groupings of the Left, so many of which indulge in needless theorizing and philosophizing, using political jargon. A schoolboy can read and understand

1. *The Myth of the Third World*, Kwame Nkrumah, Panaf 1968. Full text in *The Struggle Continues*, pp. 74–77.
2. Ibid., p. 74.
3. " p. 76–77.
4. *African Socialism Revisited*, Kwame Nkrumah, 1966. Full text in *The Struggle Continues*, pp. 78–83.

Nkrumah's books. The language is plain. Facts, ideas, policies and so on, are clearly stated; and in many of his books he includes simple charts and diagrams to illustrate the text. As he remarked, 'When I write a sentence it must be as clear as ABC.'

The two most important books he wrote in Conakry, *The Handbook of Revolutionary Warfare* and *Class Struggle in Africa* were both the shortest and contained the most diagrams of all his books. The former, sub-titled 'A guide to the Armed Phase of the African Revolution', and published by Panaf in 1968, is the only book he wrote in note form. He had been working on a manual of guerrilla warfare before the February 1966 coup took place. The manuscript was among his personal papers at Flagstaff House, so was either burnt along with the rest of his books and papers, or was probably handed by the NLC to a Western intelligence organization. One of the first targets of the coup-makers were the freedom-fighter camps which had been set up in Ghana for the organization and training of guerrillas engaged in the various liberation movements of Africa. Freedom fighters and political refugees from South Africa, Rhodesia, Mozambique, Angola, Guinea Bissau, and from other oppressed areas, who had been given sanctuary and training facilities in Ghana, were arrested and imprisoned. Many of them were then deported back to the countries from which they had escaped and where they faced almost certain death. Journalists were shown round the camps, and were told that the existence of the camps was positive proof of Nkrumah's subversive meddling in the internal affairs of other states. The African Affairs Centre and the Bureau of African Affairs were closed down, as were other concerns and organizations of a PanAfrican nature.

The importance of the new *Handbook* lies not only in its practical suggestions for the PanAfrican organizations required for the armed phase of the African Revolution, and the strategy, tactics and techniques of guerrilla warfare, but in the masterly exposition of the political conditions which necessitated the taking up of arms. Under the general heading of 'Know the Enemy' Nkrumah began the *Handbook* with a survey of the world strategy of imperialism, the need for PanAfrican political and military organization, and a summary of the main objectives of the freedom fighters of Africa. These could be summed up as national liberation, continental unification and socialism. 'These three objectives of our struggle stem from our position as people in revolt against exploitation in Africa. These objectives are closely interrelated and one cannot be achieved fully without the other.'[1] He outlined the politico-military organisation required, the formation of an All-African People's Revolutionary Party (AAPRP) and an All-African People's Revolutionary Army (AAPRA), to unify conventional and guerrilla forces to carry the armed struggle through to final victory. Controlling AAPRP and AAPRA there was to be the All-African Committee for Political Co-ordination (AACPC). For Nkrumah, the 'political' was always the supreme authority, guiding and planning policies and taking precedence over the military. The AAPRP, a people's organisation, assisted where necessary by AAPRA, would build the machinery for unification. In other words, a PanAfrican People's Party, and not heads of state and government as envisaged when the OAU was founded, would be the means through which a Union Government of Africa would be con-structed. The Central Committee of the AAPRP would, as its member-ship increased, and as it gradually came to represent the overwhelming majority of the African people, become the de facto unified governing body of Africa. In the conclusion to his last book, *Revolutionary Path*, he again clearly had this in mind when he referred to 'the new leadership which Africa so badly needs', and which might well emerge 'through the guerrilla camps, deep in the forests.'[2] One of the first things he intended to do when he returned to Ghana was to found the AAPRP, and to sum-mon a meeting of leaders of all liberation movements to form a central organization to co-ordinate strategy and tactics. Ghana would have become the secure base, and the powerhouse essential for the successful outcome of their struggle, waged not only against the remnants of colon-ialism and minority regimes but also against neo-colonialist states which were holding up progress. If Africa could not be unified by peaceful means, then it would be unified by the force of the African people themselves organized on a continental basis.

Included in the original MS of the *Handbook* was a section under the title, 'Materials for Destruction.' This contained details of the manu-facture and uses of the plastic bombs, black powder, incendiary bottles, detonators, lighting fuses, and other materials and weapons used at that time by guerrillas. But Nkrumah decided that this information should not be provided until AAPRA had been formed, and then that it should

---

1. *Handbook of Revolutionary Warfare. A Guide to the Armed Phase of the African Revolution*, Kwame Nkrumah, Panaf 1968, p. 24.
2. *Revolutionary Path*, p. 520.

be published as a separate part of the *Handbook* and distributed only to members of the freedom fighter forces. Book Three of the *Handbook*, as published in 1968, therefore, consisted of a brief Preface, under the heading 'Materials for Destruction', to indicate to the reader that there was more to come.

Nkrumah intended, on his return to Ghana, not only to call together representatives of freedom fighter organizations but members of progressive parties throughout Africa, so that a start could be made at once on the building up of the combined politico-military forces. He was also considering the possibility of forming an embryo Union Government of Africa and the providing of 'African citizenship' to members of all parties and movements which supported it. He thought that 'such a government could be established over the Heads of Independent African States.... It will work through its individual citizenship membership.'[1] Its main job would be to work with AAPRA and AAPRP.

In Conakry, Nkrumah gave much thought to the problems of Africa's professional armed forces, an increasing number of which were exercising political power as a result of military coups. Officers of these forces, built up during the colonial period to serve the interests of colonial governments, had neither the mandate nor the qualifications to govern. Nkrumah came to the view that once total liberation and an all-African Union Government had been achieved, professional armed forces should 'vanish completely', leaving the defence of Africa to rest entirely on the continent's people's militia. For in a united Africa, African would not fight African. Nor would Africans wish to attack other nations. The continental people's militia would have a purely defensive role, at times possibly assisting the police in maintaining law and order, but whose main purpose would be to protect the continent from any attack which might come from beyond its shores.

When, late in 1970, Guinea was threatened with imminent invasion from Portuguese Guinea, some units of the Guinean regular army based in Conakry were dispatched up country to help with agricultural work, leaving the defence of the capital largely in the capable, trusted hands of men and women of the people's militia. Like Nkrumah, Sékou Touré did not feel able to rely on the loyalty of professional forces.

As soon as the *Handbook* was completed, Nkrumah set to work on *Class Struggle in Africa*. His main purpose was to examine class structures

---

1. *The Conakry Years*, p. 331.

in African society: 'For the dramatic exposure in recent years of the nature and extent of the class struggle in Africa through the succession of reactionary military coups and the outbreak of civil wars, particularly in West and Central Africa, has demonstrated the unity between the interests of neocolonialism and the indigenous bourgeoisie.'[1] According to Nkrumah, at the core of the problem is class struggle. He sought to destroy myths such as African Socialism and socialism applicable to Africa alone. He states in the Introduction to the book:

> Much of our history has been written in terms of socio-anthropological and historical theories as though Africa has no history prior to the colonial period. One of these distortions has been the suggestion that the class structures which exist in other parts of the world do not exist in Africa.
>
> Nothing is further from the truth. A fierce class struggle has been raging in Africa. The evidence is all around us. In essence it is, as in the rest of the world, a struggle between the oppressors and the oppressed.

It was on the first of June 1969 that Nkrumah wrote: 'I have been thinking seriously of writing a little pamphlet on the class struggle in Africa.' He asked me to obtain books for him on the subject of class struggle in other parts of the world. It was the month when news came of the assassination of Tom Mboya, and of a coup in Sudan which Nkrumah thought was left wing: 'If the operators of the Sudan coup think they are Left Communists then the best thing for them to do is to hand over to the Communist Party of the Sudan to run the show, and they go back to their barracks. Soldiers anywhere have no right to interfere in politics.'[2]

In *Class Struggle in Africa*, Nkrumah analysed the origins of class in Africa. He wrote of communalism, slavery, feudalism, capitalism, socialism, the concept of class, the characteristics and ideologies associated with them. There are chapters entitled, 'Class and Race', 'Elitism', 'Intelligentsia and Intellectuals', 'Peasantry', 'Reactionary Cliques among Armed Forces and Police', and 'Coups d'État', revealing the impossibility of separating the interests of the African bourgeoisie from those of international monopoly finance capital. He listed the twenty-five military

---

1. *Class Struggle in Africa*, Kwame Nkrumah, Panaf 1970, Introduction p. 9.
2. *The Conakry Years*, p. 312.

coups which took place between January 1963 and December 1969, all of which, he asserted, reflected class interests, the close links between reactionary indigenous elites and foreign interests. Nkrumah concluded the book with a call for the total liberation and unification of Africa under an All-African socialist government which would, when achieved, 'bring about the fulfilment of the aspirations of Africans and peoples of African descent everywhere.' The book, only eighty-eight pages long, contains charts and diagrams and is dedicated to 'The workers and peasants of Africa.'

During my visit to Conakry (from 21 November to 9 December 1969) *Class Struggle in Africa* was finished, and typed in Villa Syli. Nkrumah remarked that he considered it the best work he had written in Conakry.

The impact made by the publication of *The Handbook of Revolutionary Warfare* and *Class Struggle in Africa* can be compared to that of *Neo-colonialism: the Last Stage of Imperialism* when it was published in 1965, and which caused such a hostile reaction from the US State Department. These books were published at a time when the international scene was changing from confrontation between the USA and the USSR to a period of détente. The Soviet Ambassador in Conakry now seldom visited Villa Syli, whereas before he had been most attentive, bringing tins of caviar and the occasional bottle of vodka, which Nkrumah used to give away. The Chinese, Cuban, Vietnamese and North Koreans remained steadfastly supportive.

On 24 June, President Kaunda arrived in Guinea. Nkrumah accompanied Sékou Touré to the airport to meet him. Then Nkrumah went with Kaunda on a tour of two regions of the country, Kankan and Labé. The visit was initially marred by an incident as the three presidents drove from Gbessia airport to the centre of Conakry. A man jumped at the car seeming to attack Sékou Touré as he stood with Nkrumah and Kaunda in the open car. Nkrumah elbowed him off. The man fell back into the crowd lining the road. The car continued on its way without stopping, and it was not until later that the three leaders were told that the assailant had been lynched.

Throughout 1968, messages and letters from individuals and organizations continued to flow into Villa Syli, most of them expressing confidence in Nkrumah's return to Ghana. Members of liberation movements throughout Africa continued to keep in touch. Nkrumah's *Africa Day Special Message* compiled in 1968, was addressed specifically to them. He was concerned particularly about the situation in central and

Nkrumah with President K. Kaunda, arriving back in Conakry
after accompanying him on tour of Guinea, 1969

southern Africa, where South Africa, Portugal and Rhodesia were co-operating to crush guerrilla liberation campaigns in their territories.[1] Nkrumah again stated the argument for Africa unity.' No part of Africa is free while any of our national territory remains unliberated.'[2]

At this time, Nkrumah was studying the strategy and tactics of both conventional and guerrilla warfare, concentrating on the experience of the Vietnam war. During the visit of President Julius Nyerere to Guinea in February 1968, Nkrumah told him that if he was not in Ghana by Easter he would go to Tanzania 'and make that my base in order to organise the freedom fighters and guerrillas into one formidable army of African liberation.' Nyerere agreed. But in a letter to me dated 24 February 1968, Nkrumah wrote that he 'could only make Ghana such a base.' He steadfastly maintained that Ghana alone had the necessary infrastructure. he added a postscript to the same letter: 'Today is February 24th, the day when the dark days in Ghana began. Two long years.'

The year 1968 was the most eventful of the whole Conakry period. Nkrumah wrote more during this year than at any other time in his life, completing seven pamphlets and working on two of his most important books, *The Handbook of Revolutionary Warfare* and *Class Struggle in Africa*. It was a year of good health and high hopes.

In the world at large, there was plenty to interest Nkrumah. It was a year which saw the young in revolt against established institutions and values. Battles between students and police on the streets of Paris almost brought down the government of General de Gaulle. Nkrumah was happy about students' actions in Paris and West Germany. 'The future is in the hands of the youth, and they must act now before the stupid old men ruin everything.'[3] In the USA civil rights confrontations reached their peak; as did anti-Vietnam war demonstrations and other protest movements throughout the world. Civil war raged in Nigeria. In Rhodesia the guerrilla war of liberation gained momentum.

There were setbacks too. News came of the murder of Congolese freedom fighter Pierre Mulele. He had been tricked by General Mobutu into returning to Zaire. There was the assassination in the US of civil rights activist Martin Luther King. Nkrumah in a letter to me dated 6th April 1968 wrote: 'Even though I don't agree with him on some of his non-violence views, I mourn for him. The final solution of all this will

---

1. *The Struggle Continues*, p. 15.
2. *Ibid.*, p. 16.
3. *The Conakry Years*, p. 234.

come when Africa is politically united.' Then came the assassination of President Kennedy. Nkrumah liked the Kennedys, having met them during a US visit when they entertained him informally in the family quarters of the White House.

On 12 June 1968, the founding date of the CPP, the Soviet ambassador to Guinea called at Villa Syli to assure him that his government fully expected him to return to Ghana soon, and that 'they will go the whole hog to help me.'[1] However, the months passed without any action in Ghana. While Nkrumah admitted to disappointment he was not discouraged. His morale and that of his entourage remained high.

I visited Conakry on four occasions during 1968, staying weeks at a time working in Nkrumah's office in Villa Syli. Looking back on that year, it is clear that it was the high point of the whole Conakry period. So much was achieved in terms of Nkrumah's writing output. There were still good grounds for optimism about an early return to Ghana. Writing to me on his birthday 21 September, he said, 'All is well. My health is really excellent.'

For Nkrumah, the year 1969 began badly. He had expected a counter-coup in December 1968, but nothing had happened.

Then early in 1969 news came of the arrest of Air Marshal Otu on suspicion of being involved in 'subversive activities.' It seemed as if the now familiar pattern of hopes and disappointments of previous years was to be repeated. Nkrumah wrote to me on 7 January 1969: 'There is a time for everything and it must fit in with the historical conditions, i.e. the concrete situation prevailing. There's not much we can do but wait and be patient.' He was becoming increasingly sceptical of those who approached him with plans for a coup. By the end of the year he severed connections with Ghanaians such as Kwesi Armah and Baidoo-Ansah, having decided to continue only with direct contacts inside Ghana.

In Guinea, in March 1969 there was an attempted coup. The plan was to capture and kill Sékou Touré and his leading ministers as they visited Labé. This was to be followed by an invasion by mercenaries and Guinean dissidents standing by in Mali and Ivory Coast. The plot was revealed, and a wave of arrests followed. I was in Guinea at the time. Nkrumah told me that one of those arrested was a senior army officer, a close friend of Sékou Touré. Nkrumah, having experienced similar betrayal from those he thought he could trust, gave encouragement and

---

1. *The Conakry Years*, p. 240.

support to the Guinean president, urging him not to show leniency. Arrests were still going on in April. 'I went to see Sékou Touré yesterday and he told me that Ghana, Ivory Coast and Mali, consorting with the Intelligence agencies of Germany, America and Britain were behind the plotters. Do these blighters think that even if they get me they will be able to alter the course of the African Revolution?'[1]

During the second half of 1969, Nkrumah was still confident of a return to Ghana. 'A lot is happening in Ghana now. I have three solid projects in the fire.'[2] This was the time of the July 1969 elections in Ghana which Nkrumah regarded as fraudulent and which ushered in the government of Kofi Busia. Mrs A. Mqotsi, the wife of a South African refugee, wrote to Nkrumah on 5 September from Lusaka: 'We are confident that the climbing of the discredited Kofi Busia to power on the shoulders of the army and police traitors and in the wake of a rigged election will not dishearten you ... we who have followed your political career closely and have derived the greatest inspiration and gained wisdom from your writings on the tasks before the African Revolution cannot lose hope in the ultimate triumph of your ideas. The future may look bleak at present, the prospects for the African Revolution may seem dim and dismal, but as they say, the darkest hour is just before the dawn.'[3] Letters such as this which continued to flow in were a great encouragement. The Busia government was established under a constitution devised by a Constitutional Commission, disguising the fact that real power still rested with the military. Furthermore, there was no lifting of the ban on political activity until after the Constituent Assembly had completed its work and the new constitution had been promulgated and imposed on the people of Ghana by the NLC. Many thousands of Ghanaians were banned for ten years from holding public office if they had been CPP office holders or members of the Party's integral wings — The United Farmers Co-operative Council, The Trades Union Congress, the National Union of Ghana Women, the Ghana Young Pioneers Movement, the National Association of Socialist Students' Organization, the League of Ghana Patriots, and the Young Farmers' League. Exemption from the Disqualification Decree could only be obtained if the Exemptions Commission was satisfied that the person was either forced into membership of the CPP or could show that he, or she, was actively opposing the Party while

1. *The Conakry Years*, p. 300.
2. Ibid., p. 323.
3.   "   p. 330.

a member of it. Nkrumah exposed the whole free elections scenario as a fraud in a statement he wrote in 1968 under the title *Civilian Rule Fraud*. He pointed out that talk of free elections was to deceive the people and to discourage resistance. Any result considered to be unfavourable to an army and police regime is declared null and void. He urged the forcible overthrow of the NLC through a mass uprising of the people, or a counter-coup.

The prolonged stay in Guinea and so many disappointments culminating in the installation of the Busia government in Ghana was beginning to affect morale among some members of the entourage. Some chose to return to Ghana, and no attempt was made by Nkrumah to stop them.

However, most of the men had adjusted well to life in Guinea, learning the local language, developing relationships with Guinean women and in some cases, fathering children.

When Nkrumah and his entourage first arrived in Guinea, Nkrumah warned the men against becoming involved with Guinean women, which might lead to friction causing problems for the Guinean government. Apparently, Sékou Touré' also foresaw possible trouble, as he instructed the police to ignore any domestic disorder involving Ghanaians of Nkrumah's entourage. They were to remember that the men were far from home, missing their families, and in the spirit of Pan-Africanism were their brothers.

Nkrumah regarded the time spent in Villa Syli as resembling a guerrillas' period in 'the forest', with all the personal discipline and organization that entailed. However, a book *The Forest*[1] impressed Nkrumah greatly, and as time went on, led to the adoption of a less strict viewpoint, though at no time were women allowed to stay within the Villa Syli compound. The book was a personal record of the Huk guerrilla struggle in the Philippines, written by an American, William Pomeroy, who had become totally committed to the movement. Pomeroy described vividly both the military and personal aspects of the lives of the men and women freedom fighters compelled to spend prolonged periods in the forest, their problems, sacrifices and courage. Nkrumah marked many passages in the book. Among paragraphs underlined is one referring to the 'revolutionary solution of the sex problem.' This was, according to Pomeroy, worked out by the Huks after lengthy discussion during

---

1. By William Pomeroy, International Publishers Inc., New York, 1963.

Nkrumah's Ghanaian entourage — Villa Syli, Conakry, 1966

In the Stadium — Conakry, Guinea 1966.
Second from left, **Camara Sana**, Guinean protocol officer

▲ Nkrumah's Ghanaian entourage demonstrating support for him at Conakry airport, 1967. OAU members had arrived to investigate whether Ghanaians were being held in Guinea against their will

▲ At Conakry airport, 1969 (L to R)Kwame Nkrumah, K. Kaunda, Ahmed Sékou Touré

one of their regular jungle conferences. They decided that extra-marital relationships were permissible 'under our circumstances', and that a man can take a forest wife if it serves the interest of the movement. However, it can only be done with the observance of strict regulations.[1] For example, there was to be no deception or promiscuity. Furthermore, forest relationships would end when it became possible for forest husband and wives to resume 'regular' married life.

Other marked passages which evidently appealed to Nkrumah when he read the book during 1969 are the following:

> Life walks always balanced on the brink of death.... We are all hostages to the great conspiracy of death that is around us. We refuse to lie down and die. How can we die? We are right, and all that we fight is wrong. That is the morality of life to us, and our tenacious reason for living. We are those who, at the fire's centre, plan for the new world to rise out of the ashes. We are a handful of people, hiding in the forest, and our enemies are on all sides of us. They are strong but it is not the strength of endurance ... They can use guns to hold on, but can guns put rice in the mouths of the restless? They talk of reforms, but can they make reforms that would interfere with their profits and their power? They talk of ending corruption, but can they end corruption that is the root and branch of the control of puppets? ... The revolutionary situation remains.... We throw down the gauntlet to the enemy.[2]

All the time he was in Guinea, Nkrumah's life was in danger in spite of strict security measures taken by the Guinean government. The Ghanaian military regimes never ceased to plot against him, doubtless assisted by staffs of Western embassies in Guinea, who were no friends of Nkrumah. Furthermore, the Guinean government was threatened from time to time by opposition elements in touch with Guinean exiles plotting in Paris. Although Camara assured me that Sékou Touré's government was safe while it was host to Nkrumah, nothing could be certain while powerful forces continued to scheme against them. The presence of Cabral in Guinea, and the support given to him by the Guinean government, also heightened tensions in Conakry. However, as events were to show, after Nkrumah's death he was the main target

---

1. *The Forest*, p. 144.
2. Ibid., pp. 134–135.

of hostile attention. Once he was removed, Cabral was assassinated in Conakry soon afterwards. Then came the death in suspicious circumstances of Sékou Touré.' Said to have suffered a heart-attack, he was flown to the USA where he died on the operating table. The funeral of Sékou Touré' in Conakry was barely over before a reactionary military coup took place.

It was towards the end of 1969 that Nkrumah's health noticeably began to deteriorate, leaving him even more dangerously exposed. Until then, he usually appeared to be in reasonable health. But after that, it was quite clear that something was seriously wrong. He rapidly began to lose weight, had frequent unexplained bowel and stomach upsets, recurring back pain and bouts of fever. At various times, Guinean, Russian, Vietnamese and Chinese doctors attended him. But the downward trend continued.

One of my arrivals in Guinea is more indelibly imprinted on my mind than any other because it marked a turning point. Instead of the usual elation at once again visiting Guinea, I felt an awful sadness and sense of foreboding. It was November 1969. We were on the approach to Conakry airport. Rain was streaming down the aircraft windows. It was only afternoon but the cabin lights had been switched on as the dark storm gathered strength. I strained to catch the first glimpse of Villa Syli. I always sat on the left side of the plane so that I would see the coast of Guinea as soon as it appeared and then Villa Syli as we came in from the sea on the final approach. The torrential rain was whipping up the sea into millions of white plumes. Then I saw Nkrumah, all in white, standing alone under the shelter of the Villa verandah. The plane banked sharply and in a flash he was gone. It seemed symbolic.

Camara was there at the aircraft steps, his mackintosh almost touching the ground, and holding an umbrella. The rain was still beating down. The walk from the plane to the terminal building was more of a paddle. The drive to the Villa was through water several inches deep. The huge concrete gutters on each side of the road were flooded. Hooded, barefoot people clothed in ankle-length grey, transparent raincoats looked like spectres with the rain streaming off them.

As soon as I saw Nkrumah I knew that all was not well. He was troubled-looking, so unlike his usual self. Apparently, he had been watching the aircraft approach through the storm and thought it might crash into the sea. We passengers also thought it highly likely, the way the plane was buffeted about as it descended lower towards the sea. The landing at Gbessia airport in the midst of the storm was the worst I had experienced. We learned afterwards that the pilot considered giving up the attempt to land in Conakry, proceeding instead to Abidjan. Because of the weather and the conditions of the aircraft, the decision was made not to proceed to Ivory Coast until the following day.

Though Nkrumah was reluctant to consider leaving Guinea for medical treatment abroad lest it should discourage the Ghanaian people, on two occasions, in 1969 and 1970, he asked the Russian ambassador to enquire if he could go to the Soviet Union for a check-up. In 1969, he suffered severe back pain. I thought he might have slipped a disc, but the Russian doctor said it was acute lumbago due to the rainy season. He administered pain-killing injections. The response to Nkrumah's request for medical help in 1970, was to send two specialists to Conakry to examine him. They advised that there was no cause for concern, and that it was politically an 'inopportune' time for him to leave Guinea.

I was not in Conakry when the specialists arrived, but Nkrumah wrote the day they left to tell me the outcome of their visit. While he was glad they had found nothing seriously wrong with him, he was disappointed that they did not seem to understand that he 'needed a change.' Whether or not on the specialists' advice I do not know, but there followed a course of injections administered by a Bulgarian doctor. The nature of the injections is unclear, but in 1971 when Nkrumah was in hospital in Bucharest, the consultant there told me that he had been given the 'exact opposite' of the treatment he required, causing whatever he suffered from — they would not give it a name — to 'spread to his whole body.' Nkrumah's son Francis, a highly-qualified doctor, told me when I visited Ghana briefly in 1972, that there was 'inexplicable medical bungling in Guinea.'

It seems inconceivable that the Russian specialists did not know that Nkrumah was seriously ill when they examined him in 1970. I suspect they did not want to offend the Busia regime in Ghana by inviting Nkrumah to the Soviet Union. The Russians had recently reopened their embassy in Accra. At that time they probably did not want him to return to power in Ghana. They disapproved of the *Handbook*, and his ideas on the need for armed struggle. For some time, even before 1966, they were concerned about what they saw as Nkrumah's leaning towards the Chinese and Vietnamese. There was much tension then between the Soviet Union and China.

Significantly, during the last weeks of 1969, Nkrumah instructed a lawyer to draw up a will to safeguard the future of his books. He appointed me sole executor, leaving me his copyright and all his books and papers, published and unpublished. This will was signed and witnessed in Villa Syli on 21 January 1970.[1] His actions indicated some doubt as to whether he would in fact ever return to Ghana. For he had, until then, left non-urgent matters to be dealt with when he was back in Accra.

It was at this time that I began to record more about Nkrumah's health in my notebooks. I noted the decline in physical activity, the longer periods of brooding quiet. The eyes, which still became concentrated and sharp in a flash, had developed a kind of sadness, a deeply meditative quality. Whereas he had formerly seldom sat for long without some kind of activity, reading, writing, searching rapidly through newspapers, he would now stare into the far distance, not dozing or closing his eyes, but sometimes sucking into his teeth as the pondered something. The small vein on his left temple had become more pronounced now that he was thinner, its throb more evident.

At these times I would sit beside him. It was usually on the terrace outside his office, or under the trees in the Villa garden. Each morning, two armchairs and a small table would be carried from the Villa and placed side by side. We would do quite a lot of work there as well as chatting and reading.

When we were there, Nkrumah could see more of the life of his entourage. He enjoyed watching them carrying out their daily tasks, often calling them over to enquire how they were getting on. He noticed if anyone was limping or seemed otherwise unwell. He would question them about their health, ask if they were taking their paludrine and so on. From where we sat he could also see when the heavily-guarded gates of the Villa were opened, noting who entered and left. I remember when he called for a car to be stopped being uncertain about the occupants. He smiled and said 'here I am my own security.'

Occasionally, he would watch intently insects, a lizard doing pressups, a butterfly, a moth or some other creature. Their behaviour interested him. I remember being surprised one day when a lizard nearby was poised ready to lick up a praying mantis. I had wanted to save the insect, but with a restraining touch of his arm he motioned me not to

---

1. In a previous will, drawn up in Ghana before Nkrumah left on the Hanoi peace mission in February 1966, he left all to the Party (CPP) asking only that the Party take care of his wife and children.

interfere with nature. His interest in animals and all forms of wild life was without affectation or sentimentality. However small or grand the creature, if it was in its natural state, he loved to see it.

There was a day when bees swarmed inside the cabinet of an old radiogram in the Villa. Camara and members of Nkrumah's entourage wanted to destroy them but he would not have them touched. He enjoyed observing them, declaring that they would make honey. Then there was a day when two of his entourage returned from fishing with a large turtle which they presented to Nkrumah, expecting him to give it to the cook for making soup. Nkrumah instructed them to place it in the small pool on the lower verandah, where it would live until his return to Ghana, when it was to be returned to the sea. He used to feed the turtle and check frequently that it had fresh sea water.

By the time of my visit from 24 July to 4 August 1970, Nkrumah's health and conditions at the Villa had worsened. There was an unfamiliar melancholy about the place, a menacing heaviness so unlike the Villa Syli of previous years. It was the rainy season, which made the general running-down process even more depressing. The electric generator no longer worked and could not be repaired. Villa Syli therefore was plunged into darkness during the frequent electricity power cuts. The air-conditioning in Nkrumah's bedroom had failed. He had to open his windows and sleep under a mosquito net. A bucket was placed in his bathroom to catch drops from a leaking roof. These and other inconveniences did not trouble Nkrumah. But the lack of maintenance on the buildings and furniture of the Villa could only have had an adverse effect on general morale. It surprised me that Camara did not do more to see that standards were maintained, though probably Nkrumah did not allow him to take action. The Guinean government was faced with enough internal and external pressures. The economic situation was difficult, but it was the threat of an armed invasion of Guinea, suspected to be timed to coincide with a domestic uprising to overthrow Sékou Toure's government which caused the most concern. There were reports of mercenaries assembling in neighbouring countries. A plot was discovered in Conakry which implicated a senior army officer, a trusted friend of Sékou Touré. A wave of arrests was followed by a tightening of security throughout the country and at Villa Syli. Bodies of the traitors were left for days hanging from a bridge in the centre of Conakry. Meantime, the Western media kept up a vicious campaign against Sékou Touré, accusing him of economic mismanagement, dictatorship

Nkrumah with the author — Villa Syli, 1970

and the barbaric treatment of political prisoners. It was reminiscent of the campaign launched against Nkrumah in the months leading up to the 1966 coup.

There were reports of trouble between Sékou Touré' and Nkrumah. A British newspaper spread a rumour that Nkrumah had been banished to an off-shore island. It was even said that Sékou Touré had congratulated Busia on winning the July 1969 election in Ghana.

In the growing tensions regarding the situation in Guinea, and the lack of progress towards a return of Nkrumah to Ghana, work continued in Villa Syli on two more books, *Rhodesia: A Case Study of Settler Politics*, and *Revolutionary Path*, a compilation of key writings and statements marking the course of Nkrumah's political struggle.

On what proved to be my last visit to Conakry, from 24 July to 4 August 1970, Nkrumah encouraged me to expand my notebook entries to include for example a full description of Villa June, which he said I might not see again. In addition, he wanted me to note details of Villa Syli. But most unexpected was a day when he asked me to witness, through the keyhole of his bedroom door, a meeting with two army men who said they intended to stir up trouble in Accra to set the ball rolling for a counter-coup. He did not tell me their names, or even if they were Ghanaian. I think he just wanted me to witness at first hand a typical encounter with such men. There had been so many similar occasions that no account of the years in Villa Syli would be complete without a description of one of them.

At that time, the situation was pretty desperate. Nkrumah was suffering terribly with what the Russian doctor had diagnosed as acute lumbago. He could hardly walk. I had helped him to dress, holding his clothes for him and putting on his socks and shoes. He stood erect, but with the bearing not of the physically fit, but of the person who cannot bend without intense pain. He did not want the soldiers to see how incapacitated he was. But he knew he could not conceal from them the fact that he had difficulty walking. So he emerged from his room keeping very erect, but taking short steps.

As I peered through the keyhole I saw the men ushered in by Camara, who then quickly withdrew. They were tall, tough-looking men, one of them bearded. Nkrumah stood stock still, smiling and extending his hand to greet them. The soldiers looked as though they had been hit between the temples. This did not surprise me. I had often seen this initial impact on people meeting Nkrumah for the first time. They shook hands.

Then Nkrumah raised the stick he was carrying and said: 'You see. I have a stick. I have some small trouble with lumbago!' The men grinned nervously. Nkrumah pointed to the chairs. 'Why don't you sit down?.'

He painfully walked to the nearest chair and sat on the edge of it, his back unbending. They were some distance away at the far end of the long sitting room. I did not hear any more that was said. But the whole scene appeared so dreadful that I felt choked. The very chairs they sat in showed the deterioration since 1966. The stuffing was sticking out through the frayed and faded covers. There was only one electric light bulb which worked. Yet there was Nkrumah, nothing like the superbly fit man he had been in 1966, but battling on with all the dignity and quiet confidence of the truly great. It all lasted less than fifteen minutes. Nkrumah stood to see them leave. Then he returned to his room. He looked drained.

The first ten months of 1970 were, however, far from being entirely negative. Nkrumah was devoting a lot of time to the compilation of his last book *Revolutionary Path*, work on which had began in 1969. It was to be a single volume containing key documents relating to the development of his political thought, which would at the same time illustrate landmarks in his life as leading theorist and activist of the African Revolution. These were to be prefaced by introductory passages. The book was well on the way to completion when Nkrumah had to leave Guinea, in August 1971, for medical treatment in Bucharest. He did not live to see the printed book. It was published by Panaf in 1973.

Another positive achievement in 1970 was the publication of *Class Struggle in Africa*, copies of which reached Villa Syli a few months before the November invasion of Guinea. Publication could not have been more timely. The validity of the analyses and conclusions reached in this book as well as in the *Handbook* were clearly demonstrated. No progressive African state was safe while the continent of Africa remained disunited and without effective unified political, economic and military structures.

The 1970 invasion of Guinea began during the pre-dawn hours of 22 November when mercenaries disembarked from Portuguese warships. A mist rising off the sea, common in Guinea during November, gave cover to the invaders who managed to get ashore and to establish bridgeheads. Their first target was the military barracks close to the presidential palace in the centre of Conakry, the presidential palace itself, and the airport. Belle Vue, a government guest house in which Nkrumah had

252 KWAME NKRUMAH, A BIOGRAPHY

spent the first few weeks of his stay in Guinea, was attacked and heavily damaged. Whether it was thought that Nkrumah still resided there is not known, but there was little point in attacking it unless the intention was to kill Nkrumah, since Sékou Touré did not live there, and there was no government guest staying in Belle Vue when the attack took place. Cabral's house in Conakry was similarly attacked. But he was out of the country.

While wave after wave of mercenaries fought their way ashore meeting fierce resistance from the Guineans, Portuguese warships shelled Conakry in an attempt to break the morale of the people. It had the reverse effect. Members of the people's militia, prepared and trained for just such an emergency, went into action. The invaders were prevented from reaching Sékou Touré's residence, and they also failed to occupy the radio station or the airport. These were key targets, and their failure to take them during the initial stages of the invasion reflects great credit on the people's militia who had quickly contained the attacks. Sékou Touré was able to broadcast to the people, calling on them to continue to rise up and crush the invaders. He warned the people of Guinea to beware of traitors inside the country.

When the first waves of mercenaries landed on the soil of Guinea, Nkrumah, having woken at the noise of gunfire, was quickly in touch with Sékou Touré by telephone. Sékou Touré instructed him to make no attempt to join him at the Presidential Palace, but to go immediately to the North Korean Embassy, a building close to Villa Syli which could be reached within a few minutes. At the time, fighting was taking place at the airport, just a mile or so along the coast from Villa Syli, and also in the streets between the Villa and the centre of Conakry. The Guinean security forces and the Ghanaians of Nkrumah's entourage took up combat positions and prepared to defend the Villa and the Korean Embassy. All through the night of the 22nd the noise of battle continued, and for a time Nkrumah was out of direct touch with Sékou Touré and dependent for news on the broadcast announcements from Guinea radio. He remained in the Korean Embassy until daylight, and then returned to Villa Syli.

The local support in Guinea which the invaders expected did not materialize. By mid-evening of the 22nd, the people of Guinea were fully mobilized to resist them. At 22.30 hours, Guinea radio announced that all strategic points in the capital were under effective control of the people.

That night, there was a further attack from the sea, and fighting continued in and around Conakry throughout the following day and night. The new landings were designed not to consolidate the aggression but to secure the retreat of pockets of mercenaries which were still able to resist the attacks of the Guinea forces. Finally, the Portuguese warships left Guinean waters and the remnant forces still left behind in Guinea were forced to surrender. Then there began the more protracted task of discovering and dealing with the local quislings who had for some time been engaged in economic sabotage in an attempt to stir up discontent.

Although suffering from acute back pain, Nkrumah accompanied Sékou Touré when the saboteurs were brought to court. They were shocked to discover during the trials that some of the prisoners had occupied key posts in the military and state apparatus. Nkrumah recognized in them the same kind of people who had supported the 24 February 1966 coup in Ghana. Among those judged guilty were seventeen government ministers, eight provincial governors, twenty members of the armed forces, forty high-level bureaucrats, fifteen political heads at various levels and seven foreigners residing in Guinea.

Documents relating to the invasion and to the attempt to bring down the PDG government of Guinea were officially published in Guinea in 1971 under the title *L'Agression Portugaise contre La République de Guinée*. Sékou Touré presented Nkurumah with a copy of the book, and wrote on the title page the following words: 'A mon ami et cher frére President K. Nkrumah — avec l'assurance de ma fidéle amitié révolutionnaire au service de la Patrie Africaine, Ahmed Sékou Touré 18-1-71'. The book ends with six political poems written by Sékou Touré, the final two under the title, *La 5ème Colome*, and *Adieu les Traitres*.

Nkrumah's health was so bad by the beginning of 1971 that doctors in Conakry, Sékou Touré and his ministers, and members of his entourage all implored him to leave at once for medical treatment overseas. For over a year I had also been pressing him to go. Convinced that he would soon return to Ghana, and that his condition was not serious, Nkrumah refused to leave Guinea. When at length, in August 1971, he was finally compelled to go, he was so incapacitated that he had to be carried on a stretcher into the curtained-off front section of the Aeroflot plane which was to take him for medical attention in Bucharest.

15

In Bucharest

Three Ghanaians of Nkrumah's entourage and
Camara Sana the Guinean protocol officer accompanied Nkrumah on the flight to Romania. The
Ghanaians were J.K. Ampah, a senior trade unionist
who had joined Nkrumah in Conakry, B.E. Quarm, a
bodyguard and personal attendant; and Nkrumah's
nephew Nyamikeh. In Bucharest, Nkrumah was
admitted to the Sanatorial de Gériatrie where Dr
Asland, a woman physician, worked. Dr Asland had
visited Ghana and impressed Nkrumah with her
knowledge of the latest medical treatments.

The move to Bucharest was kept so secret that for
a time few of those who had regularly kept in touch
with Nkrumah knew that he had left Guinea. However, reports that he was seriously ill had been pub-
licized in various newspapers throughout the world.
The UK *Daily Express* reported he had cancer. Messages of concern began to arrive in Villa Syli. These
were followed in September 1971 by birthday greetings. Both Hanna Reitsch and Douglas Rogers sent
birthday messages to Conakry, not knowing that he
was no longer there, and disbelieving media reports
which had so often in the past proved to be incorrect.

Plans had been made for me to visit Guinea in
March 1971. But shortly before I was due to leave, a
cable arrived from Nkrumah telling me to postpone the
visit. No reason was given but I feared it was because
he was very ill. I had not been to Guinea since the
1970 invasion. First, there was a cholera outbreak in

Conakry, followed by months during which the situation in Guinea in the aftermath of the invasion was such that Nkrumah decided I should not go until the trials of the traitors were over. These did not begin until January 1971. After that, Nkrumah's health rapidly worsened. I did not see him again, until as a result of a telephone call from him on 17 August 1971, he asked me to be ready to travel. I knew from the call that he was no longer in Guinea, though he did not say where he was. I assumed he must be in the Soviet Union, since that was where he originally wanted to go for a medical check-up. It was not until several weeks later that Nkrumah phoned again. This time I learned that he was in Bucharest. He gave me the address of a Party Central Committee guest house[1] in the city where I was to stay. He asked me to bring a typewriter, chocolate, biscuits, books and toiletries. From this, I thought he must be feeling better, but my hopes were short-lived. He added 'June, we must be courageous. I am not as you remember me.' I knew then that he was in deep trouble.

I found him in a VIP suite on the first floor of the Sanatorial de Geriatrie, situated in a beautiful park in Bucharest. He was sitting in an armchair, strangely with his back to windows which looked out on to a garden filled with dahlias and roses. He had been sitting there for over six weeks, it being too painful to lie in bed. His weight had dropped to under nine stone, though he looked even frailer. His legs and feet were terribly swollen from prolonged sitting. Only regular injections relieved his pain. He told me he had 'passed through hell' during the last few months. He was neither reading nor writing, and did not wish to watch TV or listen to the radio. I stayed to have a light supper with him of chicken and yoghurt. Nkrumah ate with no enthusiasm. As I left, he told me to be vigilant while in Bucharest as he could not protect me there. The agony of powerlessness, suffered since 1966, was more intense with his failing health.

Although prepared to find him changed, I was totally unprepared for the shock of seeing his condition. Quarm, Ampah and Nyamikeh were anxious I should talk to Dr Maderjac, the physician then attending Nkrumah, to find out if possible the true nature of his illness and to see if something more could be done to cure him. Camara arranged for me to see him the next day. But the meeting did nothing to relieve our anxiety. Dr Maderjac drew a sketch of a spine and spoke of 'arthrosis.'

1. Str. 6 Tolstoy N.22–24 Sector Uli, Bucharest.

There was a language difficulty which Camara did his best to overcome, but without much success. At one point I asked the straight questions, 'Is it cancer?. And if so, can you cure him?.' Dr Maderjac made a despairing gesture, asking surprisingly in English, 'Why does everyone always talk of cancer?'. He avoided the first question, but said that doctors never say that a cure is impossible. He added that if Nkrumah had been in his care two years earlier a simple operation could have cured him. But that in Guinea he had received the wrong injections and the trouble had spread to the rest of his body. He begged me not to let Nkrumah see that I was worried.

During the days which followed, Nkrumah talked about Panaf. He spoke about *Revolutionary Path*, mentioning the urgent need to draft a Conclusion. Between interruptions for medical attention he told me what he wanted to write. I made notes, as far as possible word for word, and the following day read the draft to him. He said it was all right, then after a pause, 'I could add more, but not now.' A nurse gave him a pain-killing injection, and he dozed. He did not refer to the subject again, and I did not feel I could ask him for more.

Camara and Ampah agreed with me that further medical advice must be sought urgently. Nkrumah allowed Camara to summon the Guinean Ambassador in Rome, Seydou Keita, in the hope that he might be able to arrange for a Swiss specialist to examine him. At the same time, it was arranged for me to return to London to see if Dr Stokes, chief physician at University College Hospital, would go to Bucharest to assess the situation. Dr Stokes knew Nkrumah's medical history. Not only had he been involved in the foundation of the Ghana Medical School, but he had on several occasions medically examined Nkrumah when he attended Commonwealth Conferences in London.

On returning to London I went at once to see Dr Stokes. He was distressed to hear about Nkrumah's illness, expressing the view that from what I had told him, he probably had cancer of the spine which had spread from the prostate, and into his blood, resulting in leukaemia. If that was the case, it was incurable, and Nkrumah would probably only live for another six months. He was shocked to hear that Nkrumah had been sitting in a chair for so long, and was in such pain. He said that he would certainly visit him as soon as possible in Bucharest. If Nkrumah agreed, he would arrange for him to be admitted to University College Hospital in London where he could attend him, and where he could be made more comfortable. If Nkrumah did not want to be in England then he would be able to arrange for him to enter a clinic in Switzerland where he would have the same standard of care.

Dr Stokes was ready to travel when I received a cable 'INFORM DR STOKES POSTPONE UNTIL HE HEARS FROM ME. STOP CAMARA.' I assumed that Seydon Keita had made arrangements with a Swiss specialist. But my hopes were soon dashed when Camara informed me that Nkrumah had been moved to the Central Committee Hospital in Bucharest where he had undergone an operation. Camara reported that Nkrumah was 'progressing slowly', and hoped to able soon to return to the Sanatorial. Four days later, came a typed[1] note from Nkrumah to say that he had had an operation on 2 November, that he was improving, and would ask me to go to see him as soon as he was moving about. I was told later that the operation was to help relieve the pain.

During those terrible months in Bucharest, from August 1971 to April 1972, the name 'Diallo' was, for security reasons, adopted in place of 'Nkrumah' for communication purposes. It was a name, I think, chosen by Camara, who was then our channel of contact. On 8 December 1971, Camara wrote 'As regards Mr Diallo, he is improving, but the Docs have found it necessary to give him a series of blood transfusions. However, I think the situation is not so desperate.[2] His letter increased my anxiety. I wanted to go to Bucharest at once. But it was not until 4 January 1972 that at last the cable I awaited, arrived, 'DIALLO WISHES TO SEE YOU.' I cabled back immediately that I was ready to travel. Camara specified 17 January.

Camara was at the airport to meet me and to accompany me to the Central Committee Hospital to see Nkrumah. He was alone in a ward containing three beds. He was in the central one. There was a small passageway leading from the ward to another room in which there were also three beds. Nyamikeh and Quarm lived there, on constant duty day and night, with no time off. The devotion and endurance of these two men was total. They had never left Nkrumah's side since he went to Bucharest in August 1971. I never once saw them leave the hospital or the room they occupied next to Nkrumah. They dressed all the time in pyjamas, their underclothes underneath, sandals on their feet. On top they wore thin, wool dressing-gowns provided by the hospital.

----

1. W. Sarfoh, Personal Private Secretary to Nkrumah in Villa Syli, had arrived in Bucharest. Nkrumah had sent for him when he thought he might be able to resume work on his books and correspondence.
2. *The Conakry Years*, p. 409.

The whole atmosphere of the hospital was cold-looking and grim. All was white. There were no curtains, flowers or colour anywhere. Visitors were compelled to put on ankle-length white gowns on entering the hospital, and to wear them all the time. The alienation from everything to which Nkrumah and the Ghanaians were accustomed was emphasized by the foreign-speaking doctors and nurses, who were caring but seldom smiled.

A few days before my visit a change had taken place in Ghana. On 13 January 1972, while Kofi Busia was on a visit to Britain, his government was overthrown in a military coup led by General I. K. Acheampong. Ampah assured Nkrumah that the coup was in his favour. However, Nkrumah had reservations. He asked if they had sent for him. Sadly, Ampah had to tell him that no message had come.

At the time, Nkrumah wanted above all to return to Ghana, not for reinstatement in any political role. He was far too ill for that. But just to be on Ghanaian soil and to see his mother once more. She was then in her nineties and in very poor health.

On two occasions in 1971, Sékou Touré had sent envoys to Accra to try to persuade the Busia government to allow Nkrumah to return. But no invitation was sent to Nkrumah. It seemed incomprehensible to me that the urgent appeals of the Guinean government could have been treated with such disregard. Nkrumah was clearly a dying man who would have posed no threat to the regime in Ghana, but who simply wanted to return to the land of his birth, the country which owed its independence to him.

Not long after Acheampong seized power, Kojo Botsio went to Bucharest hoping to see Nkrumah. But Nkrumah did not wish to see anyone while he was so ill. However, Botsio arranged for his wife Ruth to travel to Accra to try to persuade Acheampong to allow Nkrumah to return to Ghana. As a result, Acheampong sent Nkrumah's son Dr Francis Nkrumah to Bucharest to assess the situation. It was the first time that Francis had been to see his father since the 1966 coup. To Camara's surprise and dismay his visit was very brief. He apparently reported back to Acheampong that his father was unfit to travel, for no action was taken.

It was clear during my January 1972 visit to Bucharest that Nkrumah could not live much longer. Yet he still talked of returning to Ghana, not to lead the Party though possibly to be chairman of the Central Committee. He had then had two pain-killing operations and at times needed oxygen to relieve coughing spasms. I showed him the 1972 Panaf book list. He asked me to read it to him. For brief periods he seemed almost his old self in spirit. The day after my departure, Madame Sékou Touré and Madame Camara were scheduled to arrive to see him.

Between the second and my final visit to Bucharest I travelled, as Nkrumah wished, to East Africa. It was on Panaf business, a trip to try to drum up sales of Nkrumah's books in Kenya, Tanzania and Zambia. This had been planned some months before, but I kept postponing because of Nkrumah's health. However, when it was clear that no move could be expected from Ghana, I thought it imperative to see if either President Julius Nyerere of Tanzania or President Kenneth Kaunda of Zambia could help. One of them would, I hoped, invite him to spend the limited time left to him in their country when they knew how critically ill he was. As old friends who shared Nkrumah's PanAfrican objectives, this seemed the only chance left of fulfilling Nkrumah's longing to be once more on African soil.

I did not tell Nkrumah that I would seek their help, as I thought he might try to dissuade me, or even forbid me to make the attempt. He told me that he had often wished he could see more of East Africa, particularly when he was in Addis Ababa. But there had never been time. He hoped I would be able to promote Panaf titles and to see the Victoria Falls, a spectacle he hoped to see himself one day. I could take photographs and show them to him on my return.

Both Nyerere and Kaunda were deeply distressed to hear about Nkrumah's illness. Nyerere assured me that he would contact his envoy in Bucharest. He said it would be a great honour to have Nkrumah in Tanzania. I never heard whether an invitation was sent. There was no mention of one when, in April 1972, I saw Nkrumah again.

Kaunda seemed even more concerned about Nkrumah's condition, though he gave no assurance that an invitation would be sent. He said that a PanAfrican Centre should be founded where students could study Nkrumaism. I left his presence optimistic that at last something positive might be done to make it possible for Nkrumah to end his days on African soil. I like to think that both presidents made enquiries through their envoys in Bucharest as to whether Nkrumah was in any condition to travel. But I never heard that any message was sent to him by either president.

I spent only two weeks in East Africa. On my return to London I hoped to proceed at once to Bucharest. But once again cables arrived telling me to postpone. Clearly, Nkrumah's health had worsened. Camara cabled me on 15 December 1971, DISPATCH URGENTLY BY AIR TWO DOZEN FORTRAL. Fortral is a powerful pain-killing drug which was unobtainable then in Romania. I had difficulty in getting a supply as it was strictly on prescription only. I managed to persuade my doctor to write a prescription, though he was reluctant to do so. I did not reveal to him who the Fortral was for. I said it was for a friend who was seriously ill and in great pain in a country in Eastern Europe.

On 28 February 1972, Camara again cabled me. This time the message read: PLEASE PROCEED WITH FUNERAL DRESS AND SOME MONEY THE PRESENT STATE VERY DESPERATE STOP PARCEL AND LETTER RECEIVED GREETINGS. This cable was quickly followed by yet another telling me to postpone. Then came another, requesting a further supply of Fortral. This time my doctor refused to write another prescription. Fortunately, Kojo Botsio was in London. I contacted him and he said he would be able to obtain a supply and would despatch it urgently to Bucharest.

Eventually, a two-word cable arrived from Camara. PROCEED GREETINGS. As I quickly began to pack, yet another cable came the same day: DIALLO WISHES VISIT POSTPONED WILL INFORM NEW DATE. Worried and frustrated, there was nothing I could do but await further instructions.

It was not until 25 April that I was finally allowed to go. By then, Nkrumah had less than two days to live. The precious time I could spend at his bedside was constantly interrupted by nurses either injecting him or positioning glucose drips mixed with pain-killing drugs. Nkrumah spoke little, dozing off from time to time. I held his hand so that he knew I was there.

On the night of my arrival, Nkrumah managed to say a few words to me. According to Quarm he had not spoken or eaten for several days. He had difficulty swallowing and was heavily sedated. I told him about my East African trip and particularly about the Victoria Falls. If he had heard he made no sign. His eyes were shut and he seemed to be dozing. When I stopped speaking he suddenly opened his eyes and asked if I was hungry. He asked me to massage his legs. They were like sticks, though his feet and ankles were terribly swollen. A nurse came to administer another injection and he slept.

The following day when I arrived at the hospital a drip-feed was in operation and the doctor said that Nkrumah was under sedation and must not be disturbed. I waited by the telephone in my room at the Tolstoy guest house but no call came until the evening when I was told I could not visit as he was sleeping.

The end came the next morning at 8.45 a.m. on 27 April 1972. 'The Greatest African', the words which Sékou Touré ordered to be inscribed on his coffin, had died in a foreign land, his dearest wish to return to Africa having been denied him. The memory of the tragic circumstances of his death, in an austere hospital, a chill wind blowing outside, can never be forgotten. Nevertheless, for those who knew and were devoted to him, for PanAfricanists, and for Ghanaians in particular, 'Kwame Nkrumah never dies.'

16

Return to Africa

On 30 April 1972, three days after his death, Kwame Nkrumah returned to Africa. The Guinean government had arranged for his body to be preserved, placed in a special coffin, and flown to Conakry. In a sense Nkrumah had never left Africa. For by then, the spirit of Nkrumaism had spread throughout the continent, the diaspora and among people of the so called Third World.

For two whole days, on 13 and 14 May 1972, the people of Guinea, representatives of liberation movements, governments, progressive parties, trade unions, organizations of women, youth and so on, as well as a small delegation sent by the NRC paid tribute to Kwame Nkrumah in a series of funeral ceremonies. Most of the day of the 13th was taken up with a symposium held in the Palais du Peuple in Conakry, when speeches were made by the heads of the various delegations representing governments and peoples all over the world. It was at this symposium that Cabral declared:

> 'Kwame Nkrumah will live again each dawn in the hearts and in the determination of freedom fighters, and in the actions of all true African patriots. The immortal spirit of Kwame Nkrumah will be predominant when historians assess this decisive phase in the life of our peoples, in the struggle to the death against imperialist domination for the true progress of our

continent ... For us, the best homage we Africans can render to the immortal memory of Kwame Nkrumah is to strengthen vigilance at all levels of the struggle, to intensify it, and to liberate the whole of Africa. To succeed in the development of the economic, social and cultural progress of our peoples, and in the building of African unity; this was the fundamental objective of the actions and thought of Kwame Nkrumah; it is a vow to achieve this objective that we must all take before history and the African continent ... We are sure, absolutely sure, that surrounded by the eternal green of the African forests, flowers as red as the blood of martyrs, and yellow as the harvests of plenty, will grow on the grave of Kwame Nkrumah. For Africans will be victorious.'

In his speech to the nation, Sékou Touré said:

'Kwame Nkrumah was one of the men who mark the destiny of mankind fighting for freedom and dignity. Kwame Nkrumah lives and will forever because Africa, which is grateful to him, will live forever. The combatants of all races and colours, fighting for the independence and solidarity of all the nations of the world, will continue to live and fight for Kwame Nkrumah's ideals.'

At a mass rally in the stadium, units of the Guinean armed forces, people's militia, workers brigades, youth and women's organizations, marched past a white gun-carriage covered in flowers and draped with the Guinean flag, which bore the coffin of Nkrumah. Marching in the procession were the Ghanaians of Nkrumah's entourage[1] who had loyally remained with him at Villa Syli. They, as always when they appeared in public in Conakry, received a specially loud cheer from the crowds. The gun carriage then conveyed the coffin to a mausoleum in a park in central Conakry, where it was placed beside the tombs of Guinea's national heroes.

---

1. There were then forty-five members of the entourage who had remained loyally at Villa Syli and who had accompanied the coffin of Nkrumah when it was conveyed to Ghana following an Agreement between the Guinean and Ghanaian governments. The Roll of Honour (Appendix One) naming these men was printed in the Ghanaian newspaper *Weekly Insight* dated 22–28 November 1995. The name Boye Moses, Senior Security Officer, did not appear (it is added here for completion of record) though he would certainly have remained with Nkrumah to the end if he had not been captured and imprisoned by the NLC while on a secret mission for Nkrumah during the early part of the Conakry period.

The state funeral of Nkrumah in the stadium
— Conakry, Guinea, 14 May 1972

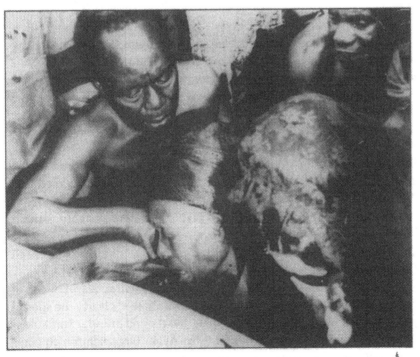

Nkrumah's mother clasping her son's coffin
at the funeral in his birthplace — Nkroful, July 1972

There it remained until 7 July 1972, when after weeks of negotiations between the Guinean government and General Acheampong's National Redemption Council, it was flown to Accra on board an Air Guinée aircraft. The Guinean government did not then anticipate that the Ghanaian government would fail to honour the Guinean conditions for the flight:

To:

1. Proclaim President Kwame Nkrumah as legitimate President of the Republic of Ghana who died outside the country, and rehabilitate the political and historic work of the great departed and his struggle for Ghana's liberation and the emancipation and unity of the African peoples.

2. Release all his comrades-in arms being detained in Ghana.

3. Lift the ban forbidding his comrades-in-arms from returning to Ghana.

4. Receive his body with all the honours due to a Head of State and accord him a funeral worthy of his gigantic work in the service of all just causes.

Sékou Touré had earlier declared that he would not oppose the return of Nkrumah's body to Ghana provided that 'the remains of the illustrious departed are received 'in dignity and rehabilitation.'

In Ghana, General Acheampong headed a long queue of people who filed past the coffin at the lying-in-state at State House. He and other members of the NRC were also present at a memorial service held in Accra. Flags flew at half mast until 6 p.m. on Sunday, 9 July. On that day, the coffin was taken to Nkroful. There it was placed in a tomb on the site of the dwelling in which Nkrumah was born. It was claimed that Nkrumah wished to be buried in Nkroful, though there is no evidence to support this claim. The family in Nkroful understandably wanted him to be laid to rest there. Furthermore, that arrangement suited the Acheampong government, as well as successive regimes which felt threatened by a revival of Nkrumaism.

Over a year after Nkrumah's death, representatives of most of the liberation movements of southern Africa showed clearly the special place occupied by Nkrumah in their hearts and minds. In Dar-es-Salaam, a film show given by the Afro-Asian Organization to commemorate the fifteen years of its existence included pictures of leaders from Lenin to Nasser, Mondlane, Nehru and Cabral. Living leaders like Sékou Touré were also shown. These were greeted with clapping. But when the picture of Nkrumah appeared, the freedom fighters spontaneously rose to their feet, and there was prolonged clapping and cheering. This was a rare tribute to a great leader who was no more with them.

Years later, at the Seventh PanAfrican Congress held in Kampala in April 1994, any mention of Nkrumah aroused spontaneous applause. The enemies of Nkrumah were never able to break his spirit. He, more than any other African leader represented the spirit of African youth determined to pursue Nkrumaist policies. 'I have often been accused of pursuing a policy of the impossible. But I cannot believe in the impossibility of attaining African freedom.'[1]

Few leaders of the quality of Nkrumah live to see the complete fulfilment of their work. Some die fighting in the guerrilla terrain of forests and mountains, or are gunned down in urban areas. Others, such as Eduardo Mondlane, Pio Pinto, Ben Barka, Ché Guevara, Martin Luther King, Malcolm X and Amilcar Cabral are assassinated. Then there are the great number like Frantz Fanon, Ho Chi Minh, Kwame Nkrumah, Sékou Touré, Samora Machel, to name a few, who die in suspicious circumstances from what are described as natural causes. Although there is a connection between the often premature deaths of such great men, and the physical demands made on them by years of selfless struggle, too many die prematurely for there not to be questions raised about the now well-known employment of insidious ways of silencing those who threaten the established order.

Sékou Touré included Nkrumah's name when listing men like Patrice Lumumba and Eduardo Mondlane whom he considered had been 'assassinated' by the enemies of the African Revolution. Amilcar Cabral certainly thought that Nkrumah was 'eliminated.' He used the term 'assassiné' in his speech at the funeral ceremonies in Conakry.

Though it may be unconstructive to speculate on the cause of Nkrumah's death, since it is unlikely to be possible to prove anything, speculation will doubtless continue. There was no post-mortem. One thing is, however, certain: he would not have died when he did, in his sixties, if it had not been for the 1966 coup in Ghana. If that had not occurred, he would not have been subjected to the strains, and exposed to security

---

1. *Africa Must Unite*, p. 170.

risks, for example over the preparation of his food while in Guinea.[1] His doctors in Ghana would have detected any early signs of illness, and he would have had instant treatment of the highest quality. In this sense, the dramatic funeral oration of Cabral, known as 'The Cancer of Betrayal' is very apt.

It was not until 1 July 1992, on the occasion of the 32nd anniversary of Ghana's Republic Day, that Nkrumah's body was reinterred in a mausoleum in a beautiful Memorial Park on the site of the old polo ground in Accra. There, on a high pedestal stands a statue of Nkrumah depicted wearing cloth, and with his right hand outstretched pointing the way ahead, indicating the CPP slogan FORWARD EVER. It is on the actual spot where he made the historic proclamation of Ghana's independence on 6 March 1957.

The coffin was lowered to rest in a deep vault within the massive mausoleum made of Italian marble, symbolizing a giant tree with a fluted base, the top cut-off like a half-felled tree. Around the mausoleum, and leading up to it, are many fountains, so that the music of falling water is always there. In the near distance is the restless pounding of the sea.

Among the distinguished visitors present on the day of reinterment were president Sam Nujoma of Namibia, Oliver Tambo, then Chairman of the ANC, and Betty Shabazz, widow of Malcolm X, representing the diaspora. Presiding was Flight Lieutenant Jerry Rawlings, Ghanaian Head of State, who had never claimed to be an Nkrumaist. He spoke of Nkrumah's vision: 'The black star of Ghana became the beacon of hope throughout Africa, throughout the Americas, throughout the world of the oppressed. We therefore honour him today as a statesman who belongs to Ghana, to Africa and to the world.' Among some of those listening there was speculation as to whether it was opportunism, from strength, or from weakness that the NDC regime had decided to respond to Nkrumaist pressures from Ghanaians and from PanAfricanists to accord Nkrumah the long overdue recognition of his greatness. Perhaps a clue may lie in the failure to arrange for the funeral procession to pass

1. Towards the end of one of my visits to Conakry, when I had shared all meals with Nkrumah, I developed severe stomach pains and fever. For over six weeks on my return to London I was seriously ill with typhoid-like symptoms which mystified my doctor. Exhaustive tests at the London School of Tropical Medicine failed to produce an explanation. Health officers visited my home to inspect taps and drains, but could find nothing to identify my illness.

◄ Marble mausoleum
("the tree cut short") —
Kwame Nkrumah Memorial Park,
commissioned in Accra, 1 July 1992

Statue depicting ▷
the CPP slogan —
FORWARD EVER
— Accra

through the streets of Accra before entering the Memorial Park, which was closed to all but authorized groups and invited guests. Such a procession would have allowed the thousands of Ghanaians who had gathered in the capital to demonstrate their deep affection and nostalgia for Osagyefo. Perhaps it was thought Nkrumaism could be finally buried with the man.

Oliver Tambo, recovering from a stroke, was too frail to speak. But Sam Nujoma gave a very inspiring address, recollecting the time when as freedom-fighter and leader of the South West African People's Organization (SWAPO), he arrived at Accra airport without any travel documents, to seek Nkrumah's support for his movement. Nkrumah saw that he was provided with the necessary documents enabling him to travel anywhere he needed to advance SWAPO. The help given by the CPP government in those early days was key to SWAPO's subsequent victory.

Betty Shabazz, in an emotional speech, said that Ghanaians had 'to share Nkrumah with millions ... he gave up the ownership of himself to Ghana and to Africa ... This will be a place of pilgrimage for all black Americans ... he will be in my mind, my heart and in my spirit for ever ... He is the father of us all.' When Malcolm X was assassinated, Nkrumah had invited Betty and her six children to live in Ghana. She regretted she did not go. It was a wonderful opportunity lost through her then lack of political awareness.

There followed other tributes, notably from the family, represented by Francis Nkrumah, and from Atukwei Okai speaking on behalf of the PanAfrican Writers Association (PAWA). In poetic language, Okai spoke of Nkrumah as a writer. He described the mausoleum as 'A huge tree cut short ... I refuse to die ... I am killed in the village but the drums still speak.'

The ceremonies were a spectacular blend of traditional funeral procedures and military ceremonial. The Ghanaian Navy, founded by Nkrumah played the central role escorting the gun carriage draped with the Ghanaian flag, and presiding over the lowering of the coffin into the vault of the mausoleum. In Accra now rest the mortal remains of three eminent PanAfricanists, W.E.B DuBois, George Padmore, and greatest of all, Kwame Nkrumah.

The following poem, written in Accra by Julia Wright after attending the commissioning of the Memorial Park on 1 July 1992, expresses the undying spirit of Kwame Nkrumah, foretelling the certain fulfilment of his vision of a free and united Africa:

THE OSAGYEFO-TREE

Children of Osagyefo
it is time for you to come
full circle
and enter at the gates
to where they finally buried him
and your independence was born

Children of Osagyefo
you will find him
under the truncated marble tree
of the Mausoleum:
he listens there,
now, at last
and for eternity
to the sound of falling water
and the liquid drumming of the sea

But he also listens for you
his children,
waiting silently at the gates
and let there be no entrance fee
for the sons and sons of sons
of the Verandah Boys
to be allowed the growth
from the independence womb
to maturity
by their father's tomb

Jose Marti said
the strongest trees grow
over dead patriots
and so,
the seed of the Osagyefo-Tree
at long last sown
in the political ground
of his beginnings —
in the ripe new earth
where the flag of independence
once grew —
will grow
timelessly tall
uniting Africa and her children,
his children,
under its shade

~~~~~~~~~~

Appendix One

Osagyefo's Men in Conakry

[As listed in *Weekly Insight* 22–28 November 1995]

1. Albert Kingsley Buah — Deputy Head of Bodyguard and Chairman of Administrative Committee
2. Moses E. Appoh — Special Intelligence Officer and Deputy Chairman of Administrative Committee
3. Alfred Quaye Codjoe — Functions Officer and Member of Administrative Committee
4. Mathew Ackah Mensah — Head of Special Intelligence Unit and Member of Administrative Committee
5. Emmanuel Kwadjo Obeng — Bodyguard, Member of Administrative Committee. Financial Clerk and Household affairs; i/c of Administrative Committee Office
6. Jacob Ohene — Member of Administrative Committee, Bodyguard and Transport Officer
7. John Borlebo Mensah — Special Intelligence Officer and Member of Administrative Committee
8. Frantz Wulf-Tagoe — Member of Administrative Committee
9. Wellington Sarfo — Personal Private Secretary to the President
10. E.Q. Lamptey — Bodyguard
11. N.K. Lartey — Bodyguard
12. A.C.K. Baah — Bodyguard

13. B. Etie Quarm — Bodyguard and Personal Attendant to President
14. J.K. Ackon — Functions Officer
15. Henry Ketibuah — Bodyguard
16. E.R. Amoah, Jnr. — Bodyguard Driver
17. A.C.K. Amoabeng — Bodyguard Driver
18. E.K. Baah — Bodyguard Driver
19. P.K. Amoo — Bodyguard Driver
20. Bannerman Smith — Bodyguard Driver
21. E. Ebuley Ediem — Bodyguard Officer
22. Ambrose Yankey Snr. — Personal Assistant to President
23. Ambrose Yankey Jnr. — Special Intelligence Officer
24. Leonard Moses Blay — Special Intelligence Officer
25. Samuel A. Buah — Bodyguard
26. Benjamin Kanga Forjoe — Bodyguard
27. Francis Adiah — Bodyguard
28. Francis Abekah — Bodyguard
29. Adayi Quarm — Bodyguard
30. Ambrose Akorsey — Bodyguard
31. Paul Kojo Amoah — Bodyguard and President's Photographer
32. J.H. Anaman — Bodyguard
33. Isaac C. Ackah — Bodyguard
34. P. Alphonse Quaicoe — Bodyguard
35. Daniel Kweku — Bodyguard
36. Samuel Kwame Koomson — Protection Officer
37. Nyamikeh Nganyah — Personal Attendant to President and Nephew of President
38. David Ghartey — Special Intelligence Officer
39. Moses Awoonor-Williams Jnr. — Special Intelligence Officer
40. George Kwamina Bartles — Special Intelligence Officer
42. Thomas Rees Amonoo — Special Intelligence Officer
42. J.K. Mensah — Special Intelligence Officer
43. Moses Ovate — Special Intelligence Officer
44. Etienne N. Mobil — Special Intelligence Officer
45. J.K. Okyere — Special Intelligence Officer

In addition:
Boye Moses — Senior Secutirt Officer (see fottnote, p. 264)

Appendix Two

Address to the Conference
of African Heads of State and Government —
Addis Ababa, 24 May 1963

On the eve of the foundation of the Organization of African Unity
(OAU) Kwame Nkrumah addressed the Heads of Independent
African States who, on 25 May 1963 signed the OAU Charter in
Addis Ababa

~~~~~~~~~~

YOUR EXCELLENCIES, COLLEAGUES,
BROTHERS AND FRIENDS

I am happy to be here in Addis Ababa on this
most historic occasion. I bring with me the hopes and
fraternal greetings of the Government and people of
Ghana to His Imperial Majesty Haile Selassie and to all
Heads of African States gathered here in this ancient
capital in this momentous period in our history. Our
objective is African Union now. There is no time to
waste. We must unite now or perish. I am confident
that by our concerted effort and determination we shall
lay here the foundations for a continental Union of
African States.

At the first gathering of African Heads of State,
to which I had the honour of playing host, there were
representatives of eight independent States, only.
Today, five years later, here at Addis Ababa, we meet
as the representatives of no less than thirty-two States,
the guests of His Imperial Majesty, Haile Selassie, the
First, and the Government and people of Ethiopia. To
his Imperial Majesty, I wish to express, on behalf of the

Government and people of Ghana my deep appreciation for a most cordial welcome and generous hospitality.

The increase in our number in this short space of time is open testimony to the indomitable and irresistible surge of our peoples for independence. It is also a token of the revolutionary speed of world events in the latter half of this century. In the task which is before us of unifying our continent we must fall in with that pace or be left behind. The task cannot be attacked in the tempo of any other age than our own. To fall behind the unprecedented momentum of actions and events in our time will be to court failure and our own undoing.

A whole continent has imposed a mandate upon us to lay the foundation of our Union at this Conference. It is our responsibility to execute this mandate by creating here and now the formula upon which the requisite superstructure may be erected.

On this continent it has not taken us long to discover that the struggle against colonialism does not end with the attainment of national independence. Independence is only the prelude to a new and more involved struggle for the right to conduct our own economic and social affairs; to construct our society according to our aspirations, unhampered by crushing and humiliating neo-colonialist controls and interference.

From the start we have been threatened with frustration where rapid change is imperative and with instability where sustained effort and ordered rule are indispensable.

No sporadic act nor pious resolution can resolve our present problems. Nothing will be of avail, except the united act of a united Africa. We have already reached the stage where we must unite or sink into that condition which has made Latin-America the unwilling and distressed prey of imperialism after one-and-a-half centuries of political independence.

As a continent we have emerged into independence in a different age, with imperialism grown stronger, more ruthless and experienced, and more dangerous in its international associations. Our economic advancement demands the end of colonialist and neo-colonialist domination in Africa.

But just as we understood that the shaping of our national destinies required of each of us our political independence and bent all our strength to this attainment, so we must recognize that our economic independence resides in our African union and requires the same concentration upon the political achievement.

The unity of our continent, no less than our separate independence, will be delayed if, indeed, we do not lose it, by hobnobbing with colonialism. African Unity is, above all, a political kingdom which can only be gained by political means. The social and economic development of Africa will come only within the political kingdom, not the other way round. The United States of America, the Union of Soviet Socialist Republics, were the political decisions of revolutionary peoples before they became mighty realities of social power and material wealth.

How, except by our united efforts, will the richest and still enslaved parts of our continent be freed from colonial occupation and become available to us for the total development of our continent? Every step in the decolonization of our continent has brought greater resistance in those areas where colonial garrisons are available to colonialism and you all here know that.

This is the great design of the imperialist interests that buttress colonialism and neo-colonialism, and we would be deceiving ourselves in the most cruel way were we to regard their individual actions as separate and unrelated. When Portugal violates Senegal's border, when Verwoerd allocates one-seventh of South Africa's budget to military and police, when France builds as part of her defence policy an interventionist force that can intervene, more especially in French-speaking Africa, when Welensky talks of Southern Rhodesia joining South Africa, when Britain sends arms to South Africa, it is all part of a carefully calculated pattern working towards a single end; the continued enslavement of our still dependent brothers and an onslaught upon the independence of our sovereign African states.

Do we have any other weapon against this design but our unity? Is not our unity essential to guard our own freedom as well as to win freedom for our oppressed brothers, the Freedom Fighters? Is it not unity alone that can weld us into an effective force, capable of creating our own progress and making our valuable contribution to world peace? Which independent African State, which of you here will claim that its financial structure and banking institutions are fully harnessed to its national development? Which will claim that its material resources and human energies are available for its own national aspirations? Which will disclaim a substantial measure of disappointment and disillusionment in its agricultural and urban development?

In Independent Africa we are already re-experiencing the instability and frustration which existed under colonial rule. We are fast learning that political independence is not enough to rid us of the consequences of colonial rule.

The movement of the masses of the people of Africa for freedom from that kind of rule was not only a revolt against the conditions which it imposed.

Our people supported us in our fight for independence because they believed that African Governments could cure the ills of the past in a way which could never be accomplished under colonial rule. If, therefore, now that we are independent we allow the same conditions to exist that existed in colonial days, all the resentment which overthrew colonialism will be mobilized against us.

The resources are there. It is for us to marshal them in the active service of our people. Unless we do this by our concerted efforts, within the framework of our combined planning, we shall not progress at the tempo demanded by today's events and the mood of our people. The symptoms of our troubles will grow, and the troubles themselves become chronic. It will then be too late even for PanAfrican Unity to secure for us stability and tranquillity in our labours for a continent of social justice and material well-being. Unless we establish African Unity now, we who are sitting here today shall tomorrow be the victims and martyrs of neo-colonialism.

There is evidence on every side that the imperialists have not withdrawn from our affairs. There are times, as in the Congo, when their interference is manifest. But generally it is covered up under the clothing of many agencies, which meddle in our domestic affairs, to foment dissension within our borders and to create an atmosphere of tension and political instability. As long as we do not do away with the root causes of discontent, we lend aid to these neo-colonialist forces, and shall become our own executioners. We cannot ignore the teachings of history.

Our continent is probably the richest in the world for minerals and industrial agricultural primary materials. From the Congo alone, Western firms exported copper, rubber, cotton, and other goods to the value of 2,773 million dollars in the ten years between 1945 and 1955, and from South Africa, Western gold mining companies have drawn a profit, in the six years between 1947 to 1951 of 814 million dollars.

Our continent certainly exceeds all the others in potential hydro-electric power, which some experts assess as 42 per cent of the world's total. What need is there for us to remain hewers of wood and drawers of water for the industrialized areas of the world?

It is said, of course, that we have no capital, no industrial skill, no communications and no internal markets, and that we cannot even agree among ourselves how best to utilize our resources for our own social needs.

Yet all stock exchanges in the world are pre-occupied with Africa's gold, diamonds, uranium, platinum, copper and iron ores. Our capital flows out in streams to irrigate the whole system of Western economy. Fifty-two per cent of the gold in Fort Knox at this moment, where the USA stores its bullion, is believed to have originated from our shores. Africa provides more than 60 per cent of the world's gold. A great deal of the uranium for nuclear power, of copper for electronics, of titanium for supersonic projectiles, of iron and steel for heavy industries, of other minerals and raw materials for lighter industries — the basic economic might of the foreign Powers — come from our continent.

Experts have estimated that the Congo Basin alone can produce enough food crops to satisfy the requirements of nearly half the population of the whole world and here we sit talking about regionalism, talking about gradualism, talking about step by step. Are you afraid to tackle the bull by the horn?

For centuries Africa has been the milchcow of the Western world. Was it not our continent that helped the Western world to build up its accumulated wealth?

It is true that we are now throwing off the yoke of colonialism as fast as we can, but our success in this direction is equally matched by an intense effort on the part of imperialism to continue the exploitation of our resources by creating divisions among us.

When the colonies of the American Continent sought to free themselves from imperialism in the 18th century there was no threat of neo-colonialism in the sense in which we know it today in Africa. The American States were therefore free to form and fashion the unity which was best suited to their needs and to frame a constitution to hold their unity together without any form of interference from external sources. We, however, are having to grapple with outside interventions. How much more, then do we need to come together in the African unity that alone can save us from the clutches of neo-colonialism and imperialism?

We have the resources. It was colonialism in the first place that prevented us from accumulating the effective capital; but we ourselves have failed to make full use of our power in independence to mobilize our resources for the most effective take-off into thorough-going economic and social development. We have been too busy nursing our separate states to understand fully the basic need of our union, rooted in common purpose, common planning and common endeavour. A union that ignores these fundamental necessities will be but a sham. It is only by uniting our productive capacity and the resultant production that we can, amass capital. And once we start, the momentum will increase. With capital controlled by our own banks, harnessed to our own true industrial and agricultural development, we shall make our advance. We shall accumulate machinery and establish steel works, iron foundries and factories; we shall link the various states of our continent with communications by land, sea and air. We shall cable from one place to another, phone from one place to the other and astound the world with our hydro-electric power; we shall drain marshes and swamps, clear infested areas, feed the under-nourished, and rid our people of parasites and disease. It is within the possibility of science and technology to make even the Sahara bloom into a vast field with verdant vegetation for agricultural and industrial developments. We shall harness the radio, television, giant printing presses to lift our people from the dark recesses of illiteracy.

A decade ago, these would have been visionary words, the fantasies of an idle dreamer. But this is the age in which science has transcended the limits of the material world, and technology has invaded the silences of nature. Time and space have been reduced to unimportant abstractions. Giant machines make roads, clear forests, dig dams, lay out aerodromes; monster trucks and planes distribute goods; huge laboratories manufacture drugs; complicated geological surveys are made; mighty power stations are built; colossal factories erected — all at an incredible speed. The world is no longer moving through bush paths or on camels and donkeys.

We cannot afford to pace our needs, our development, our security, to the gait of camels and donkeys. We cannot afford not to cut down the overgrown bush of outmoded attitudes that obstruct our path to the modern open road of the widest and earliest achievement of economic independence and the raising up of the lives of our people to the highest level.

Even for other continents lacking the resources of Africa, this is the age that sees the end of human want. For us it is a simple matter of grasping with certainty our heritage by using the political might of unity. All we need to do is to develop with our united strength the enormous resources of our continent. A United Africa will provide a stable field of foreign investment, which will be encouraged as long as it does not behave inimically to our African interests. For such investment would add by its enterprises to the development of the continental national economy, employment and training of our people, and will be welcome to Africa. In dealing with a united Africa, investors will no longer have to weigh with concern the risks of negotiating with governments in one period which may not exist in the very next period. Instead of dealing or negotiating with so many separate states at a time they will be dealing with one united government pursuing a harmonized continental policy.

What is the alternative to this? If we falter at this stage, and let time pass for neo-colonialism to consolidate its position on this continent, what will be the fate of our people who have put their trust in us? What will be the fate of our freedom fighters? What will be the fate of other African territories that are not yet free?

Unless we can establish great industrial complexes in Africa — which we can only do in a united Africa — we must leave our peasantry to the mercy of foreign cash crop markets, and face the same unrest which overthrew the colonialists. What use to the farmer is education and mechanization, what use is even capital for development; unless we can ensure for him a fair price and a ready market? What has the peasant, worker and farmer gained from political independence, unless we can ensure for him a fair return for his labour and a higher standard of living?

Unless we can establish great industrial complexes in Africa, what have the urban worker, and those peasants on overcrowded land gained from political independence? If they are to remain unemployed or in unskilled occupation, what will avail them the better facilities for education, technical training, energy and ambition which independence enables us to provide?

There is hardly any African State without a frontier problem with its adjacent neighbours. It would be futile for me to enumerate them because they are already so familiar to us all. But let me suggest to Your Excellencies that this fatal relic of colonialism will drive us to war against one another as our unplanned and unco-ordinated industrial development expands, just as happened in Europe. Unless we succeed in arresting the danger through mutual understanding on fundamental issues and through African Unity, which will render existing boundaries obsolete and superfluous, we shall have fought in vain for independence. Only African Unity can heal this festering sore of boundary disputes between our various states. Your Excellencies, the remedy for these ills is ready in our hands. It stares us in the face at every customs barrier, it shouts to us from every African heart. By creating a true political union of all the independent states of Africa, with executive powers for political direction we can tackle hopefully every emergency, every enemy, and every complexity. This is not because we are a race of supermen, but because we have emerged in the age of science and technology in which poverty, ignorance and disease are no longer the masters, but the re-treating foes of mankind. We have emerged in the age of socialized plan-ning, where production and distribution are not governed by chaos, greed and self-interest, but by social needs. Together with the rest of mankind, we have awakened from Utopian dreams to pursue practical blueprints for progress and social justice.

Above all, we have emerged at a time when a continental land mass like Africa with its population approaching three hundred million are necessary to the economic capitalization and profitability of modern productive methods and techniques. Not one of us working singly and individually can successfully attain the fullest development. Certainly, in the circumstances, it will not be possible to give adequate assistance to sister states trying, against the most difficult conditions, to improve their economic and social structures. Only a united Africa functioning under a Union Government can forcefully mobilize the material and moral resources of our separate countries and apply them efficiently and energetically to bring a rapid change in the conditions of our people.

If we do not approach the problems in Africa with a common front and a common purpose, we shall be haggling and wrangling among ourselves until we are colonized again and become the tools of a far greater colonialism than we suffered hitherto.

Unite we must. Without necessarily sacrificing our sovereignties, big or small, we can here and now forge a political union based on Defence, Foreign Affairs and Diplomacy, and a Common Citizenship, an African Currency, an African Monetary Zone and an African Central Bank. We must unite in order to achieve the full liberation of our continent. We need a common Defence System with African High Command to ensure the stability and security of Africa.

We have been charged with this sacred task by our own people, and we cannot betray their trust by failing them. We will be mocking the hopes of our people if we show the slightest hesitation or delay in tackling realistically this question of African Unity.

The supply of arms or other military aid to the colonial oppressors in Africa must be regarded not only as aid in the vanquishment of the freedom fighters battling for their African independence, but as an act of aggression against the whole of Africa. How can we meet this aggression except by the full weight of our united strength?

Many of us have made non-alignment an article of faith on this continent. We have no wish, and no intention of being drawn into the Cold War. But with the present weakness and insecurity of our States in the context of world politics, the search for bases and spheres of influence brings the Cold War into Africa with its danger of nuclear warfare. Africa should be declared a nuclear-free zone and freed from cold war exigencies. But we cannot make this demand mandatory unless we support it from a position of strength to be found only in our unity.

Instead, many Independent African States are involved by military pacts with the former colonial powers. The stability and security which such devices seek to establish are illusory, for the metropolitan Powers seize the opportunity to support their neo-colonialist controls by direct military involvement. We have seen how the neo-colonialists use their bases to entrench themselves and even to attack neighbouring independent states. Such bases are centres of tension and potential danger spots of military conflict. They threaten the security not only of the country in which they are situated but of neighbouring countries as well. How can we hope to make Africa a nuclear-free zone and independent of cold war pressure with such military involvement on our continent? Only by counter-balancing a common defence force with a common desire for an Africa untrammelled by foreign dictation or military and nuclear presence. This will require an all-embracing African High Command, especially if the military pacts with the imperialists are to be renounced. It is the only way we can break these direct links between the colonialism of the past and the neo-colonialism which disrupts us today.

We do not want nor do we visualize an African High Command in the terms of the power politics that now rule a great part of the world, but as an essential and indispensable instrument for ensuring stability and security in Africa.

We need unified economic planning for Africa. Until the economic power of Africa is in our hands, the masses can have no real concern and no real interest for safeguarding our security, for ensuring the stability of our regimes, and for bending their strength to the fulfilment of our ends. With our united resources, energies and talents we have the means, as soon as we show the will, to transform the economic structures of our individual states from poverty to that of wealth, from inequality to the satisfaction of popular needs. Only on a continental basis shall we be able to plan the proper utilization of all our resources for the full development of our continent.

How else will we retain our own capital for our development? How else will we establish an internal market for our own industries? By belonging to different economic zones, how will we break down the currency and trading barriers between African States, and how will the economically stronger amongst us be able to assist the weaker and less developed States?

It is important to remember that independent financing and independent development cannot take place without an independent currency. A currency system that is backed by the resources of a foreign state is *ipso facto* subject to the trade and financial arrangements of that foreign country.

Because we have so many customs and currency barriers as a result of being subject to the different currency systems of foreign powers, this has served to widen the gap between us in Africa. How, for example, can related communities and families trade with, and support one another successfully, if they find themselves divided by national boundaries and currency restrictions? The only alternative open to them in these circumstances is to use smuggled currency and enrich national and international racketeers and crooks who prey upon our financial and economic difficulties.

No Independent African State today by itself has a chance to follow an independent course of economic development, and many of us who have tried to do this have been almost ruined or have had to return to the fold of the former colonial rulers. This position will not change unless we have a unified policy working at the continental level. The first step towards our cohesive economy would be a unified monetary zone, with, initially, an agreed common parity for our currencies. To facilitate this arrangement, Ghana would change to a decimal system. When we find that the arrangement of a fixed common parity is working successfully, there would seem to be no reason for not instituting one common currency and a single bank of issue. With a common currency from one common bank to issue we should be able to stand erect on our own feet because such an arrangement would be fully backed by the combined national products of the states composing the union. After all, the purchasing power of money depends on productivity and the productive exploitation of the natural, human and physical resources of the nation.

While we are assuring our stability by a common defence system, and our economy is being orientated beyond foreign control by a Common Currency, Monetary Zone and Central Bank of Issue, we can investigate the resources of our continent. We can begin to ascertain whether in reality we are the richest, and not, as we have been taught to believe, the poorest among the continents. We can determine whether we possess the largest potential in hydroelectric power, and whether we can harness it and other sources of energy to our own industries. We can proceed to plan our industrialization on a continental scale, and to build up a common market for nearly three hundred million people.

Common Continental Planning for the Industrial and Agricultural Development of Africa is a vital necessity.

So many blessings flow from our unity; so many disasters must follow on our continued disunity, that our failure to unite today will not be attributed by posterity only to faulty reasoning and lack of courage, but to our capitulation before the forces of neo-colonialism and imperialism.

The hour of history which has brought us to this assembly is a revolutionary hour. It is the hour of decision. For the first time, the economic imperialism which menaces us is itself challenged by the irresistible will of our people.

The masses of the people of Africa are crying for unity. The people of Africa call for the breaking down of the boundaries that keep them apart. They demand an end to the border disputes between sister African states — disputes that arise out of the artificial barriers raised by colonialism. It was colonialism's purpose that divided us. It was colonialism's purpose that left us with our border irredentism, that rejected our ethnic and cultural fusion.

Our people call for unity so that they may not lose their patrimony in the perpetual service of neo-colonialism. In their fervent push to unity, they understand that only its realization will give full meaning to their freedom and our African independence.

It is this popular determination that must move us on to a Union of Independent African States. In delay lies danger to our well-being, to our very existence as free states. It has been suggested that our approach to unity should be gradual, that it should go piece-meal. This point of view conceives of Africa as a static entity with 'frozen' problems which can be eliminated one by one and when all have been cleared then we can come together and say: 'Now all is well, Let us now unite.' This view takes no account of the impact of external pressures. Nor does it take cognizance of the danger that delay can deepen our isolations and exclusiveness; that it can enlarge our differences and set us drifting further and further apart into the net of neo-colonialism, so that our union will become nothing but a fading hope, and the great design of Africa's full redemption will be lost, perhaps, forever.

The view is also expressed that our difficulties can be resolved simply by a greater collaboration through co-operative association in our interterritorial relationships. This way of looking at our problems denies a proper conception of their inter-relationship and mutuality. It denies faith in a future for African advancement in African independence. It betrays a sense of solution only in continued reliance upon external sources through bilateral agreements for economic and other forms of aid.

The fact is that although we have been co-operating and associating with one another in various fields of common endeavour even before colonial times, this has not given us the continental identity and the political and economic force which would help us to deal effectively with the complicated problems confronting us in Africa today. As far as foreign aid is concerned, a United Africa should be in a more favourable position to attract assistance from foreign sources. There is the far more compelling advantage which this arrangement offers, in that aid will come from anywhere to a united Africa because our bargaining power would become infinitely greater. We shall no longer be dependent upon aid from restricted sources. We shall have the world to choose from.

What are we looking for in Africa? Are we looking for Charters, conceived in the light of the United Nations example? A type of United Nations Organization whose decisions are framed on the basis of resolutions that in our experience have sometimes been ignored by member States? Where groupings are formed and pressures develop in accordance with the interest of the groups concerned? Or is it intended that Africa should be turned into a loose organization of States on the model of the Organization of American States, in which the weaker States within it can be at the mercy of the stronger or more powerful ones politically or economically and all at the mercy of some powerful outside nation or group of nations? Is this the kind of association we want for ourselves in the United Africa we all speak of with such feeling and emotion?

Your Excellencies, permit me to ask: Is this the kind of framework we desire for our United Africa? An arrangement which in future could permit Ghana or Nigeria or the Sudan, or Liberia, or Egypt or Ethiopia for example, to use pressure, which either superior economic or political influence give, to dictate the flow and direction of trade from, say, Burundi or Togo or Nyasaland to Mozambique or Madagascar?

We all want a united Africa, united not only in our concept of what unity connotes, but united in our common desire to move forward together in dealing with all the problems that can best be solved only on a continental basis.

When the first Congress of the United States met many years ago at Philadelphia one of the delegates sounded the first chord of unity by declaring that they had met in 'a state of nature'. In other words, they were not in Philadelphia as Virginians, or Pennsylvanians, but simply as Americans. This reference to themselves as Americans was in those days a new and strange experience. May I dare to assert equally on this occasion. Your Excellencies, that we meet here today not as Ghanaians, Guineans, Egyptians, Algerians, Moroccans, Malians, Liberians, Congolese or Nigerians but as Africans. Africans united in our resolve to remain here until we have agreed on the basic principles of a new compact of unity among ourselves which guarantees for us and our future a new arrangement of continental government.

If we succeed in establishing a New Set of Principles as the basis of a New Charter or Stature for the establishment of a continental unity of Africa and the creation of social and political progress for our people, then in my view, this conference should mark the end of our various groupings and regional blocs. But if we fail and let this grand and historic opportunity slip by then we shall give way to greater dissension and division among us for which the people of Africa will never forgive us. And the popular and progressive forces and movements within Africa will condemn us. I am sure therefore that we shall not fail them.

I have spoken at some length, Your Excellencies, because it is necessary for us all to explain not only to one another present here but also to our people who have entrusted to us the fate and destiny of Africa. We must therefore not leave this place until we have set up effective machinery for achieving African Unity. To this end, I propose for your consideration the following:—

As a first step, Your Excellencies, a declaration of principles uniting and binding us together and to which we must all faithfully and loyally adhere, and laying the foundations of unity should be set down. And there should also be a formal declaration that all the Independent African

States here and now agree to the establishment of a Union of African States.

As a second and urgent step for the realization of the unification of Africa, an All-Africa Committee of Foreign Ministers be set up now, and that before we rise from this Conference a date should be fixed for them to meet.

This Committee should establish on behalf of the Heads of our Governments, a permanent body of officials and experts to work out a machinery for the Union Government of Africa. This body of officials and experts should be made up of two of the best brains from each independent African State. The various Charters of the existing groupings and other relevant documents could also be submitted to the officials and experts. A Praesidium consisting of the heads of Governments of the Independent African States should be called upon to meet and adopt a Constitution and other recommendations which will launch the Union Government of Africa.

We must also decide on a location where this body of officials and experts will work as the new Headquarters or Capital of our Union Government. Some central place in Africa might be the fairest suggestion, either at Bangui in the Central African Republic or Léopoldville in Congo. My Colleagues may have other proposals. The Committee of Foreign Ministers, officials and experts should be empowered to establish:

(1) a Commission to frame a constitution for a Union Government of African States;
(2) a Commission to work out a continent-wide plan for a unified or common economic and industrial programme for Africa; this place should include proposals for setting up:
   (a) A Common Market for Africa;
   (b) An African Currency;
   (c) An African Monetary Zone;
   (d) An African Central Bank, and
   (e) A continental Communication system.
(3) a Commission to draw up details for a Common Foreign Policy and Diplomacy.
(4) a Commission to produce plans for a Common System of Defence.
(5) a Commission to make proposals for a Common African Citizenship.

These Commissions will report to the Committee of Foreign Ministers who should in turn submit within six months of this Conference their recommendations to the Praesidium. The Praesidium meeting in Conference at the Union Headquarters will consider and approve the recommendations of the Committee of Foreign Ministers.

In order to provide funds immediately for the work of the permanent officials and experts of the Headquarters of the Union, I suggest that a special Committee be set up to work out a budget for this.

Your Excellencies, with these steps, I submit, we shall be irrevocably committed to the road which will bring us to a Union Government for Africa. Only a United Africa with central political direction can successfully give effective material and moral support to our freedom fighters, in Southern Rhodesia, Angola, Mozambique, South-West Africa, Bechuanaland, Swaziland, Basutoland, Portuguese Guinea, etc., and of course South Africa. All Africa must be liberated now. It is therefore imperative for us here and now to establish a liberation bureau for African freedom fighters. The main object of this bureau, to which all governments should subscribe, should be to accelerate the emancipation of the rest of Africa still under colonial and racialist domination and oppression. It should be our joint responsibility to finance and support this bureau. On their successful attainment of Independence these territories will automatically join our Union of African States, and thus strengthen the fabric of Mother Africa. We shall leave here, having laid the foundation for our unity.

Your Excellencies, nothing could be more fitting than that the unification of Africa should be born on the soil of the State which stood for centuries as the symbol of African independence.

Let us return to our people of Africa not with empty hands and with high-sounding resolutions, but with the firm hope and assurance that at long last African Unity has become a reality. We shall thus begin the triumphant march to the kingdom of the African Personality, and to a continent of prosperity, and progress, of equality and justice and of work and happiness. This shall be our victory — victory within a continental government of a Union of African States. This victory will give our voice greater force in world affairs and enable us to throw our weight more forcibly on the side of peace. The world needs peace in which the greatest advantage can be taken of the benefits of science and technology. Many of the world's present ills are to be found in the insecurity and fear engendered by the threat of nuclear war. Especially do the new nations need peace in order to make their way into a life of economic and social well-being amid an atmosphere of security and stability that will promote moral, cultural and spiritual fulfilment.

If we in Africa can achieve the example of a continent knit together in common policy and common purpose, we shall have made the finest possible contribution to that peace for which all men and women thirst today, and which will lift once and forever the deepening shadow of global destruction from mankind. Ethiopia shall STRETCH forth her hands unto God.

AFRICA MUST UNITE.

~~~~~~~~~~

The Independent countries which signed the Charter:

Algeria	Mauritania
Burundi	Morocco
Cameroun	Niger
Central African Republic	Nigeria
Congo (Brazzaville)	Rwanda
Congo/Zaire (Léopoldville/Kinshasa)	Senegal
	Sierra Leone
Dahomey	Somalia
Ethiopia	Sudan
Gabon	Tanganyika (Tanzania)
Ghana	Tshad (Chad)
Guinea	Togo
Ivory Coast	Tunisia
Liberia	Uganda
Libya	UAR (Egypt)
Malagasy	Upper Volta
Mali	(Burkina Fasso)

~~~~~~~~~~

Index

Kaunda, Kenneth 87, 220, 236, 237, 243, 260
Keita, Modibo 89, 90, 91, 140, 148, 186, 206, 207
Keita, Seydou 257, 258
Kennedy, John F. 111, 239
Kenyatta, Jomo 24, 26
Ketibuah, Henry 274
King, Martin Luther 77, 238, 267
Koi, Ansah 64
Koomson, Samuel Kwame 274
Korle Bu Hospital 60
Kosi, John Ketsowo 213
Kotoka, Colonel E.K. 177, 179, 182, 183, 219
Kwame Nkrumah Foundation, Accra, 1987 38
Kwame Nkrumah: The Political Kingdom in the Third World (Rooney) 31
Kweku, Daniel 274

L

Labour Monthly 231
Labour Party (UK) 14, 25, 28, 155
Lamptey, E.Q. 273
Lamptey, Obetsebi 41, 45, 58, 172
Lartey, N.K. 273
Legislative Council 36, 55
Liberia 77, 83
Libya 83
Lie, Trygve 63
Lincoln University (USA) 7, 10, 11, 18, 61, 63, 227
Liverpool 9, 10, 32
London School of Economics (LSE) 21
Lumumba, Patrice 87, 92, 94, 95, 144, 146, 148, 150, 176, 227, 267
Lusaka Conference, 1970 139
Lyttleton, Oliver 63

M

Maderjac, Dr. 256, 257
Makeba, Miriam 228
Makonnen, Ras..T. 22, 24
Malcolm X 135, 136, 148, 227, 229, 267, 268, 270
Manly, Florence 22
Mao Tse Tung 215
Mboya, Tom 87
McDowell Presbyterian Church, Philadelphia (USA) 18
Medlock, Julie 201
Mensah, J.K. 274
Mensah, John Borlebo 273
Mensah, Mathew Ackah 217, 273
Message to the Black People of Britain, Kwame Nkrumah 1968 229
MI5 29
Milliard, Peter 23, 24
Milne, June 22, 25, 26, 32, 111, 112, 162, 163, 196
Milne, Van 78
Mobil, Etienne N. 274
Mobutu, General Sese Seko 146, 175, 176, 238
Mohammed V, King of Morocco 92
Mondlane, Eduardo 148, 266, 267
Monrovia Conference 92, 93
Morocco 83
Morrow, Dr. 13
Moses Blay, Leonard 274
Moses, Boye 204, 217, 218, 264, 274
Motion of Destiny 57, 65, 66
Movement for the Liberation of Angola (MPLA) 152
Movement National Congolese (MNC) 87
Moxon, James 215
Mozambique 109, 141, 152, 160, 232
Murby, Leslie 78
Murumbi, Joseph 101
Mussolini, Benito 10
Mutesa II, King Fred, The Kabaka of Buganda 78

Sukarno, President of Indonesia 137, 138

Swahili 14

T

Tambo, Oliver 268, 270

The Forest (W. Pomeroy, 1963)241, 244

The Spark 121, 153, 215

Thomas Nelson and Sons 78

Tito, President of Yugoslavia 137, 138

Tolbert Jnr, W. S. 77

Trades Union Congress (TUC) 204

Tshombe, Moise 144, 146, 150

Tsiboe, Nancy 38

Tsikata, Capt. Kojo 225

Tunisia 83

U

Unilateral Declaration of Independence (UDI) 101, 102, 151, 154, 155, 159, 164

Union of African States 88, 89, 94, 109

Union of African States (UAS) 89

United Gold Coast Convention (UGCC) 31, 32, 34, 36, 37, 38, 39, 40, 41, 42, 43, 45, 46

United Nations (UN) 63, 77, 78, 93, 127, 139, 142, 144, 148, 149, 155, 185

United Party 169

University College of the Gold Coast, Achimota 60

University of Ghana 45, 86, 128, 130, 132, 133, 180

Urban League, USA 14

V

Villa Syli 191, 193, 195, 202, 203, 209, 212, 213, 217, 219, 226

Voice of Africa 153

Volta Dam 110, 111, 114, 175, 215

Volta Lake 166

Volta River Project (VRP) 61, 63, 108, 110, 113, 166

W

Wachman, Dr. Martin 227

Watson, Aiken KC 42

Watson Commission 45, 46

Watson Report 45

Welbeck, N.A. 49, 180

West Africa (Magazine) 25, 199

West African Monitor (Magazine) 51

West African National Secretariat (WANS) 24, 25, 26, 27, 28, 29

West African Students' Union (WASU) 21, 22, 26, 27, 28

West African Youth League (WAYL) 9, 33

Williams, Franklin 182

Wilson, Harold 25, 155, 156, 159, 163, 174

Women's Council 204

Workers' Brigade 204

World Bank 103

World Federation of Trades Unions (WFTU) 76

Wright, Julia 202, 270

Wright, Richard 133, 202

Wulf-Tagoe, Frantz 273

Y

Yameogo, President of Burkina Fasso 98

Yankey Jnr, Ambrose 274

Yankey Snr, Ambrose 274

Yeboah, Lt. Moses 219

Young Pioneers 204

Z

Zaire (Congo) 238

Zambia 159, 161, 162, 163, 260

Zanerigu, Colonel 177

Zimbabwe 87, 101, 141, 153

Zimbabwe African National Union (ZANU) 152, 153

Zimbabwe African People's Union (ZAPU) 152, 153

Printed in the USA
CPSIA information can be obtained
at www.ICGtesting.com
LVHW051022120823
755047LV00038B/375